Transformed by the Evidence

Testimonies of Leading Creationists

Edited by Doug Sharp, B.S.
and Jerry Bergman Ph.D.

Leafcutter Press, Publisher

Leafcutter Press, PO Box 102, Southworth, WA 98386. Published in the United States of America.

Library Catalog Data

Bergman, Jerry R. (1946 -) Editor
Sharp, Doug (1950 -) Editor

ISBN 13 978-0-9818734-9-7
ISBN 10 0-9818734-9-9

1.   Evolution vs. Creation
2.   Christianity
3.   Evidence for Creation
4.   Science and Design

Book design and cover by Kevin H. Wirth and Lori A. McKee
Book cover image by Kevin H. Wirth

Table of Contents

Acknowledgements

The editors wish, first of all, to thank the Creation Research Society for their help and encouragement for this now decade old project. Secondly, we must thank each of the contributors for their chapters and willingness to go through multiple revisions and rewrites to achieve the finished product, which we can be justly proud of. Last, we thank our editors, including Marilyn Dauer, Wayne Frair, and MaryAnn Stuart, for their careful review of the manuscript.

We would also like to acknowledge David Bump who originally suggested the idea for this book on CRSnet.

Preface by Doug Sharp

One of the reasons for the increase in skepticism about the veracity of the Bible today is the fact that many people often do not observe a clear difference between church attenders and non-believers. The apostle Paul challenges us in Romans 12:1-2:

> I beseech you therefore, brethren, by the mercies of God, that ye present your bodies a living sacrifice, holy, acceptable unto God, which is your reasonable service. And be not conformed to this world: but be ye *transformed* by the renewing of your mind, that ye may prove what is that good, and acceptable, and perfect will of God.

Consider what the unbelieving world sees: a church whose leadership and members are often just as skeptical of the straightforward reading of Genesis as any agnostic or atheist. The foundational teachings of Genesis are too often dismissed in our churches or presented as myth. And without this foundation, God's good, acceptable, and perfect will remains a mystery for too many seekers.

In this volume, Dr. Jerry Bergman and I are pleased to present testimonies of those who have encountered the tough questions concerning faith, science and the Bible. Many of the writers have conducted investigations to determine if the evidence supports a straightforward understanding of the Scriptures. As a result, their lives were transformed from atheist to Christian, from nominal Christian to active Christian, or from an active Christian to a more committed Christian. Thanks to their interest in science and the clear evidence that the Creator has left for us, they have become new creatures in Christ.

Some of these testimonies involve events that caused intensive personal sacrifice, pain, and despair. But not one of these authors would return to a life of unbelief, doubt and less commitment to Christ. Knowledge of the scientific evidence for a Creator who loves us keeps us vitalized and encouraged even in difficult times.

Many people who are strong believers in Jesus Christ and the Bible, but do not have any interest in science, base their faith in Christ on other facets of His Word and their personal experiences. They may never have encountered situations where they were tested in this area, and God has blessed them. But for many of those who recount their experiences in this book, the challenges presented by the theory of evolution and the notion that life is billions of years old have become stumbling blocks that were difficult to overcome. At the very least, this experience had created a major test of their faith; and in some cases was a stumbling block that prevented them from accepting the creation worldview. The fact is, evolution is often the doorway to atheism.

Transformation is not Without Tests

As you read about their struggles with this issue, and how those struggles were resolved, I invite you to examine your own beliefs concerning Creation. Has your life been transformed by the renewing of your mind to the point where the good, acceptable and perfect will of God in your life is evident to those around you?

In our chapter in this book, Rich Geer and I recount the tragic event that struck at the very heart of our beliefs and challenged the faith of our families, our group of friends, and the churches that were involved. Not only were we faced with choices that were severe and difficult to make, but these challenges continue to raise questions that we can't fully answer. The comfort we have is in the fact that we know enough of the tough questions were answered for us long before the tragic event, and though we do not like going through this difficult time, we can still praise God for many things.

We have found that God, who prepared our hearts over the years by giving us a factually based foundation, both in the Bible and scientific evidence, provides a deep, overflowing well from where we draw the pure living water that refreshes us when we traverse the sometimes difficult times in our lives. The experiences He has brought us through may be subjective and meaningful only to us, but when coupled with rock-solid testable, repeatable and observable, scientific evidence they intertwine to create a dynamic cord that cannot be broken, even by the most difficult test of our faith.

This is the difference I believe most people are thirsting for, but because some churches offer little more than dust or mud, the thirsty are turned away. We must offer answers to the tough questions, believing in a God who works miracles and offers both abundant life here on earth and, later, everlasting life.

Our main objective in this book is for each of the contributors to reveal the scientific and other evidence that transformed their perspective on science and faith in God. We believe that God has revealed Himself and His nature through His creation. The skeptics dilemma is, in order for a person to be skeptical of God as creator, he must become a true believer in something else, and that is why evolution is for them virtually a religious faith.

There exists a vacuous argument that claims belief in creation is not scientific. This argument is refuted by an examination of scientific facts. The accounts in this book show that, if one allows for the possibility of a Creator God and His Word and the Bible is true, then not only can answers be found to the tough questions, but also a transformed life results.

Why do we Resist Transformation?

Even if you're already a solid believer in the person and work of Jesus Christ, you are likely to find this book personally transformational. We live in a hostile, dangerous world full of traps, many of which seem quite innocent on the surface, but underneath lie trouble. As I edited the testimonies, my eyes were opened to the areas of my life where I have resisted His transforming power. It is these ingrained habits and gray areas that are the most difficult to extract from our lives. They are like near neutral genetic mutations that accumulate and, as a set, eventually cause problems. As some note, "When God uses your wife—or someone else—as a mouthpiece, why do you get annoyed?"

One of the reasons why evolution is appealing is that it does not make any such demands. Evolutionary change is due to chance, random mutations, the outworking of natural law, plus time, lots of time. But since God created us for His purpose, He wants the best for us, and that normally means we must be willing to let go of the things that do not meet His ideals. If we have spent a lot of time, study, and money on a belief, change is hard to achieve. If a person publishes an opinion based on an incorrect premise, its change is resisted, a condition that is difficult to eradicate. The accounts in this book are about those who have used their scientific training in support of receiving the transforming power of Jesus Christ.

How about you? Perhaps you have one or two questions you haven't been able to answer that cause you to stumble in your Christian walk. Perhaps you are not ready to receive all that God has available for you because you cannot move past these questions. The hope is that our experiences in seeking answers will not only encourage you in your faith, but will also transform your life.

Why Educated People Reject the Darwinian Worldview

Dr. Jerry Bergman gives an overview of the testimonies in this book and examines the reasons why intelligent people reject the Darwinian worldview.

As I edited these testimonies, several themes stood out. One was the positive change that resulted in the lives of those who accepted the creation worldview. This change often involved, not just a new view of origins, but also a change that positively affected their goals and even one's relationships with family and friends. Another theme was the fact that rejecting, or even questioning, evolution often resulted in intolerance by dogmatic atheists and fundamentalist Darwinists. When these factions reared their ugly head persecution commonly began.

The testimonies included in this volume were those of persons who have studied both sides of the creation-evolution issue, and concluded that the creation worldview had the edge, not only based on the facts of science, but also for other reasons. To sort out the reasons is no easy task and, as true of any worldview, many reasons always exist, some of which even the persons themselves cannot always clearly articulate because, in the end, personal reasons dominate.

Most of the subjects in this collection were college educated, and many had graduate degrees. Most were professionals, and many were college professors, teachers or scientists. All of them put a great deal of thought into making their decision, a concern because they were forced to go against, not only the scientific consensus, but also the academic and secular media consensuses. In addition, of the over 50 court cases fought over this question since the Scopes trial, the courts have, in every case without exception, sided with those who held the Darwinian worldview. It is not easy to buck the system. The main things we have on our side are the scientific facts, and I do not make this assertion lightly.

I have taught biology, genetics, chemistry, biochemistry, anthropology, geology, and microbiology at the college level for over 43 years. I was a research associate in the department of experimental pathology at the Medical College of Ohio, and taught at the University of Toledo for six years and for seven years at Bowing Green State University. I am also a graduate of the Medical College of

Ohio, Wayne State University in Detroit, The University of Toledo, and Bowling Green State University. In addition, I have completed 40 graduate hours in the department of chemistry at Miami University in Oxford Ohio, and studied geology, philosophy, nutrition, and chemistry at the University of Wisconsin, Madison, Wisconsin. I have, so far, earned nine degrees.

My conclusions have been published in over 940 publications, mostly in the science area, in 12 languages and 32 books and monographs. My work has been published by Houghton Mifflin, Greenwood Press, Syracuse University Press, Columbia University Press, Prometheus Books, and the State University of New York University Press. I was also a consultant for over 20 science textbooks, mostly in the area of biology and biochemistry.

In addition, I have presented over one hundred scientific papers at professional and community meetings in the United States, Canada, Europe, and Africa. To discuss my research, I have been a frequent guest on radio and television programs. My research has made the front page in newspapers throughout the country four times, has been featured by the Paul Harvey Show several times, and has been discussed by David Brinkley, Chuck Colson, and other nationally known commentators.

I have been listed in *Marquis Who's Who in the Midwest* since 1992 *Marquis Who's Who in America* since 2000, in *Marquis Who's Who in Education* since the 6th Edition, *Marquis Who's Who in Science and Engineering* since the 8th edition, *Marquis Who's Who in Medicine and Health Care* since 2005, and *Who's Who in Theology and Science*, and *Who's Who in America*. I had the honor of being selected by my students for *Who's Who Among America's Teachers* for the years 2000 and 2005.

I will now attempt to summarize below what I have concluded from my over 40 years research. Evolution is rarely defined, so to insure readers know what we are talking about, evolution, as used in this book, is defined as follows:

> Evolution has produced one species who has the need to take a look around and wonder where it came from. Fellow humans, how did we get here? Charles Darwin compiled mountains of evidence to demonstrate how all living creatures are connected, how each species ends up with unique defining features that distinguish each from every other, and through the process of selection, this wonderful precision and diversity emerges with no one in charge of the design. Chance mutation, competition, and evaluation, the fittest possibilities surviving—this is what makes for multifarious and infinite living world. The genius of the idea of evolution is that so simple a process can explain so much (Rothenberg, 2011, p. 3).[1]

---

1   Page 3 in David Rothenberger. 2011. *Survival of the Beautiful: Art, Science, and Evolution.* New York, NY: Bloomsbury Press.

In short, evolution is from goo to people by way of the zoo purely by natural forces such as gravity, electromagnetic force and time, enormous amounts of time. Another definition shows that Darwinism is directly connected to materialism

Well-known philosopher Harry A. Overstreet wrote that materialism had

> its roots in the science of the late 19th century, and … began with the publication of Darwin's "Origin of Species." Materialism, or the belief that matter … is the sole type of existence in the universe … was backed by all the contemporary science of the late 19th century. Its main support was, however, derived from the inductive investigations on biology and psychology[2]

He wrote that, in order

> to explain the whole process of development that has led from the amoeba to man, including also the development of intelligence in man, they found it necessary to invoke neither mind nor purpose, neither creative force nor divine agency; they relied solely upon the operation of natural forces. Darwin ascribed the development to chance variations of which the fittest survived.[3]

The Foundation of Evolution, Mutations, Has been Falsified

Close to thirty years ago I would have bristled at a book title such as *Darwinian Evolution: Science Fiction*. After studying this issue in depth for forty years, and having taught biology for as long, I now agree with this title. The simple fact is, from all we know about physics, chemistry and biology, evolution - defined as the upward progression from simple molecules, such as carbon, oxygen, hydrogen and water, to humans - never could have happened, and never did happen.

Survival of the Fittest and Arrival of the Fittest

It is obvious that life more fit to survive will be more likely to survive. The problem with evolution has never been the survival of the fittest, but the arrival of the fittest and this is still by far the most serious problem today with Darwinism. The main theory of the source of phenotype variations for natu-

---

2   Page 2375 in Harry Overstreet. 1944. "The Philosophy of Materialism," pp. 2875-2877 in Volume 5 of *The Popular Educator Library*. New York: National Educational Alliance Incorporated.
3   Page 2375 in Harry Overstreet. 1944. "The Philosophy of Materialism," pp. 2875-2877 in Volume 5 of *The Popular Educator Library*. New York: National Educational Alliance Incorporated.

ral selection to select from is macro-mutations. Professor Richard Mayer wrote that

> evolution by natural selection…is not predetermined. It is heavily dependent on the variations to be found between members of the species. All variations between species and between individual members of species can ultimately be sourced to random mutations. In effect, whenever a mutation occurs, it is checked for effectiveness with effective mutations leaving more offspring and ineffective mutations leaving fewer or even no offspring.[4]

The late Harvard Professor, Ernst Mayr, wrote that "Ultimately, all variation is due to mutation" The late Professor Theodosius Dobzhansky wrote "mutation is the only source of the raw materials... and hence of evolution"[5] and added that "mutation... is only the source of the raw materials of evolutionary change... Without mutation all evolution would eventually stop."[6]

Evolution True, but Going the Wrong Way

Research has shown the vast majority of mutations, over 99.99 percent, are either near neutral, mildly deleterious or clearly harmful.[7] As one cell biologist concluded "some years ago it was discovered that human DNA has a high mutation rate and is deteriorating at an alarming rate."[8] The result is a steady accumulation of damage to the genome, eventually causing genetic catastrophe, then mutational meltdown and species extinction. As Lynch and Blanchard wrote

> It is well established on theoretical grounds that the accumulation of mildly deleterious mutations in nonrecombining genomes is a major extinction risk in obligate asexual populations. Sexual populations can also incur mutational deterioration in genomic regions that experience little or no recombination, i.e., autosomal regions near centromeres, Y chromosomes, and organelle genomes.[9]

In each new generation of humans an estimated 100 to 200 new mutations are added to the human gene pool.[10] Professor Michael Lynch et al., wrote "a parent can never produce an offspring with fewer deleterious mutations than

---

4   Mayer, 2005, p. 23
5   1957, p. 385.
6   1974, p. 315
7   Aims and Gold, 2002
8   Beardsley, 1990, p. 32, 36
9   1998, p. 29
10   Meisenberg, and Simmons, 2008, p. 153

it carries itself."[11] The number of new harmful mutations varies, but they always increase and never decrease. Darwin was correct when he titled his 1871 book *The Descent of Man* and not *The Ascent of Man,* which, incidentally, was the title of evolutionist Jacob Bronowski's book on human evolution. The fact is, we are descending genetically as the Scriptures teach, and not ascending upward biologically, as evolutionism claims. For this reason evolution is true, but is going the wrong way, as Judaism and Christianity has taught since almost the beginning of humankind's sojourn on earth.

A History of Macro-Mutation Theory Failure

Lamarckianism remained strong long after Darwin died, especially among paleontologists. It was the strongest around 1900 when Dutch botanist Hugo De Vries (1848-1935) proposed "mutation theory as a plausible ... explanation for the evolution of species." The problem was

> Classical Darwinism seemed discredited, because it had no mechanism for preserving variations. ...Lamarckianism was discredited by the work of August Weissmann. What was the alternative? Biologists all over Europe and America were scrabbling to try to come up with some answer. If you read scientific papers from this period, you'll just see them struggling with what possibly could be the cause of variation and inheritance, and therefore, evolution. How could the whole process work? "We believe in evolution, but we really don't have a clue of what mechanism is plausible." [12]

The result was De Vries "came up with a possible solution, and that was mutation theory" which also had "its problems" but in the 1900s every evolution theory

> had its problems. People were looking for alternatives. ...De Vries proposed a rather radical solution. He proposed that mutations ... would be so significant, the mutations... so discontinuous, that they would create a big "jump;" ... not slightly better talons, but dramatically better talons, dramatically changed eyes; dramatic changes. That was implausible enough, but then he added that they would be widespread enough to happen throughout a population, or at least a significant minority in a population.[13]

---

11   1995, p. 1067.
12   Larson, 2002, pp. 108-109
13   Larson, 2002, pp. 108-109

The result was the

affected population would almost abruptly form a breeding population of a new variety of species. These seem like broad claims, and they were … To him, natural selection still existed, but it really wasn't central. For him, it operated mostly to preserve beneficial mutations. Interest soon passed among scientists.[14]

Professor Hugo De Vries first demonstrated from his research on the evening primrose that, in his words, dramatic new life varieties and traits can arise suddenly and without explanation.[15] He and others believed that the explanation for the new traits was macro-mutations that finally gave evolutionists a mechanism for producing new genetic traits in plants and animals.

Further research found that De Vries' results were not due to mutations, but rather were a result of the fact that the evening primrose has an unequal chromosome number that caused hybrid plants to *appear* to produce new varieties. In fact, a rearrangement of existing genetic variation was the cause of the plant's putative new physical appearance, not mutations as De Vries postulated. Larson noted that: "It created an initial stir in mutation theory, but within half a generation, interest in mutation theory had pretty well passed. It left a legacy and influence however.[16]

Early Opposition to Mutation Theory

The opposition to the mutation theory as the origin of variation for natural selection to select from has a long and complex history. As early as 1925 Harvard University Biology Professor Edward Jeffery recognized that mutations could not be a significant source of new genetic varieties. He wrote that for

two decades the hypothesis of mutation or the salutatory origin of species has enjoyed a large vogue in America biological laboratories… First formulated… as the result of the investigations of the Dutch physiologist, De Vries, on Lamarck's evening primrose, *Oenthera lamarckina*. In this species De Vries … observed the appearance of a relatively small number of [new] forms from seed, which differed in marked degree from the parent species.[17]

---

14   Larson, 2002, pp. 108-109
15   De Vries, 1910
16   2002, p. 109
17   Jeffery, 1925, p. 3

Jeffery carefully researched this example, finding that the variety produced was not due to mutations or "salutatory" evolutionary jumps as De Vries proposed, but rather it is now "conceded, even by geneticists and physiologists, that the species of the genus Oenothera … [is] of hybrid origin, and the mutability frequently found in their offspring receives its obvious explanation as the result of previous crossing."[18]

Jeffery added that "It has since become increasingly obvious … that large numbers of species of plants are of hybrid origin and that these hybrid species, as well as known hybrids, give rise" to phenomena exactly similar to those found in Oenothera and Drosophila.[19] Professor Jeffery concluded from examining several hundred divisions of the *D. melanogaster* spermatocytes that the "cytological investigation of *Drosophila melanogaster* seems accordingly to establish beyond any reasonable doubt that the species is hybrid origin."[20]

Thus, neither case was an example of new species due to mutations, but simply common hybrids of existing species. Jeffery concluded in 1925 that the mutation theory is dead, and in the future this theory will be an embarrassment to science:

> The Morgan hypothesis of mutation based on the study of *Drosophila mela-nogaster* by contrast runs counter to practically all the inductive conclusions of the biological sciences… science appears to warrant no expectation of long life for the mutation hypothesis. It is, moreover, inconceivable that a science… should itself progress by unreasoning revolution and the subversion of the fundamentals of the biological sciences. It is in fact not impossible that before many years have elapsed the doctrine of mutation will appear to the eyes of men as fantastic Fanta Morgana.[21]

Unfortunately, Dr. Jeffery's prediction about the demise of the mutation doctrine, although fully valid, has not yet come true after almost 100 years of new research has verified his conclusions. This is in spite of the fact that the evidence is now overwhelming that mutations did not, and cannot, evolve simple organic compounds into people. Evolution by mutations is accepted in spite of the fact that no other hypothesis has been able to replace the mutation theory, thus it has not yet suffered the fate that Professor Jeffery has predicted.

---

18   Jeffery, 1925, p. 4
19   Jeffery, 1925, pp. 4-5
20   Jeffery, 1925, pp. 4-5
21   Jeffery, 1925, p. 25

Hopeful Monsters

The macro-mutations theory was briefly resurrected in the 1940s by University of California Berkeley geneticist Richard Goldschmidt. Goldschmidt concluded that the origin of major new animal and plant varieties was due to single mutations that caused large and complex changes which happened to produce more successful life forms than those without these new macro-mutations. Such creatures Goldschmidt called "hopeful monsters."

Research has now confirmed that large mutations do not produce hopeful monsters but rather hopeless monsters as a result of causing major genetic damage. Since then no satisfactory mechanism to produce progressive upward molecules to human evolution by macro-mutations has been proposed by modern neo-Darwinists.

The fact is, as Darwin's son Leonard Darwin wrote, "how evolution ... came about is still a matter of dispute and is likely to remain so for some time."[22] Jeffery is correct, and Leonard Darwin's conclusion is still fully valid today.

The Altenberg Conference

Presentations at the famous Altenberg 16 Conference by 16 of the worlds leading evolutionists admitted the fact "that the theory of evolution which most biologists accept and which is taught in the classrooms today, is inadequate in explaining our existence."[23] Altenberg 16 attendee, evolutionist Dr. Jerry Fodor, added, "I don't think anybody knows how evolution works."[24]

Stanford University Biophysicist Howard Pattee, referring to natural selection and chemical evolution, wrote that evolution could not have begun from random molecules nor DNA sequences as evolutionism, then and now, teaches.[25] All of the other mechanisms postulated to cause macro-evolution have also been falsified. Thus, the main mechanism of producing genetic variety required for evolution, random mutation, has also been falsified.

The more rational evolutionists have known for years that neo-Darwinism cannot work, but have been reluctant to openly say so. It is becoming increasingly difficult for them to suggest a mechanism for evolution that would not imply, or point to, intelligent design. Mutations have failed as a source of genetic variation used to produce phenotype variation, and, as discussed, this fact was

---

22   Quoted in Miller, 1925, p. 43
23   Quoted in Mazur, 2010, p. 29.
24   Quoted in Mazur, 2010, p. 24
25   1961, p. 683.

known as early as 1925. In 2012 the distinguished Professor of Biological Sciences, Austin Hughes, wrote that of

> all the fads and foibles in the long history of human credulity, scientism in all its varied guises—from fanciful cosmology to evolutionary epistemology and ethics—seems among the more dangerous, both because it pretends to be something very different from what it really is and because it has been accorded widespread and uncritical adherence. Continued insistence on the universal competence of science will serve only to undermine the credibility of science as a whole. The ultimate outcome will be an increase of radical skepticism that questions the ability of science to address even the questions legitimately within its sphere of competence. One longs for a new Enlightenment to puncture the pretensions of this latest superstition.[26]

A conversation recounted by Victoria University Adjunct Biology Professor John Ashton summarized the modern state of affairs. He wrote, while sitting around the lunch table with his colleagues, he

> asked the research scientist in charge of the plant-breeding project a question. "Do mutations ever give rise to new purposeful genetic information?" His answer was immediate. "Of course—yes!" "Can you give me an example?" I then asked. He thought for a moment and replied along the lines of "Um, I can't think of a specific example right now but ask our geneticist … he will be able to." Later that afternoon I caught up with the senior genetics researcher in the university plant-breeding department and asked him the same question. His reply was just as quick, but the very opposite! "Never!" Surprised, I pressed him further. He explained that mutations always lead to damaged DNA, which usually results in the *loss* of genetic information. He knew of *no* instances where new purposeful genetic information arose, either by a natural process or through a mutation induced chemically or with radiation.[27]

The Problem with Extrapolating Microevolution to Macroevolution

We now know that far more then a few mutations are required to produce the changes required to evolve a new animal order—actually many hundreds or thousands would usually be required. Many evolutionists today postulate that a large number of very small mutations, and not the macro-mutations that De

---

26   2012, p. 50
27   Ashton, 2012, pp. 15-16.

Vries and Goldschmidt postulated, can account for macro-evolution. This conclusion is not based on experimental evidence, but on the assumption that the evidence for micro-evolution (which creationists call variation within the genesis kinds) can be extrapolated to macro-evolution.

The empirical evidence, however, is clear—neither macro-mutations nor micro-mutations can provide a significant source of new genetic information: The fact is "Mutation accumulation does not lead to new species or even to new organs or tissues."[28]

What mutations eventually lead to is sickness and death because, as noted, the vast majority, over 99.99 percent, are near neutral or harmful. Professor Lynn Margulis, when president of Sigma Xi, the honor society for scientists, added that "many biologists claim they know for sure that *random mutation* (purposeless chance) is the source of inherited variation that generates new species of life… No I say."[29] The question now asked is "Due to "Contamination of Genome by Very Slightly Deleterious Mutations: Why Have We Not Died 100 Times Over?"[30]

Both Creationists and Intelligent Design advocates conclude that the only plausible source of genetic information is intelligence. Because the estimated 100 to 200 new mutations that are added to the offspring, compared to the parents, 99.99 percent are near neutral or harmful, Intelligent Design postulates only an intelligent source of genetic information can explain what exists in the natural world. Creationists conclude the source is an Intelligent Creator we call God.

In contrast to the facts, contemporary evolutionary theory involves primarily the accumulation of genetic mistakes called mutations that are selected by natural selection. They believe that, in essence, the evolution of humans from molecules such as carbon, hydrogen, water, and nitrogen, occurred by the accumulation of DNA copying mistakes and mutations. Thus, humans are the result of the accumulation of many billions of mistakes. As noted, the problem has always been the vast majority of mutations are near neutral or harmful, even lethal, causing disease, including cancer and about 5,000 other diseases.

One study of 15, 336 genes from 6,515 individuals concluded that, given Darwinistic assumptions, 73 percent of the protein coding single nucleotide variants and about 86 percent of these predicted to be deleterious arose in the past 5 to 10 thousand years.[31] Thus, the human genome is rapidly accumulating deleterious mutations that has a "profound effect" on increasing the burden of deleterious single nucleotide variants in humans.[32]

---

28   Margulis and Sagan, 2002, p. 11
29   Margulis and Sagan, 2002, p. 11
30   Kondrashov, 1995, p. 583.
31   Fu, et al,. 2013, p. 216.
32   Fu, et al,. 2013, p. 216

Conclusion

Evolution is true, but the clear trend is, it is going the wrong way. The problem is the vast majority of mutations are near neutral, i.e., mildly deleterious, and most of the rest are worse. Life is gradually accumulating these deleterious mutations and is facing genetic catastrophe and mutational meltdown, eventually causing extinction. The fact is, never did a

> mutation make a wing, a fruit, a woody stem, or a claw appear. Mutations, in summary, tend to induce sickness, death, or deficiencies. No evidence in the vast literature of heredity changes shows unambiguous evidence that random mutation itself, even with geographical isolation of populations, leads to speciation.[33]

Over 5,000 genetic diseases are now known and the number is growing for several reasons, one of which is the accumulation of deleterious mutations. As Professor Ashton wrote "What we observe in research laboratories today is DNA deteriorating, not new DNA evolving. This means we actually observe the very opposite of evolution.[34] The evidence is clear: evolution is true, but it is going backward.

---

33   Margulis and Sagan, 2003, p. 29
34   2012, p 132.

References

Ames, Bruce and Lois Gold. 2000. "Paracelsus to parascience: the environmental cancer distraction." *Mutation Research*. 447:3-13

Ashton, John. 2012. *Evolution Impossible: 12 Reasons Why Evolution Cannot Explain the Origin of Life on Earth*. Green Forest, AR: Master Books.

Ayala, Francisco José. Theodosius Grigorievich Dobzhansky. 1974. *Studies in the Philosophy of Biology: Reduction and Related Problems*.

Beardsley, T. 1999. "Mutations Galore: Humans Have High Mutation Rates. But Why Worry?" *Scientific American*, 208 (4) 32,36.

Darwin, Charles. 1871. *The Descent of Man*. London: John Murray.

De Vries, Hugo. 1910. *The Mutation Theory. Experiments and Observations on the Origin of Species in the Vegetable Kingdom. Vol. 2 The Origin of Varieties by Mutation*. Chicago, IL: The Open Court Publishing Company.

Dobzhansky, Theodosius. 1957 "On Methods of Evolutionary Biology and Anthropology." *American Scientist*, 45(5):381-392. December.

Fu, Wenqing, Timothy D. O'Connor, Goo Jun, Hyun Min Kang, Goncalo Abecasis, Suzanne M. Leal, Stacey Gabriel, David Altshuler, Jay Shendure, Deborah A. Nickerson, Michael J. Bamshad, NHLBI Exome Sequencing Project, and Joshua M. Akey. 2013. "Analysis of 6,515 Exomes Reveals the Recent Origin of Most Human Protein-Coding Variants." *Nature*, 493:216-220, January 10.

Hughes, Austin L. 2012. The Folly of Scientism. *The New Atlantis; Journal of Technology and Society*. pp. 32-50. Fall.

Jeffrey, Edward. 1925. "Drosophila and the Mutation Hypothesis". *Science*. July 3, G2 (1592): 3-5.

Kondrashov, Alexey. 1995. "Contamination of the genome by very slightly deleterious mutations: Why have we not died 100 times over?" *Journal of Theoretical Biology*. 175:583-594.

Larson, Edward. 2002. *The Theory of Evolution: A History of Controversy*. Chantilly, VA: The Teaching Company.

Lynch, Michael; John Conery; Reinhard Burger. 1995. "Mutational Meltdowns in Sexual Populations." *Evolution*, 49(6):1067-1080.

Lynch, Michael and Jeffrey L. Blanchard. 1998. Deleterious mutation accumulation in organelle genomes. *Genetica* 102/103: 29–39.

Margulis, Lynn. 2006. "The Phylogenetic Tree Topples" *American Scientist*. May-June Vol 94:194.

Margulis, Lynn and Dorion Sagan. 2008. *Acquiring Genomes: A Theory of the Origin of Species*.

New York: Basic Books

Mayr, Ernst. In Moorehead, Paul S. and Martin M. Kaplan, eds., 1967. *Mathematical Challenges to the Neo-Darwinian Interpretation of Evolution.* Philadelphia: Wistar.

Mayer, Richard E. 2005. *The Cambridge Handbook of Multimedia Learning.* New York Cambridge University Press.

Mazur, Suzan. 2010. *The Altenberg 16: An Exposé of the Evolution Industry.* Berkeley, CA: North Atlantic Books.

Meisenberg, Gerhard and William Simmons. 2006. *Principles of Medical Biochemistry.* Philadelphia, PA: Mosby.

Miller, Arthur. 1925. "Evolution and Education in the Tennessee Trial." *Science.* July 17. 62(1591): 43.

Pattee, Howard. 1961. "On the Origin of Macromolecular Sequences." *Journal of Biophysics.* 1(8):683.

A Zealous Atheist and Evolutionist

By Tom DeRosa[35]

Richard D. Lumsden Ph.D was Professor Emeritus of Parasitology and Cell Biology and Dean of the Tulane University Graduate School. He has a B.S. and M.S. in Zoology from Tulane University, was awarded a traineeship in Cell Biology at Harvard, earned a PhD. in Biology from Rice University, and was a Post-Doctoral Research Fellowship in Medical Pathology from Tulane University School of Medicine. He received over 21 Research Grants and contracts, including from the National Institutes of Health, The National Science Foundation, and the FDA, trained 30 Ph.D.s., was the winner of the highest award for his parasitology research, published some 90 peer-reviewed scientific papers, mostly in parasitological journals, often describing new species, and presented over 100 program abstracts. He was awarded the Henry Baldwin Ward medal, the highest award in parasitology.

The Challenge

If Dr. Richard Lumsden's (1938–1997) biography was on a theater marquee, it would read, "A Zealous Atheist and Evolutionist." In 1986, Professor Lumsden decided to use the last lecture in a course he was teaching that semester to launch a direct assault on Creationism. He did this in retaliation for the Louisiana state law, that would later be declared unconstitutional, requiring that Creationism be taught alongside evolution. Lumsden had been angry with God for a long time, and this law caused him to rant that it was an act of "stupidity" and evil. Now, armed with his evolutionary biology, he was going to use the lecture hall to declare war on the God of Creation. He would show that, without any doubt, evolution was the absolute truth. In his own words, "I mentioned Genesis with all the mockery, sarcasm and cynicism I could bear, quoting Darwin and others with the fervor of a Baptist minister attempting to demolish everything that had to do with the God of Creation." After the lecture, he received a standing ovation of appreciation;

35   Professor DeRosa is now Executive Director and Founder of Creation Studies Institute. 1-800-882-0278 info@creationstudies.org. Their website is www.creationstudies.org. Dr. Lumsden's testimony can be found at www.creationstudies.org/Education/seed_of_indoctrination.html

however, he had no idea that his world, consisting of evolution, atheism, and his ingrained Darwinian philosophy, would be turned upside down that same day.

After the lecture, he was approached by a young lady with a yellow legal pad. "Doc, Doc, Doc, terrific lecture! Doc, I have a bunch of questions that I would like to ask you." He had high regard for her because she was his top "A" student for that year. In his own words, "I was flattered with this student's positive approach," so he agreed on a time to meet in his office. Perhaps her positive approach led him to think she was going to applaud him for his impassioned statements made during the lecture and he felt it was his obligation to spend time with her. Maybe the questions she posed would be supportive of his anti-creationism stand.

She was also an excellent student, and an excellent prospect for graduate school. He dutifully made an appointment that afternoon. When she appeared punctually at his office, she had a yellow legal pad filled with questions and a stack of reference books in tow. He had no idea that this meeting would last over three hours and would transform his life forever.

Eloquently Making a Case

She came prepared with thoughtful science questions and a strategy to avoid going down the emotional pathway of the creation vs. evolution debate. There was too much at stake. It was evident from the morning lecture that Lumsden was vested, heart and soul, in evolution. For this reason, she decided to preempt any argument by stating, "Doc, I don't want to present an argument about today's lecture this morning; I just want to get my science straight." In a previous Evolutionary Biology course, where she was also an "A" student, as reported by her professor, she "drove her professor nuts" on the issue of evolution being scientific. She was so academically skilled that she would go on to study medicine and become a medical missionary.

She challenged him with questions that were qualified by research in the pertinent literature and relevant to the courses she was taking. Basically, Lumsden had to validate what he taught that morning and, more importantly, his approach to biology and the very core of his life's philosophy. If you believe you are a product of chance, then there is little or no meaning to life. However, if you are a product of design by a Creator, then there is very clear purpose for life.

She started going down a long list of questions on her legal pad with the first question dealing with the origin of life. At that time, it was believed that life came from inert lifeless particles of earth called amino acids, and that they could assemble themselves into the building blocks of life called proteins. Not many realized that the basic chemical equations found in the textbooks that were used by Lumsden and many others did not work. In fact, these formulas defied the laws of chemistry. This astute student pointed this out to Lumsden and it was very difficult for him to defend. Why were these incorrect formulas in the textbooks and why were so many scientists continuing to use these reactions to explain the origin of life? The answer lies in their deep blind faith in evolution. If you state unequivocally that evolution began from inert matter and all the laws of chemistry and physics negate that possibility, then no explanation apart from divine intervention can explain it. Lumsden had known there was a problem here, but like so many others, he simply overlooked it, because of his evolutionary indoctrination.

Even though she basically dismantled the professor's morning lecture, she did not stop there. The molecules-to-man scenario has been doomed since its inception. It is refuted by the very laws of chemistry and physics that are foundational to all of the sciences. With the utmost respect for her professor, she steadfastly moved on to the area of probability. Being a math minor in college, she demonstrated clearly that these preliminary particles, amino acids, could not just randomly come together to build a living organism. She impressed the professor with her mathematics and the conclusions were clear. It would be impossible for life to come into existence by chance. She came prepared with the scientific literature that cited the statistical improbabilities of producing life from the materials found in soil.

One of those sources was Cambridge University's eminent astronomer and mathematician, Fred Hoyle. He is famous for comparing the evolutionary origin of life to a tornado sweeping through a junkyard and assembling a fully operational Boeing 747 from the materials therein. In the scientific journal, "The New Scientist," in November 1981, Hoyle compared the statistical probability of life arising by purely natural processes by using the analogy of a blind person solving a Rubik's cube puzzle. He wrote, "Now imagine 10^{50} blind persons, each with a scrambled Rubik's cube, and try to conceive of the chance of them all simultaneously arriving at the solved form."

Simply stated, the possibility of life being formed from the inert particles called amino acids would be like the chances of that number of blind people, essentially equaling twice the number of stars in the universe with all of them simultaneously solving the Rubik's cube. Such a statistical improbability brings us to the evident conclusion again, that the evolution of life on earth is impossible to the highest degree.

As the young student meticulously used the sword of science to shred away the professor's evolutionary philosophy, she then took aim at beneficial mutations. She reminded him of what he said in a previous class, "Doc, you mentioned most mutations are destructive to the species, then how does it cause evolution." A mutation is a change in the deoxyribonucleic acid (DNA) code that can result in missing or malformed proteins that may lead to disease. One such genetic mutation causes sickle cell anemia (SSA). This type of anemia is a multigenerational disease that has its origin in Africa. It causes a person's red bloods cells to become stiff, sticky, susceptible to rupture, and far less permeable than normally flexible biconcave-shaped red cells. This distortion gives the red blood cells their typical crescent moon appearance. When sickling occurs, they can block blood flow in the smaller blood vessels called capillaries. An attack causes severe pain, depriving tissues and organs of oxygen-rich blood, and can lead to serious organ damage, especially in the lungs, kidneys, spleen and brain.

In countries without advanced medical facilities, sickle cell disease is often a fatal hemoglobinopathy. It is considered a "beneficial" mutation, because people with the sickle cell trait (carriers as well as those with the disease) do have some increased protection against malarial infection. The decreased permeability in their red blood cell's membrane makes those cells more resistant to invasion by the malarial parasite. Is sickle cell anemia really beneficial to the human race? No, this mutation can be lethal. Is having the "trait" really beneficial? Perhaps it is to you, but not to your children. Two parents with the trait are destined to pass the trait on to three out of four of their children, with the fourth inheriting the deadly form of SSA. That cannot be considered beneficial by anyone's definition. If one parent has the disease and the other is a carrier, the morbidity rate for your children increases to 50 percent and the remaining 50 percent becoming carriers.

It cannot be truly beneficial if you might escape a malarial infection, only to die from SSA. Losing information never benefits the original overall design of any organism. This is what we observe today as many different species have become extinct. Lumsden could easily identify with this example, because he was recognized for his work on organisms like the female Anopheles mosquito, the genus that carries the malarial parasite.

The Humbled Professor

After three hours, the student graciously thanked him, but he was intellectually devastated. The altar Lumsden had built for evolution had been demolished. He described the experience as follows, "It was worse than the oral defense for his doctrinal dissertation." For the first time, he heard himself answering those questions and realized how void of science evolution truly was. According to Lumsden, evolution was "a bankrupt theory" worse than any pseudoscience or science fiction.

For the first time, he was being truly challenged. If evolution was not the answer, he would be faced with the only alternative, other than a race of creator-aliens, and that was God. After a year, his daughter invited him to church and he accepted Christ as his Savior. In his own words, "With flesh protesting every inch of the way, I found myself walking forward, down to the altar. And there, I found God! Truly, at that moment, I came to know Him, and received the Lord Jesus Christ as my Lord and Savior." That student who questioned him had prayed for all her professors, but she gave Lumsden special attention.

After becoming a new creature in Christ, it was difficult for Professor Lumsden to continue at Tulane University. His vocal conversion resulted in his expulsion from the science faculty. Soon after, he took a position as Director of Biology at the Institute of Creation Research and began teaching at the Master's College from 1990 to 1996. Dr. Lumsden went home to be with the Lord at age 59. He left a legacy of a vibrant professor who, especially at the end of his life, was always excited about God's glory as evidenced through His Creation.

Dangerous Indoctrination

One of the most revealing aspects in Dr. Lumsden's testimony is from early in his life. As a child who loved science and regularly attended Sunday school, he had numerous questions about apparent contradictions between science and the Bible. When he sought answers from his Sunday school teachers and pastors, they were not forthcoming. When he saw Adam and Eve being depicted as beautifully human in his Sunday school, he compared them with the gross pictures of prehistoric man found his textbook. Because the church never addressed his needs, he went with evolution. Lumsden defined this as the seed of indoctrination. Everything around him, in all the materials he read, the instruction in the classroom, the public media and almost everywhere else he looked, evolution was spoken as a fact. If God is censored out of the explanations, and the brainwashing mantra is constantly repeated, "everything comes from evolution," what else can you expect? The salient point was, as a youngster in church, his questions went unanswered. Rather than giving him the clear logic of God's Word and truly biblical answers, he was indoctrinated into a hostile atheistic worldview by which he was blinded to the truth of God.

We can't be idle when so many young lives are being taken hostage by the lie of evolution. I have written a book, *Evolution's Fatal Fruit: How Dar-*

win's Tree of Life Brought Death to Millions, in which I present Darwin, the man, and his dangerous theory of evolution. The book identifies Darwin's key disciples; men who were needed to carry and pass the torch of this dark lie to Hitler and others who would ultimately bring death to millions. Todd Friel, who has dynamic insight in these issues, has produced an exciting two DVD documentary series entitled, *What Hath Darwin Wrought?* This film chronicles the dreadful results of evolution's twisted ideas. It features Dr. John West, Dr. Richard Weikart and Dr. David Berlinski. This two-hour series will definitely open your eyes to the atrocities that evolution has brought, and continues to bring, on our society.

Evolution: The Origins Myth of our Age

The cosmology claims of evolutionism has been dominated by the Big Bang theory. Dr. Humphreys examined the evidence and compiled a long list of processes that favor an age for the earth much less than billions of years. Though he did not grow up in a Christian home and was taught evolution as fact, Dr. Humphreys changed his mind when he uncovered this evidence.

Every age of mankind has had its *origins myths*, stories by which people put themselves into the context of space and time. The Egyptians pictured their god Ra-Atum as emerging from a watery abyss long ages ago and making the world to ease his loneliness. The Vikings teach that the present world came from the body of the frost giant Ymir after Odin and his brothers killed him. The Greeks spoke of the goddess Gaia coming out of Chaos and bearing a son, Uranos, who shaped the earth into the form we know it today.

Myths about origins can mold the thought and culture of a nation. Here I am using the word "myth" in its oldest sense, that of an archetypal narrative that may or may not be true. Today the word also can imply falsity, as in "fable," so I will use the more neutral term "worldview." Since every adult has formulated some opinions about the world, we all live and think within a worldview of some sort. However, many persons may never consciously think about such things. The worldview we adopted as we grew up is simply the way things are, and many people never consider the possibility that their worldview might not be valid. Adopting a worldview is like putting on sunglasses; after getting used to the changed colors, we no longer consciously notice them.

For nearly two millennia, the Bible, including the account of creation in Genesis, shaped the prevailing worldview in the Western world. However, in the nineteenth century, the Western view of origins began to change. The psychologist C. G. Jung commented that most of his twentieth-century European patients were no longer seeing the world through the eyes of the Bible or Christianity, and that this was also true of him. But Jung knew that humans, including himself, cannot function without some kind of worldview, and so the old origins worldview must be replaced by a new one. He asked, "What is the myth through which I myself see the world?"

Though Jung was a perceptive thinker, he was not able to perceive one myth, evolutionism, which deeply shaped both his own thinking and that of the world around him. But once it is pointed out, it should be clear to any student of his writings and of modern history: the prevailing origins myth of our age is *evolutionism*.

Evolutionism and Its Various Forms

By "evolutionism" I mean the story that the world grew, or was developed, into its present state over a period of billions of years purely by natural law. The tale has several parts, physical science and life science, and there are several versions of each part. Here is an outline of the various versions of evolutionism.

For the past few decades, the physical science part of evolutionism has been dominated by the *Big Bang* theory. It pictures the cosmos as having evolved into its present galaxies, stars, and planets out of a cataclysmic explosion of space-time and matter-energy many eons ago. Some big-bang theorists are *naturalistic*; they do not want to even consider the possibility of any possible supernatural intervention. Others are *deistic*; they think that in the beginning some sort of deity put enough design into the natural laws of the cosmos for it to develop on its own by means of those laws. (more on deism below). Yet other Big Bang theorists are *theistic*; they believe that God frequently intervened to achieve the present degree of organization that we see in the physical cosmos.

The life science part of evolutionism has a greater diversity of versions, each clamoring for acceptance. The *Darwinists* portray the present complexity of the biological world as having emerged very gradually from non-living molecules during the last few billion years. *Punctuated equilibrium* theorists claim such evolution happened, not gradually, but in spurts during billions of years. Both versions are naturalistic, asserting that the emergence and development of life occurred by entirely natural processes without any help from a deity. Life "just happened" by a series of accidents, they claim.

A relatively scarce subspecies of biological evolutionists alleges that ages ago, a deity of some sort started up the cosmos, establishing physical laws and natural processes. After that, this group claims, the deity left the cosmos alone to evolve living things entirely by means of those natural processes. This "absentee landlord" view of a god is essentially the same as eighteenth-century deism, so I call this group of theorists *deistic evolutionists.*

Lately, a new movement called *intelligent design* theorists has rightly questioned the notion that life could ever come into existence, or develops upwards from single cells to humans by natural processes alone. They assert that great intelligence is required to design living things. This large umbrella group contains people with very diverse beliefs. Many of them still subscribe to physical and biological development of life during billions of years.

Among the long-age design theorists are many Christians. Some of them are *theistic evolutionists*, believing that the God of the Bible instigated and supervised gradual evolution. More recently some with similar beliefs call themselves *progressive creationists*; the main distinction is their assertion that God developed or created things, not gradually, but in spurts, during billions of years. The latter two views are variations of the old *day-age* theory, in which the days of Genesis chapter one were really long ages of time, millions or billions of years.

Gap theorists are yet another type of Christian design theorists, who say there was a "gap" of billions of years before the first Genesis day. While chapter one of Genesis does not explicitly mention such a gap, they assert that a gap is implicit in the passage somewhere between the first and fifth verses. An older version of the gap theory puts the formation of the fossil-bearing geologic layers into the gap, but a more recent version does not.

All the above origins theorists never seem to question one central claim: the supposed reality of the billions of years. Onto the framework of those assumed eons, they distribute the alleged events of physical and biological evolution. Included are the Big Bang theory, formation of stars, galaxies, and planets, then the appearance of early life on earth. Next, more complex life, such life being captured and preserved over millions of years as fossils in the geologic strata. The common denominator of these theories is the billion-year backdrop on which the various events are painted. Thus an essential element of the world's present origins myth is the notion of *long ages of time.*

Most of the Evidence Favors a Young World

You may have noticed that in a few of the paragraphs above I resumed using the word "myth" in spite of its negative connotations today. The reason is because the observed data have convinced me that the alleged billions of years claim is a modern fable, an incorrect myth. I once believed the myth myself — but what transformed my mind was the *scientific evidence*, not the Biblical evidence, although much exists.

Let us now survey that evidence. In three decades of study, I have found only a few hundred physical processes that one could use to estimate the age of the earth. I have been continually astounded by the fact that *over ninety percent of the processes favor an age much less than billions of years.* Here are a dozen examples of the 90 percent majority of evidence pointing to a young world along with brief explanations:

1. The rapid accumulation of **mud on the ocean floor**, versus the slow removal of it by plate tectonic subduction.

2. The presence of **carbon 14** well above the detection limit **in all fossils**, from those that are supposed to be 2 million years old down to the deepest, allegedly 560 million years old. Yet the decay half-life of carbon 5,730 years, is so short that no carbon 14 atoms would be left in any fossil that was more than a million years old. This is strong evidence that all the fossil-bearing geologic layers are only thousands, not millions, of years old

3. The great excess of **helium** still retained **in** tiny radioactive **zircon crystals** in the granite of the earth's crust, where the helium is formed by the emission of alpha particles from atomic nuclei. The helium diffusion age of deep-core samples of these zircons turned out to be 6000 (± 2000) years.

4. The rapid accumulation of **sodium in the sea,** versus its slow removal by various processes, such as the evaporation of shallow seas.

5. The rapid decay of the energy stored in the **earth's magnetic field**, especially during the periods of very rapid direction reversals recorded in geologic strata.

6. Evidence throughout the geologic strata of very rapid deposition of **continent-scale sedimentary rocks** by waters moving at meters per second — the results of a worldwide catastrophic flood. Nowhere on earth are such events happening today.

7. Many **multiple-layer fossils** worldwide, such as fossil trees projecting through two or more strata. Conventional geology says a tree should rot away long before a second layer buries it.

8. **Fossil "graveyards"** of billions of creatures buried in the sedimentary geologic strata throughout the world. Nothing like that is happening today.

9. Evidence for **tight folding and bending** of large geologic strata while they were still wet and soft (during the Genesis flood).

10. The presence of **DNA and soft tissue**, even **in fossils** that are allegedly hundreds of millions of years old. An example is blood vessels and blood cells found in the marrow of a Tyrannosaurus Rex leg bone that is allegedly 70 million years old.

11. The extreme **scarcity** (thousands) **of stone-age burial sites** compared to the abundance (billions) of sites that should exist if the Stone Age had lasted 100,000 years or more.

12. The **recentness of agriculture and recorded history**, and the dispersion of people, civilization, and languages from a small region in the Middle East.

Explanation and documentation for all but items 7 and 8 are in a June 2005 *Impact* article, "Evidence for a Young World," that I wrote for the Institute for Creation Research.[36] Remember, *most* of the evidence favors a young world. All of this evidence can be found scattered throughout secular scientific literature, but rarely with its young-world significance pointed out. As far as I know, secular news and secular scientific media have never publicized such evidence, and certainly not its implications. As a consequence, the public, and even most scientists, are unaware of most of this data — especially the fact that such data are the rule, not the exception.

However, many thousands of scientists worldwide, including myself, have been convinced by these evidences that has transformed our thinking. The usual name for us is "young-earth creationist." I prefer the term "young-world creationist," or simply *creationist*.

Evidence for an Old World is in the Minority

At first glance, less than ten percent of the several hundred processes seem to support the long-age chronology of today's origins myth. Dating methods based on those processes are familiar to many people because the secular news media have widely publicized them. Most of them fall into two classes:

(A) **Radiometric** (nuclear decay) methods, such as carbon-14, potassium-argon, rubidium-strontium, uranium-lead, etc.

(B) **Cosmological** methods, such as how long it might take light from distant galaxies to reach us.

---

36   available online at http://www.icr.org/article/evidence-for-young-world. For items 7 and 8, see the list of articles on the Genesis flood at http://creation.com/noahs-flood-questions-and-answers. For a list of 101 items of young-world evidence, along with explanations and references see http://creation.com/age-of-the-earth.

Clearly, the first-glance implications of the majority and the minority of the data cannot both be correct. Either the world is billions of years old, or it is not. Of course we should examine all the data for loopholes. But where should we look first for a solution? Wouldn't the most scientific approach be to "go with the flow" of the majority data and look for better interpretations of the minority data? That is the working hypothesis creation scientists have used, and with great success I might add. The Radioisotopes and the Age of the Earth (RATE) creationist research initiative (see participants in Figure 1) developed very good answers to the methods of class (A).

Figure 1. RATE participants. Front row, left to right: John Baumgardner; Larry Vardiman; Russ Humphreys, Gene Chaffin. Middle row, left to right: Andrew Snelling, Steve Austin, Don DeYoung. Back row, left to right: John Morris, Ken Cumming, Bill Hoesch, Steven Boyd.

See RATE resources at <http://www.icr.org/rate>. A book I published in 1994, *Starlight and Time*, was the first in a series of young-universe creationist cosmologies based on Einstein's general theory of relativity that deal with class (B) dating methods.[37]

Thus creation science offers positive evidence for a young-world re-interpretation of the seemingly old-world minority of data. That would resolve the conflict in favor of a young cosmos.

Why Most Scientists Believe the World is Old

There is an irony in this controversy about the age of the world. The majority of scientists — the evolutionists — rely on a *minority* of the relevant data. Yet a minority of scientists — the creationists — rely on the *majority* of the relevant data. Adding to the irony is the public's wrong impression that it is the other way around. If these ideas are new to you, you may be asking yourself the question: If the evidence is so strong for a young earth, why do most scientists believe otherwise? The answer is simple:

> *Most scientists believe the earth is old because they believe most **other** scientists believe the earth is old!*

They are trusting in a circular argument, not data. Here's one example. In March of 1987, I presented to a young geochemist at the National Laboratory where I then worked the data to support item four above: the rapid

---

37   See the list of articles on such topics at http://creation.com/astronomy-and-astrophysics-questions-and-answers.

accumulation of sodium in the ocean. His specialty was appropriate for such a discussion, since much of geochemistry deals with chemicals in the ocean. I wanted to see what objections he could put on the table before a co-author and I completed a scientific paper on the topic. (The paper is available online at <http://www.icr.org/article/sea-missing-salt>.) We went around and around for an hour. Finally he admitted he knew of no way to remove sodium from the sea fast enough. But then he said,

> "Since we *know* from other sciences that the ocean is billions of years old, such a removal process must exist."

I questioned whether we "know" that and started to mention some of the other evidence for a young world. He agreed that he was not familiar with most of this data, since the science journals he depended on did not discuss it. He did not want to examine the evidence for himself, because, he said,

> "People I trust don't accept creation."

I asked him which people he was relying on. His answer was, "I trust Steven Jay Gould!"

Thus, he revealed his main reason for believing that the earth is old: "*people I trust*", i.e., the scientific authorities had declared it. I was surprised that he didn't see the logical inconsistency of his own position. He trusted Gould, a famous evolutionist, and other authorities not to be doing the very thing in their fields that he was doing in his own field — ignoring highly relevant data!

Perhaps the young geochemist thought it so unlikely the earth is young that he wasn't going to waste time investigating the possibility for himself. But if that were the case, then it shows one way the old-world myth perpetuates itself — by intellectual inertia.

I remember having similar attitudes when I was a graduate student in physics while still an evolutionist. I was wondering about a seeming inconsistency in biological evolutionism. But, I told myself, surely the experts know the answer, and I've got my dissertation research to do. I had no idea that (a) the experts had no answer for it, and (b) the implications were extremely important, affecting my entire worldview.

Before I became a Christian, I would have resisted evidence for a recent creation because of its spiritual implications. It may be that the geochemist also was resisting such implications, and was merely using scientific authority as a convenient excuse.

My point is that many scientists are not the independent seekers of truth the public imagines. For a variety of reasons, they depend on other scientists to be correct, even when they themselves have some reason for doubt. Unfortunately, as most creationist scientists can tell you, this young man's reaction is not at all exceptional. Many scientists trust their training and the mainline sources of information. However, I'm happy to report that others, when presented with these data, have become very interested in it, and are investigating it.

The Early Training of an Evolutionist

One reason most scientists believe the world is old is that they rely on their training. I will show how that indoctrination takes place using my own experiences as an example. The general course of my training is similar to that of many evolutionists. The particular details will help you understand, in the phrase of the sixties, "where I'm coming from." Some of those details involve my encounters with Christianity that are quite relevant to the attitudes of many evolutionists.

During childhood, family, school, and other influences are all critical. My father was a chemist and a naturalistic evolutionist. When I was young I asked him how old the earth is. He answered in a very matter-of-fact way, "five billion years". My mother, a public school science teacher, was also college trained in chemistry and also an evolutionist. She re-affirmed my father's teaching. My public school education also reinforced it. Most general science textbooks I read taught the then-standard story: gradual upward evolution of the cosmos and life, a natural process taking billions of years.

In the fifth grade, I found in the school library several geology books for children, including one called *The Earth for Sam.* They fascinated me. A drawing in one showed geologic time as a spiral, bedecked with various fossils, uncoiling backwards into a dim and misty past long ages ago. The idea of mysterious eons of geologic time strongly attracted me, offering an emotional connection to the past, and the reasons why I existed.

The Walt Disney movie, *Fantasia*, was another early influence. Near the middle of the movie is a sequence promoting evolutionism to the music of Stravinsky's *Rite of Spring*. It depicts a nebulous formation of the solar system, then a volcanic proto-earth. Next, it showed life gradually evolving from single cells in the ocean to the dinosaurs that died and were then fossilized.

My parents took me to see the movie in my early elementary school years, but I did not become fully conscious of the deep influence it had on me until years later when I saw it again as an adult. I realized then that some of my mental visualizations of evolution came straight from *Fantasia*. It is interesting that Disney, as a master storyteller, recognized the mythological potential of the evolution story well enough to put it among other powerful narratives, right between *The Sorcerer's Apprentice* and Greek myths.

My family members were not Christians. My father was an atheist and my mother rejected the Baptist training of her youth. But I did experience a few Christian influences outside of our family: a first-grade felt board artist presenting the Easter account, the first chapter of Genesis in a vacation Bible school, and a children's' Bible story book my mother bought me as a result. However, none of the Christians I encountered tried to connect those things with the world of science into which I was being initiated. By the time I reached high school I thought of evolutionism as The Way Things Are, and of Christianity as a fable, no longer of much interest to me.

As a high-school senior I became one of the forty finalists in the 1959 Westinghouse National Science Talent Search. At that time science was very much in fashion, and nationwide over 16,000 high school seniors entered the contest every year. The finalists were all sent to Washington to compete for various prizes, a visit to President Eisenhower in the White House, a tour the National Bureau of Standards, and the privilege of talking with various scientists. Since I was the first such finalist ever to come from the state of South Carolina, there was quite a bit of local hoopla. It was a heady experience for me, as were my contacts with other science-minded students and with senior scientists that confirmed my confidence in evolutionism. As far as I knew, everyone I met believed in the billions of years and all that followed. Nobody had offered me evidence against this worldview. It was "in the air" and nobody thought to question it.

The College Training of an Evolutionist

My undergraduate college education at Duke University continued to solidify the evolutionary worldview I had acquired. Though a course in Christianity was required by the trust fund financing the university, it became clear to me that the religion professor teaching the course was what I would now call a theological liberal. That is, he did not believe the Bible — at least not in the straightforward sense we would normally read any other non-fiction book. I now feel contempt for what seemed the hypocrisy of collecting a salary to teach a story one did not believe.

Some students in my physics classes were Christians, but I dimly perceived that they were all theistic evolutionists, though I couldn't have labeled their views then. That caused me to lump them, perhaps unfairly, into the same category as the liberal religion professor. It seemed plain to me that the history of the world as written in the Bible completely disagreed with the history of the world as written in science textbooks. I thought of all Christians as compromisers, unable or unwilling to recognize that evolutionism contradicted their beliefs. I was not at all attracted to that kind of Christianity, and I then knew of no other kind.

There is a lesson here for those well-meaning Christians who think that mixing long ages into the Bible makes the gospel more palatable. The lesson is that, for at least some unbelievers, a seeming compromise of Christianity with evolutionism is not attractive. As applied to me, theistic evolution proved to be an ineffective tool for evangelism.

None of my professors openly mocked Christianity. That trend came to most colleges a decade later. There was even one professor who must have been a Christian, a Roman history teacher I respected. In a mid-term exam he asked his class, "What was the most important historical event during the reign of Augustus Caesar?" All of us answered something like, "The founding of the Roman empire." But the professor said, "No, it was the birth of Jesus Christ!" We were shocked, first because neither he nor the textbook had mentioned that hitherto, but, more importantly, because none of us had connected the required "religion" course with events in real history. He made an unforgettable impression, but I didn't follow up on it then.

The reason I didn't pursue the matter was that I still had my faith in evolutionism. All my other courses seemed to support it. For example, my undergraduate nuclear physics textbook[38] had a section describing theories about the origin of the elements. These theories depended on knowledge of the age of the solar system, which Evans set at three billion years, saying it was "based on radioactivity studies of terrestrial and meteoritic samples ... This age scale is confirmed by many other types of evidence and is also in agreement with the cosmic time scale derived from the Hubble red shift."[39]

At that time I had no reason to doubt Evans' billions of years date, because they were consistent with the worldview in which I had been immersed since childhood. When I graduated from Duke with a B.S. in Physics in 1963, I still had the same opinion.

In graduate school, at the Department of Physics and Astronomy at Louisiana State University, I began learning experimental physics research. After doing my course work, the Ph. D. dissertation research involved a large cosmic-ray observatory project to be built in the mountains of Colorado. In 1968, accompanied by my wife and our two small children, I moved to Colorado to help build the observatory and set up the experiment. By then I was well educated in the wisdom of evolutionists. If anyone had told me that in less than three years I would cease to believe in the billions of years, I would have dismissed the thought as completely impossible.

---

38   *The Atomic Nucleus*, by R. D. Evans,
39   p. 282.

I mention these personal details to show how pervasive the concept of long ages is in our scientific culture. There were some ideas I was skeptical about, such as the accepted interpretation of quantum mechanics, but I never dug into the details of either physical or biological evolutionism, the actual evidence on which the theories are based. Most scientists today have not done so either.

How an Atheist became a Christian

Creationism is not identical to Christianity. For example, many orthodox Jews and conservative Moslems are creationists, and many genuine Christians are not creationists. Some people, including a number of Russian scientists in the late 1980s, have become convinced of the truth of creation science and then became Christians afterward.

One American example of that sequence is Dr. Richard Lumsden, whom I was privileged to know in the 1990s, when we were both serving on the board of directors of the Creation Research Society. He was a biology professor and academic dean at Tulane University, and now he is with the Lord. While he was teaching a class on evolutionism, a student began politely but persistently asking him for evidence that evolution had actually occurred, or could occur. After several days Dick found that he knew of no such evidence, and he realized living things had to be created. About six months later, he accepted Jesus Christ as his personal savior, thereby becoming a Christian but only after he had become a creationist.

I followed a different sequence, becoming a Christian first and then becoming a creationist several years later. When we arrived in the mountains of Colorado in 1968, my wife, who had become a Christian some time previously, wanted to attend a small independent Bible church near where we lived. When the pastors of the church found out that I was an atheist, they offered to give us a Bible study in our home. I accepted, relishing the opportunity to argue with some Christians. However, these believers were different than the others I had encountered. These two were not at all ashamed of the Bible and boldly proclaimed what it says. They didn't know much about origins issues, but they did take the Bible seriously. They referred me to the various verses involved, and then got back to the essentials.

As a result of the Bible study, and unknown to me, the prayers of the church, I became well aware of the basic teachings of the Bible. Because my Duke University religion course had taught that Mark was the oldest of the four gospels, I began studying it for myself. I asked God — whom I had known to exist — that if He had anything to do with Jesus Christ and the Bible, to convince me of it.

He convinced me and I still don't fully understand how, but within a month I knew that the gospel of Mark is true. It is important to understand at that point I was not yet a Christian. Knowing the truth and obeying it are two different things, and for about a month I was miserably aware of the difference. Finally, in July 1969, alone in a pine forest near Frisco, Colorado, I asked Jesus Christ to save me from my sins and come into my life. At that instant, things began to change — for the better — within me and in my life around me. I was transformed.

I have never regretted that decision. Instead I have delighted in it, and the boundaries of my life have continually been expanding from that day to now. In John 10:10, Christ says, "I am come that they might have life, and that they might have it more abundantly." That is what happened to me.

How a Christian became a Creationist

For the next year or so, I was a Christian but not a creationist. I began studying the whole Bible for myself, beginning in the Old Testament with Genesis. I tried to read evolutionism into the first eleven chapters, but the fit wasn't good. I decided I would leave the origins questions open and continue with the rest of Scripture. I read a book called *God, the Atom, and the Universe*, by James Reid, and its theistic evolutionism seemed concordant with my desire to reconcile evolutionism with my newfound faith. However, its muddled approach to Scripture seemed inconsistent with the straightforward way I was trying to understand the Old Testament, so I wasn't really satisfied.

That winter I met a creationist at a church dinner. He was a young man my age visiting from Denver, full of the evidence that he had picked up at a recent creation seminar. When I started explaining my stumbling attempts at theistic evolutionism, he assumed I was the enemy and began arguing with me. New enthusiastic creationists take note: he probably set me back about six months in my Christian walk!

Not long after that, I discovered in the church library a book briefly referring to salt entering the sea as evidence for a young world. I was not highly impressed by it, mainly because it was a layman's outline and did not appear to consider the possibility that salt might also somehow be leaving the ocean. One piece of data, not very scientifically explained, was not sufficient for me to question what I had been taught for a lifetime.

In the spring of 1970, my family and I moved back to Louisiana so that I could write my Ph.D. dissertation. We joined a church that turned out to be outstanding, and there I learned much more about the Bible. The adult Sunday school class was working its way through Genesis, verse by verse. By summer we got to the Genesis flood, in chapters 6 through 9. The teacher remarked that many Bible scholars think the flood was a worldwide catastrophe with major geologic consequences. That was a new thought to me. That fall, the pastor, an old-time gap theorist, passed along to me a creationist book he had been given. He said he wasn't too sure about it himself, but he felt the Lord wanted me to have it.

Was he ever right! The book was *Biblical Cosmology and Modern Science*, by Dr. Henry Morris, one of the founders of the modern creation science movement. It is not one of his better-known books, but it was enough to make me realize that I never had delved into the actual evidence for evolutionism or long ages. Reading the evidence it mentioned, I had a strong feeling that this was the scientific answer I had been looking for.

A few months later, a friend introduced me to the Creation Research Society and its quarterly scientific journal. By the time I received my Ph.D. in physics in 1973, the scientific evidence I had come across had thoroughly convinced me that nothing like evolution ever occurred, and that the "billions of years" claim is fiction. I was transformed, and was no longer a theistic evolutionist, but a young-world creationist. Forty years of research, much more evidence, and many encounters with evolutionist scientists, have resoundingly confirmed that change in my worldview. I listed some of the evidence that transformed me at the beginning of this chapter.

Two Paradigm Shifts

I'm describing these biographical details to help you understand how important a scientist's worldview is to how he interprets the scientific data. In his book, *The Structure of Scientific Revolutions*, science historian Thomas S. Kuhn speaks of scientific *paradigms*; worldviews and models that scientists use to interpret data. The origins myth of our age, evolutionism, is an example. Kuhn points out that a scientist who has never shifted paradigms is one that views the data as invincible. He is as unconscious of his paradigm as the person who has forgotten his glasses are tinted. But a person who has changed paradigms is much more aware of the powerful effect such a worldview can have.

I am such a person. I have seen the world through three different scientific paradigms. First I was a well-trained atheistic evolutionist. Then, after I became a Christian, I was a theistic evolutionist for about a year. Now I'm a young-world creationist, and have been one for over four decades. Since I have been in the shoes of each type of scientist, I know how each type thinks. My thinking as a naturalistic evolutionist was quite narrow and cloudy. As a theistic evolutionist, it was still rather darkened, but much less so than before. As a creationist, my intellectual horizons have been continually widening, and to see each new piece of the scientific puzzle falling into place gives me great joy.

On the other hand, many evolutionists have never shifted paradigms. I have found that they have tremendous difficulty understanding the science of creationists. In judging this clash of paradigms, you might assume that those who have made at least one paradigm shift are more likely to be closer to the truth than those who have not made any.

Of course, there are some who have shifted paradigms the other way. Many of the most vehement atheists seem to have had some bad experience with a Judeo-Christian childhood background, against which they are rebelling. Some theistic evolutionists appear to have come from a Christian upbringing with a naïve creationism, without much emphasis on evidence, or much training in what evolutionists teach. When they meet ridicule in college, often they abandon what little they knew in favor of theistic evolutionism, which has the advantage of not contrasting on the scientific level with naturalistic evolution. Both these types often appear to be clinging to their view very emotionally, perhaps because to them it seems to be a last resort. You can learn from them primarily by asking, "Why all the fervor? Isn't it just a matter of science?"

Of course, it isn't just a matter of science. A person's worldview is foundational to his life, whether he is a scientist or not. It affects very profoundly how he views his place in the cosmos and his destiny. All of us tend to defend our worldviews with tenacity, often even fighting against the evidence. But, from experience, I can assure you that there is life after a paradigm shift!

Why a Young World is Important to You

You may now be asking, "since shifting worldviews is so painful, why is this author trying to inflict that kind of pain on me?" The answer is I have seen knowledge of the recentness of creation bear good fruit in the lives of many people. It changes our attitudes toward three of the wellsprings of life:

1. **Scripture.** The most questioned part of the Bible is its short time scale for the history of the world, which clearly is at odds with the alleged billions of years. Most people respond either by discounting scripture, or by imagining it as much more mysterious than it really is, not meaning what it appears to be saying. But if the scientific evidence strongly supports the Biblical time scale, then the problem is solved. To the reader whose eyes are opened, the Bible becomes alive and clear. Scripture becomes a reliable source of wisdom and knowledge, direct to you from the living Creator of the cosmos!

2. **God.** The time scale affects our deepest feelings toward God. If the universe were old, God would be remote and cold, not caring about inflicting misery on his creatures for billions of years before man's sin. Such a god would be unlikely to answer our individual prayers now, or to come to earth anytime in the next few billion years. But the God of a young creation is loving and active, inflicting pain on His creation only as a necessary response to human sin. He has intervened recently and strongly in the world's history and on our behalf individually, making it very likely that he will return soon.

3. **The gospel.** If physical death had existed for billions of years before man's sin, it would be hard to understand what the problem is with the world and us, and to understand God's solution for the problem, the good news (gospel) about Jesus Christ. But the Biblical account of a *recent* creation puts the whole gospel into context. Physical death entered the cosmos only because of the first Adam's sin. The physical death of the second Adam, Christ, makes it possible for redeemed humans to live forever in a new cosmos without sin or death.

As I implied in item 1, Scripture very emphatically declares the world is young. If you are not sure about that, or if you are one of those fortunate people who are inclined to take the Bible at face value regardless of what "science" might say, then at this point you may want to go to one of the many creationist websites, such as <creation.com>, and look up the Biblical evidence for a young world. However, I think most people already suspect that the Scriptural time scale is short. The big problem is with what they think "science" says about the matter. If you are in that majority, then I invite you to search creation websites for young-world scientific evidence. My hope is that you soon will be rejoicing with me, having discovered that real science resoundingly supports the young world of Scripture knowledge that will transform your life as it did mine.

Chemist and Computer Scientist

"I want to know what is true, about God, the Bible and evolution, even if it means all I have learned and cherish turns out to be wrong". When Royal made this scary decision at the age of thirteen, his parents feared he might bitterly regret it later. Living in several countries exposed him to many plausible sounding viewpoints in many areas, which were nevertheless contradictory. So he learned that a worldview must be more than just plausible and should be analyzed in depth.

He spent many years examining the naturalist claims, for the origin of life, of complex biological novelty, the workings of the mind and belief in God. He ended up soundly rejecting these naturalist claims. The reasons were primarily scientific, and secondarily theological.

Ever wonder what the toughest job in the world might be? Perhaps it would be a gladiator, a contortionist in a Chinese circus or a sanitary engineer at a leprosy station? No. People with the right training handle these jobs quite well.

My parents decided that they would pursue their calling in the most challenging career available. In their early twenties, with virtually no money and four babies, they became Christian missionaries. Their destination was the Indian village of Temuco in Southern Chile, where they did not even speak the language.

These kinds of missionaries face challenges that would, without Divine intervention, break mortals. They faced sickness, contempt from their families and former friends, constant concern about the children, incomprehensible language and culture, no retirement plan, and no assurance that they would even have the money to bail out and get back home. They faced an Enemy with thousands of years of experience in human psychology.

Christian Influences, Warnings about Science

My parents were convinced of the truth of the Bible and willing to submit to God's authority. This was based not so much on intellectual arguments, but personal experience. They told me I was precocious and had "asked Jesus into my heart" at the age of three and a half. This I can't remember, but I can vividly remember at the age of seven wanting to make sure my salvation had been settled. Alone, and with no prompting, I asked Jesus to forgive all my sins, and asked to be given the gift of salvation. This was an experience so meaningful that it transformed me. I used all opportunities to tell friends how they too could keep from landing in hell.

After moving to the capital, Santiago, I attended an elite high school where we were taught that man had descended from the apes. Not as theory, but as fact. Every scientist supposedly believed this. God was not necessary to explain where we came from. My heart revolted at this claim. I knew this could not be true, but did not know how to defend myself. I was a straight A student, but how much does a young kid really know?

I also had the soul of an empirical scientist. I would collect all the fuels I could find, place them in identical little jars, light them at the same time, and determine which would burn the longest. I used to plant beans at strategic locations in the proximity of a solid wall to determine the effect of varying amounts of sunlight on plant growth. I also read everything I could get my hands on pertaining to the creation-evolution controversy.

My father urged me in the strongest terms to stay away from science. I had the naïve belief many have, that science offers objective truth waiting to be discovered, tools scientists simply need to apply. But if the Bible was God's word, then it could not contradict scientific truth! I could not accept the possibility of contradiction and that I would have to believe contrary objective evidence.

Beware of peer influences

As teenagers, we went to a Christian English-speaking summer camp. One day we participated in a complex treasure hunt. The third clue consisted of a hidden note we had found with a verse in rhyme containing the phrase, "How far the sun to see." We were baffled until someone looked up, saw a Spanish sign for a city by the ocean: "Mirasol", or "look (to the) sun." We rushed to the sign trying to figure out what the clue meant. Suddenly someone had an idea and everyone raced off down the road after him. My heart yearned to follow the crowd and participate in the excitement. What was more important, these wonderful friends or some stupid misgivings they were wrong?

But I stopped. Why should the majority be right? I didn't know what the others were up to, and didn't like the idea of going along without knowing what their reasoning was. On the other hand, most were older than me. This was my very first treasure hunt, and they were all very experienced in this game. But surely there was something to be learned from this sign. With a heavy heart I watched those rich kids (none a poor missionary kid like me) disappearing in the distance, the members of the "popular clique." I went back to the sign, totally alone. Actually, being with that crowd was more important to me than solving the treasure hunt. Maybe I still could catch up to them… But I continued to look for clues at the sign. At first it looked like I was going to make a fool of myself; no hidden trapdoors, no scribbled messages. After much effort I finally found a tiny stub sticking out of the ground, containing a rolled up paper with the next clue.

I strolled casually towards the others, who were now looking confused. Without saying anything I showed them the paper. I thought to myself, "You guys are rich, beautiful, confident and lots of fun. But all of you were wrong." This experience was helpful in future discussions over creationism: the majority, even when brilliant, older and more experienced, are not always right and going along with the rich and powerful would be so easy, and could be so wrong.

Marxist controversies: a foretaste of future controversies

The late '60s to early '70s was a time of intense Cold War conflict. Many Marxist terrorist groups were wreaking havoc on South American economies. As Lenin taught, "Conflict breeds change." Where the population is reasonably content revolution is unlikely. Valuable economic capital, such as power stations, would be damaged, and the next day one could read freshly painted signs on walls like, "What an incompetent government. It can't keep law and order."

At this time Americans were supposedly hated as likely CIA agents and representatives of those exploiting the third world. But this was not my experience. Maybe our enemy was too busy with the grown-up missionaries. I was easily the most popular kid in the school. How could you not love an MK? We were all great soccer players!! Today, some 40 years after having left Chile, I still get e-mails and telephone calls from former classmates.

During the late '60s and early '70s a Marxist view circulated throughout South America that Chileans were poor *because* the USA and Western countries were rich. In a supposedly zero-sum-game, the rich were exploiting the natural resources of the poor and stealing them dry. Emotions were at a fever pitch. This was the period when the Russians and Americans were competing to be the first to land a man on the moon, and playing James Bond all over the world.

During these years, Chilean strangers would approach me to tell me what they thought was "the truth about what was going on in Chile" at the time. The views ranged from extreme Marxism to right wing fanaticism. Everyone was persuaded they had a proper understanding of the historical roots of poverty, injustice and ignorance. They thought they knew what should be done to solve these problems. I discovered that among divergent views often lie correct facts that can be interpreted or weighted differently. A particular viewpoint was often justified (and developed) by ignoring some factors.

In South America back then, the probability of growing up to enjoy a high social economic status depended primarily on the family that one was born into. During the 1500s, the original *Conquistadors* were assigned *huge fundos*, which provided their descendants with overwhelming economic advantages. The Spaniards and Portuguese mercilessly enslaved the Indians, exploited their gold and silver mines, murdered their leaders, and destroyed their cultures. Raw materials and precious metals were shipped back to Europe as the Crown demanded, and little investment was made locally because many of the adventurers intended to return to Europe and live as nouveau rich.

I evaluated the historical and political data, and understood these different perspectives. But I realized that not all proposed solutions were equally valid. Taking over the copper mines in Chile without compensating the investors could not (and did not) work. The engineering and management skills were missing, the owners retaliated in the world courts, and the markets sought other sources of copper.

I also learned some general principles that later helped me in the creation / evolution controversy. One must accept true facts and judge fairly the interpretations others make of these. It is easy to develop a large number of models by selective use of data. Another problem is, one's own perspective can be strongly biased by beliefs passed on from parents or influential mentors. If I were the illegitimate son of a Mapuche Indian housemaid, I might agree that the risks inherent in a Marxist revolution were perfectly acceptable. What would I have to lose? Why should I be destined to misery, with no options to improve my lot?

Salvador Allende, an absurdly rich medical doctor who presented himself as the savior of the poor and downtrodden, became the Marxist leader in Chile in 1970. Party activists at the grass-roots level made impossible and contradictory promises. To the pro-Israel supporters he promised tolerance and brotherhood among all people, including protection of Jews. To the pro-Arab people, he promised the destruction of Israel. Upon learning that one family in our church liked Americans, the neighborhood cadre told them that all Americans supported Allende. Sensing our surprise, the family sought clarification, and was told that all *educated* Americans supported the Marxist —both my parents have university degrees.

The copper miners, like many factory workers, had been promised personal ownership of the means of production, implying immediate wealth. Within months the story was modified to "the Chilean government, as representative of the working class, was now the owner of the means of production." The miners rioted, and production came to a standstill.

By 1972 the economy was in free-fall. Farmers were butchering their cattle and sowing fewer crops to avoid being attractive for expropriations. Truckloads of farm workers would simply go to a well-managed farm, chase off or shoot the owners, tie Chilean flags on the fences, and make themselves at home. This meant a long fiesta until all the animals had been eaten, and then they moved on to find another farm. It did not seem to occur to very many of them to work the new farms because the farm down the road offered some excellent wine.

At this time the risk of civil war was steadily increasing. The government had announced that, since the constitution had been written by and for the bourgeoisie, it did not apply to a revolutionary people's government. Heavily armed right and left wing paramilitary groups were active, and the average mood was utter depression.

We then were getting telephone death threats, and giving thought to routes to smuggle out of the country, since we'd been trying unsuccessfully for over a year to leave. The US embassy managed to arrange for a legitimate flight out of the country, and, with little forewarning, we headed for the airport. Many of my classmates met us there, andwith tears begged me not to forget them. And, of course, when I got to the States I did not to forget to "tell the truth about what was happening in Chile"! There are so many perspectives and interpretations, and I would be careful to be as objective as possible.

I Decide to Become a Scientist

A short time later, my parents went to Argentina as missionaries, and I remained behind to complete high school. I had noticed that in most missionary families, in our mission at least, one child graduated valedictorian from high school. Perhaps the extra challenge of coping with multiple change and cultures was a good thing. My mother also had graduated valedictorian, and I was happy to continue the family tradition at the same high school.

Now I was free (although dirt poor) to decide exactly what to do with my life. No pesky parents, no roots, no responsibilities, and lots of confidence. A chance to reevaluate everything I had concluded so far. I could even decide how long to grow my hair. Fortunately, my conviction of the accuracy of the Scriptures was still intact. Dad wanted me to study Bible at some institute and music on the side. This was all totally unacceptable to me. I wanted to go into science—they never did find out what area I graduated in until it was too late!

I was burning to learn new scientific things. I had decided to examine carefully what science had to say about the origin of life. I felt it would be statistically absurd to expect that all my beliefs in theology, psychology, and politics, all passed on from my parents, should be right. If the creation report in Genesis was true, this had to be reflected in objective, scientific studies.

For the next nine years, I attended various universities for 12 months a year, including summer school. Chemistry was my first choice, and I figured I could get a second degree in psychology. But with more experience, I began to realize that "the experts" in psychology were not able to provide the kinds of conclusive answers that I had assumed were possible. Especially during various psychology courses, I would hear plausible sounding theories, but was left with the question, "How do they know (and how do we test) if this theory is true?" How did Freud know for sure the symbolic meaning of various dreams?

During one course a major jolt occurred as we learned about the 16 different mutually exclusive theories for the cause of child autism. It was easy for me to earn an A in psychology courses, and my last instructor stated repeatedly in class how bright she thought I was. But I knew that no one had a clue about the answers to the questions I had, such as:

1. Exactly how are memories stored and retrieved? How does the mind decide the desired memory was successfully retrieved?
2. How do people translate concepts between languages? A "meta language" seems to capture the concept, which must then be expressed in different languages. What compares whether the phrases in different languages indeed express the same underlying thought, and how is this done?
3. What is the physical nature of choice and will?
4. What guides the mental process to develop new cognitive models, alternative manners to "understand" or solve a problem?
5. What is this "aha" feeling that exists when we have finally understood something?

I feared if my colleagues, mostly psychology majors, were typical of the "experts" I hoped would provide such answers, then I knew I was going to be bitterly disappointed. As a result I did not take any more psychology courses. I then dedicated myself to "real science," based on hard facts not open to speculation. I did not want to waste time on required subjects I could learn on my own. So I read the various university text books parallel to my normal courses and took CLEP, MLA and other certification examinations to gain college credit without having to sit in the classroom.

At age 20 I had finished bachelor degrees in chemistry and computer science. I realized that I was not ready to start my PhD in chemistry yet, and canceled my graduation for a year to take more science courses to help me decide what to do with my life. During the latter bachelor years (and later in graduate school) I would frequently ask my colleagues if they believed in the theory of evolution. Most said they did. When I asked why, they answered that everyone knew it was true because it had been proven true in other disciplines: the chemists said the biologists and geologist had proven it true. The geologists, however, claimed the paleontologists had actually demonstrated it. The paleontologists said the chemists had shown how life evolved from simple chemicals. It was pure herd instinct. Through my Ph.D. program I never met anyone who had *hard evidence* for neo-Darwinism.

The Question of Origins

Only in graduate school did I finally understand enough about fundamental principles (such as in thermodynamics and kinetics) to feel competent to ask the right questions. Years of training in organic chemistry reaction mechanisms showed me how a mixture of deterministic principles plus stochastic/statistical effects provided a clear understanding of how chemistry works. I realized that putting the correct building blocks together and stirring them in a warm flask was never going to produce life. In fact, many of our chemistry bottles showed a lot of polymeric oxidized "gunk" at the bottom. We had to use careful intelligent guidance using the skills we had learned that permitted us to bring the correct reagents together under the right conditions and timing, then to isolate and protect the intermediate desired, and to continue with the next carefully planned step.

I learned that proteins and sugars must be built with optically pure starting materials, and natural chemical processes cannot generate these without intelligence. Isolating these from living sources showed that they soon racemized to a worthless mixture of mirror images, deadly for biological purposes. In addition, I learned about the vast number of chemical reactions possible for different functional groups of molecules, and the sheer endless number of isomers that can be generated using amino acids plus simple cyanides, aldehydes and other building blocks. The desired biochemicals would be surrounded by virtually 100 percent worthless "gunk" in a putative original pea-soup ocean, especially since the necessary components for life are not favored thermodynamically or kinetically.

For example, the production of polypeptide chains under the aqueous conditions proposed by origin of life chemists is chemically nonsense. The amino acids are present in far too low a concentration; other amines and carboxylic acids interfere; water would hydrolyze the amide bonds; and any developing chains would immediately produce the intramolecular product, in which the amine at one end reacts with the carboxylic acid of the other. The cyclic product can no longer polymerize as necessary to produce proteins. This is easily demonstrated in a laboratory.

So, I now was fully persuaded that a naturalistic source of life without divine intervention would not work, but was not entirely sure about the details. As my parents had feared, my Christian beliefs had been strongly assaulted in the university setting. When I was 19, one of my instructors told us in class that males had to become sexually active or risk becoming impotent. Other professors made it clear that, to be considered real scientists and be accepted among the important insiders, one cannot believe in a miraculous creation.

During the next years the thought kept coming back: how is it possible that so many brilliant scientists are convinced that the theory of evolution is true? *What do they know that I don't?* Have I managed to overlook overwhelming and clear evidence? Do I simply believe what I wish to believe, what I was brought up to believe? In the final analysis, I feared that my belief in God and the truth of the Bible seemed akin to a feeling. I no longer believed that feelings and conviction could be scientifically analyzed.

After I completed my Ph.D., I joined a huge multinational corporation where I was able to work in many areas of chemistry, especially surfactant chemistry, and with a wide range of computer technologies. The firm financed an MBA from the University of Michigan at Ann Arbor and a permanent transfer to the mother company in Europe followed. This permitted me to get involved in many business issues in several countries.

Intensive Study of the Creationist and Evolutionary Literature

I decided to read all the major university textbooks on cell biology, and also the evolutionary technical literature. It became obvious that the endless dogmatic statements in these textbooks, such as, "In the course of evolution this enzyme developed diffusion controlled perfection" were unsupported. Most cellular functions require an average of more than ten different complex proteins, and the proportion of individual polypeptides able to perform some useful biological function is negligible. Getting whole ensembles to work together without intelligent guidance was not possible. I was not willing to follow the herd. I had almost made that mistake earlier, in Chile. Darwinism by natural selection was clearly synonymous with "a miracle." This knowledge transformed me from doubt to firm conviction that evolution was scientifically impossible.

My training as a chemist had taught me to examine fine detail, such as exact electronic and geometric structures of reaction mechanisms. A key question was always, "Exactly how does this work?" In biochemistry and especially cell biology, where the subject material is more complex and involves many interacting components with feedback regulation, the explanations tend to be very superficial and descriptive. An ancient genetic replicater existing about three billion years ago was supposed to have undergone continual Darwinian selection leading to additional novel genes and integrated *de novo* biological functions.

It all sounds so easy until one examines the details critically. Each of the 64 codons of the genetic code must be accounted for by t-RNAs or as deliberate 'Stops', or the message will have gaps and be terminated. Until this scheme is functional, no natural selection can act. And afterwards the translation must be close to perfect. Even if all the necessary enzymes were available, and the incredibly low one percent error rate in translation or transcription could be achieved, macroevolution could never work. The reason is because almost all genes have more than 100 bases and hundreds of genes are required for life to exist. Each protein copy from the same mRNA would be different for each gene. This would lead to chaos in the cell, and no consistent factor for natural selection to select. The process could, additionally, never start until the dozens of proteins and RNA strands needed to produce ribosomes worked flawlessly.

The conceptual problem is that all these molecular machines are also coded for by genes, which themselves cannot work unless their products are already present and the genetic code fully developed. Whole metabolic networks are also necessary to generate the activated amino acids, which will be linked together to produce proteins in the order needed to function. All these complex components need to be concurrently present in the same cell environment.

I came to realize that, just as I noted in psychological theories, evolutionists were relying heavily on plausible sounding stories and scenarios. With little data, and selective use thereof, one could always come up with some kind of "just-so" story, to use Stephen Jay Gould's term.

An example is the commonly told story of how bird flight may have developed:

> Once upon a time, there were creatures that liked to climb trees. Of course, some were clumsy enough to fall off of branches, terminating millions of years of hard won evolutionary effort, leaving no progeny. Others, however, were endowed with some convenient membrane-like material in their extremities, just enough so that as they desperately flapped their paws in midair, their flight downwards was slowed enough to enhance their survival odds. After a few million years, natural selection determined that, of all-important events in the lives of these creatures, this would be a particularly attractive one to fine-tune. Gliding was followed by features and before long birds had evolved. The mutations needed for the additional new nervous system, brain structures and instincts are minor detracting details.

Of course, we could easily also invent a theory for how membranes and proto-gliding could have been *removed* by natural selection as "predicted" by evolutionary theory:

> Once upon a time, there were creatures that liked to climb trees. This was back in the pre-Devonian when landphilic creatures were still carting around superfluous fins. Gene sequence analysis extrapolations show they have a close resemblance to modern "flying fish." Fossils of extinct creatures known as "birds" are universally believed to have shared a common ancestor with the tree-climbing creatures under discussion. Fatty pouches were also known to be present on some of their extremities.
>
> Trees offered both predator and prey strategic advantages. However, prey could avoid becoming a one-time amino acid source by jumping down from branches when attacked. The predator would follow in hot pursuit. Now, as fate would have it, some members of both populations were endowed with just a little less membrane and hindering finny material, permitting a more streamlined descent and a selective advantage. Analogous to an arms build-up, this effect was mutually reinforcing such that a faster predator would be ever more likely to catch those less competent prey, and the resulting average faster prey population would be more likely to starve out the slower predator lineages after a few million years of natural selection… and so what we observe is the expected outcome of natural processes. Today, of course, we realize that "birds" were an unsuccessful evolutionary attempt, and show many maladaptive features, which surely contributed to their demise.

There are endless variants to the story-telling theme. Why should proto-gliding or proto-flying be the selected trait?

> Once upon a time, there were these creatures, which liked to climb trees. Of course, as fate would have it, some were clumsy enough to fall off of branches terminating millions of years of hard evolutionary effort and leave no progeny. Others, however, were endowed with a slight more level of intelligence. The less gifted would fall off branches more often and earn their just reward that Darwinian theory reserves for the natural loser. After a few million years of natural selection etc., and so what we observe is the expected outcome of natural processes, namely high intelligence!

I came to realize that an "explanation" could be thought-up for any fact contradicting an evolutionary claim. Highly conserved genes must be so because functional constraints prevented most mutations from being tolerated in that gene. Unexpected similar structures in unrelated organisms are the effect of "convergence." What would guide hundreds of genes, modified by random mutations, along a relentless path leading to very similar morphological features, is not questioned—and, in my opinion, is an absurd proposal.

Years of intensive reading led me to the conviction that "the emperor is naked." Computer models designed to show how neo-Darwinian theory does the job are hopelessly unrealistic, but commonly accepted and quoted as having provided proof by those who do not understand the details because they are unknown. Evolutionary theory does not explain the origin of what Professor Behe calls "irreducible complexity," nor does it explain the origin of increasing complexity. It creates some very disturbing questions as to our human identity and characteristics, even under a theistic evolutionary framework:

1. Are our minds no more than the physical brain performing various chemical and electrical operations? Why do we believe that neurons firing under control of thermodynamic and kinetic processes plus chance provide a reliable picture of external reality?
2. Is human reasoning the result of chance mutations across thousands of genes followed by natural selection for some unknown criteria, such as minimal energy requirements?
3. What integrates signals coming from our sense organs into a logical model of the external world in a fraction of a second? How could an uncoordinated ensemble of proteins in various cells produce life?
4. Is there an objective basis for morality, or is survival of the fittest the ultimate good? Was Hitler right?

These kinds of questions illustrate the far-reaching effects of believing in this materialistic reductionistic theory: who are we, where did we come from, and are we someday going to be accountable to our Creator?

In my studies, I reviewed research data that can be accommodated into an evolutionist worldview. It is not correct that all facts point unambiguously and exclusively to a Creator. Data does not speak for itself, as I used to think many years ago. In fact, until an interpretative framework is in place, a scientist can look at a list of numbers or some object, and remain fully disoriented. This interpretative model also leads to selective use and exclusion of raw data, often unconsciously. Some data is deemed "obviously wrong" and never reported. The challenge, however, is for scientists to search for the outliners in an attempt to develop models that incorporate as much truth as possible.

Integrating Biblical Evidence with Scientific Data

I became so convinced that the various evolutionary theories can't explain much more than some rather trivial micro-evolutionary details, that I now believe I could not accept any of them even were I not a Christian. I know many scientists who don't want to accept the possibility of a God, but openly admit that the evolutionary theories being taught in schools and universities as fact *cannot* be correct. These colleagues are willing to admit that they don't have a clue as to why life exists.

The age of the earth and the Flood were also important topics for me. As a scientist, I recognized how new conceptual models may inspire novel explanatory theories. The details matter, and I did not wish to embark on a false framework. Some models can conflict with claimed data, which therefore need to be reexamined. For example, I never questioned the accepted date for when the Cheops pyramids were built (allegedly 3,100 B.C.), but a universal Flood between then and now, as a straightforward reading of Genesis indicates, poses considerable problems. Creationist studies now provide good evidence that multiple Egyptian dynasties were parallel and not sequential, demanding reevaluation of their history.

At this time the most satisfactory scenario implies a Creation date in the low thousands of years and a universal Flood about 2500 B.C. As a natural scientist by nature, I do not fear examining controversial claims. If data is discovered that contradicts biblical claims, then God will understand if an honest researcher is faced with doubts. Is this not reasonable? If He put these stumbling blocks in my path, does He also carry some responsibility to help bail me out? It is possible my views may be modified someday. This is the risk I have to take since I decided I would expose myself to the possibility of being wrong.

New horizons for scientists

In science, the most interesting models are those making unique predictions, being able to direct research in novel and unexpected directions. This offers Young Earth Creationists unique opportunities. This particular framework predicts very rapid speciation, for which causal mechanisms based on pre-loaded information must be found. For example, all bear kinds (and dogs/wolves; and horses/zebras) are predicted to have arisen within 4500 years. Apparent ages in radioactive studies and population genetics need to be reexamined based on genetic bottlenecks (a single starting location using miniscule population sizes). I believe these endeavors will be more fruitful than the naturalistic approach that has dominated the last century of biological research.

CHAPTER 5: JAMES WIGHT[40]

From Plastic Ambiguity to Genuine Answers

As a youth, James Wight inhaled the world like a suffocating man, one hurried draft after another. James questioned little, just took in as much as he could get. He even accepted his biology teacher's glib explanation of human origins without question. When James researched it himself, however, his mind and life were changed forever.

There was a time when I believed there was no absolute rule or standard by which all others must follow. My church said God made the world, but my school said we evolved from animals, therefore it must be true. There must be some compromise because, after all, *anything* can be correct if one was open-minded enough. It just took a bit of compromise to make it happen.

This was my belief coming out of public high school. At school I was taught evolution. Not just 'animals change' evolution, but flat-out, no-holds-barred, amoeba-to-mankind evolution. I studied rows of carefully arranged skulls, grotesque animal skeletons, and chads of white paper sprinkled over black construction paper to learn about natural selection. I believed without question that we evolved from animals. I didn't ask about the difference between micro and macro, I just believed. I saw no reason to *question*. In fact, I was not encouraged to question anything, and so I didn't. I lived my life content with the knowledge that the world was plastic and everyone was right in some way. It was the time of compromise. There were no absolutes, and to me this fact was *absolutely* certain.

I graduated high school full of all the knowledge of the world, and very little knowledge of the church, and lived my life accordingly. I led a promiscuous lifestyle, complete with alcohol and rock-n-roll. I started a rock band and traveled around in Michigan playing in bars and clubs. My drum set was my voice and I cared little for talking about the *larger* questions of life. I was more concerned about my next girlfriend, or where my band would play next. I saw no conflict between evolution and Christianity; in fact, I saw no conflict between any of the world religions. I was taught moral relativism and, like most students who are taught it, I believed it. There was no absolute right or wrong. It all depended on the situation and not on some outside, outdated authority like the Bible. This belief deeply affected my behavior and I lived true to my beliefs.

---

40   James Wight is a pen name. He is a public school teacher whose job could be in jeopardy if he used his real name.

Then, something amazing happened that transformed me forever. My love for reading had not diminished, despite my education, and a friend gave me a book to read titled, *Scientific Creationism* by Dr. Henry Morris. The Bible's creation story, could it be supported by science? I was intrigued. Every page was totally new to me. I had never even considered the idea that Creation explained the world *better* than evolution! As I turned each page I would shake my head in disbelief. I would wonder why I had not heard of this before. *Why has this been kept from me?*

I lay awake that first night, huddling under the soft glow of my bedside lamp, and read until the wee hours of the morning. I read about the importance of origins, and I immediately could see it. I understood how a person's belief influenced their behavior. I remember repeatedly nodding my head until my neck ached. Visions of friends and relatives from years past floated in front of me, and I could hear the catch phrases about Biblical error fall to the floor.

After the importance of origins discussion, Henry Morris explained the two choices about the origin of matter, energy, and natural law. Either there was an all-powerful Creator, or it was all the result of a natural process. I immediately understood that the Bible had a clear and consistent explanation involving an all-powerful Creator that exists outside of the creation. A naturalistic explanation fell flat on its face in light of scientific knowledge of the laws of thermodynamics. I was hooked.

As I raced through the book *Scientific Creationism* and read about the complexity of living systems and the argument from design, I began to see the bigger picture. I finally realized the debate over origins is not a science versus religion debate, but rather is about two different conclusions being reached with the same evidence! I felt that this was a fair way to view a contentious topic. Both sides are looking at evidence, and both sides have reasons for believing different things.

For example, a creationist views the evidence of the complexity in nature and concludes: *design.* An evolutionist looks at the same evidence and concludes: *natural process.* While reading this book, I began asking, "Which conclusion is the best one?" And I repeatedly came to the conclusion that *design* is far better supported. This was not based on my religious convictions, because at the time I was a staunch evolutionist! I had naturalistic tendencies because that was all I had been taught. In fact, I became a bit upset at this fact.

I asked my pastor why I had not been taught that the creation account was supported by scientific observations. He seemed puzzled over the question, and did not give a satisfactory answer. I do not hold anything against this man of God; he eventually became one of my first advisors when I started my own ministry, Creation Science Ministries. The idea that I could grow up in a church and not believe that God created the world in the way the Bible says is sadly true for many Christians in today's world.

Because of *Scientific Creationism,* I became convinced the Bible is literally true. When I finished reading it, I was in a conundrum. Here I was, playing drums in a rock band and doing things I shouldn't, and now I was totally convinced I had believed a lie that mankind had evolved from animals. I realized this lie had affected the way I was living my life, and I knew I needed to be transformed, but didn't know how. I did know I needed to pray, and pray I did. The world around me did not immediately change, but I surely did.

My eyes were opened to the truth of God's Word, and I knew that the world was not made of plastic. There were certain truths in the world that were based on the Bible and the teachings of Jesus, and these were immutable. I saw the progression of the world as all-important: The creation of a perfect world, the fall and curse because of sin, and the subsequent need for salvation. This helped explain the condition of the world for me, and I saw the sinful state as a result of humans initial fall from grace. The evidence for creation helped build this worldview for me that now is the basis of my personal ministry.

After my initial introduction to creation science, I began to focus my voracious reading solely on creation books. I stormed through such creation classics as: *The Genesis Flood* by Henry Morris, *The Answers Book* by Ham, Sarfati, and Wieland, *In Six Days* by John Ashton, and *In the Beginning* by Walter Brown, among many others. I discovered that there were numerous books on creation and that the more I read the more my interest grew. It became an obsession. I read everything I could get my hands on and enjoyed every page of it.

During this time my life was getting straightened out. I no longer played drums in bars and clubs, but instead played for my local church. I was reading my Bible and devoting my life to Christ, and I even went back to college full-time. This transition took nearly ten years and has totally redirected my life. It was a good thing, too. College was to challenge me like I had never been challenged before. My beliefs were challenged, my belief in creation, in Christ, and in the Bible were all tested, mocked, and ridiculed. I found out that at the secular university the world *is* plastic; there was no absolute right or wrong because everything was relative and all views acceptable, except Christianity, of course.

In my first year at Grand Valley State University I started a speaking ministry on creation. I had seen a few good creation speakers and really felt drawn to it. I realized many people believed in evolution for the same reason I did; that's all they were taught! I began to practice speaking, sometimes for hours a day, and my home pastor was kind enough to give me pointers and allow me to speak to Sunday school groups. This advanced to Wednesday night services for adults and recommendations to other churches. During this first year, I also was confronted with academia's attack on the Bible.

I was taught in my philosophy class that humans had invented God, and in science class I was taught that science had disproved His existence. Many of my professors were very adamant against the Bible and the Christian faith. I was doing enough study of the matter by this time to be able to adequately defend my faith, but I was concerned for the other students who were not able to do so. Many students would approach me after a particularly intense discussion with the professor who declared that "belief in God is now relegated to children and the infantile."

The students who talked to me afterwards would nearly always express their appreciation for how I had defended Christianity and the Bible, and explained that they were too afraid to say anything during class. I could understand, but not fully respect, their timidity. A secular university is not an especially comforting place for a Bible-believing Christian to be. However, it was the evidence for creation and the Bible that kept my faith strong and, as a result of the ferocious attacks on anything 'Christian,' my personal belief solidified into a coherent and thorough position resting squarely and soundly on the Bible. This knowledge of creationism had truly transformed me!

I was encouraged by my experiences in college and started to pursue my speaking ministry with more effort. I even publicly debated a kind, but atheist, professor of evolution when I was still a student. I was growing in confidence and knowledge about the creation and evolution controversy. I continued to read, study, and speak as my college years passed. After graduation, I found myself looking for a job and, at the same time, speaking on a regular basis. I was now a frequent guest speaker at various churches and my family became more involved in my ministry.

Now, as I smooth the wrinkled pages of *Scientific Creationism*, I often think about the transformation in my life that it caused. The words on the pages of this worn book in my hands did not transform my life, but rather it was the message they contained that did. The message was that God's Word is scientifically sound, relevant and powerful in today's world. When this message hit my heart I was left breathless and overcome with the desire to take this message to others. I know I have found my calling. It is to tell people the world is not plastic and the evidence is clear: God, as recorded in Genesis, created the world. This evidence has the power to transform lives as it has my own.

"Do not conform any longer to the pattern of this world, but be transformed by the renewing of your mind." Romans 12:2a

How I was drawn into the Creation/Evolutionism Debate

Steve Miller's fascination for astronomy led him to investigate the claims made by the Big Bang theory and stellar evolution, but he had always had nagging doubts about their explanatory power.

Member of Creation Research Society, Former President, Calumet Astronomical Society, and Young Universe Creationist!

For several reasons the evolutionary paradigm has never persuaded me. When I was very young, our neighbor, Mrs. Pearl Carpenter, was always talking about the Lord Jesus, and how He suffered and died for our sins. The result is the fact that I never questioned the creation account in the Bible, and creation has always made more sense to me than evolution.

In my first year of Junior High School, I remember studying the nebular hypotheses theory of how the solar system was formed. The billions of years required for the formation of the universe and the solar system were explained in detail in class. The time element was in direct conflict with the Biblical account, and the only explanation for why I did not believe it was the Lord kept His hand on me, and did not allow atheistic naturalism to triumph. Moreover, this was when I made my personal commitment to follow the Lord Jesus.

In my sophomore year in High School, Biblical Special Creation came into direct conflict with the evolutionary paradigm. Mr. Herbert Schmidt was my biology teacher. The puzzling thing is, I remember him to this day as my favorite and most challenging teacher in high school. In fact, he scared me. He expected something out of all of us and he was not going to take any excuses. I remember many times locking horns with him over evolutionism and did not realize at the time that the underlying principle of the evolutionary paradigm was atheistic naturalism. However, there have been many occasions now when I wished I could go back to lock horns with Mr. Schmidt again. Nevertheless, I will always respect Mr. Schmidt, because he actually cared about us and how we were going to manage in life. I will always admire him for that.

Fortunately, by the time high school was over, I had made a decision to attend a Christian university, Tennessee Temple in Chattanooga, Tennessee. The college had only one class that dealt with worldviews and evolutionism on the college level. The class was "Bible and Science" and the teacher was Dr. Phillips. In the class I received answers to my many questions about the evolutionary paradigm and evolutionism. These issues never came up until I was elected President of the Calumet Astronomical Society in 1989.

The event that shifted me into amateur astronomy was the return of Halley's Comet. At the age of five, Saturn was the first astronomical object I ever saw in a telescope. Saturn was awesome! My dad and granddad often talked about Halley's Comet. Granddad had seen the 1910 return of Halley's, and told us how great it was to see it. Dad wanted to see Halley in its 1985-1986 return, but died at the young age of forty-eight, a month before Apollo 11 landed on the moon. When 1985 rolled around, there was a telescope under the Christmas tree for me. Things have never been the same. This telescope and what I learned about astronomy transformed me.

There was no local astronomy group in our area. In 1986 we went to the Lake County Fair and met Mr. Earl Delong, a member of the Calumet Astronomical Society. I joined the club later that year. In 1989, I was elected president when the club was down to four active members and broke. By 1994, when I stepped out of the presidency, the club was blessed with 120 dues-paying members and over 40 active members. We had a public outreach program at Lemon lake County Park, along with an operational observatory and member's only observing sessions on Friday night at Lemon Lake. The checking account had over $1,200, and many members plunked down $1,000 to $1,500 on new telescopes during this time.

This is significant because of what I was falsely accused of since. If the accusations were true, how could I have been elected as president five times or have been so successful? We did an indoor amateur astronomy forum in 1998 and the guest speaker was John Dobson himself. John Dobson, the inventor of the Dobsonian Telescope, was on the Johnny Carson show twice. He was then probably the most famous amateur astronomy buff in the world. I was the director of programs for the club at this time and played a major role in arranging this event. This occasion is so important because John Dobson is also a Hindu monk, and he believes in the steady state theory for how the universe began. I never censored other points of view, and even encouraged other points of view to be discussed in the CAS. In John's talk at Purdue University Calumet, he blasted the Big Bang theory in front of all the CAS club members.

Here is where the real rub of evolutionism came into conflict. In the Calumet Astronomical Society, many of the members had gone to secular colleges or schools, and they were taught the only way to look at the universe was with the evolutionary mindset, which is nothing more than atheistic naturalism. The CAS members may think evolutionism is science, but it is the religious dogma of *atheistic naturalism* running beneath the radar screen in the stealth mode of evolutionary science. Evolutionism is Atheistic Naturalism, and it is a religion just as Christian Theism is.

What nearly all the people are never told is that there are many astronomical evidences that point to a recent creation. All they get to hear are the ad-hoc special pleading storytellings, which were invented to cover up for anything that will show the evolutionary paradigms and time scales were wrong. For example, the Oort cloud was invented to explain away short lives of comets over billions of years. Astronomers know comets have a finite life span, and they know if the earth has been here for billions of years, comets cannot last nearly that long. The Oort cloud was invented to continually provide new comets in the solar system to save the billions of years time frame. Even Carl Sagan stated that there was not one shred of scientific evidence for the existence of the Oort cloud.

Another example of this type of thinking is found in the galaxy-winding problem. Astronomers know that galaxies rotate or spin. They know the stars closer to the core of a galaxy are moving faster than the stars out on the spiral arms. Spiral galaxies over billions of years would have "wound up" after so much time; therefore density waves were invented to explain spiral structure. The problem with this explanation is the fact that there is no direct hard scientific evidence for the existence of density waves except in evolutionary astronomers' minds. In addition, another example of this type of thinking is how evolutionary astronomers try to get around the problem of galaxy clusters and the overall structure of the universe. Observations document that galaxies are grouped together, but are moving apart. Astronomers know there is not enough visible matter to hold these clusters together for billions of years by the power of gravity alone. In other words, there must be something we cannot see that holds the star clusters together for billions of years. Enter Dark Matter. If the universe is young, such inventions are not needed because there has not been enough time for the clusters to fly apart.

Another major problem is the observational fact that both galaxies that are very near to us, and those at the outer edges of the universe, look very much the same. For example, galaxy NGC 1300 in the Fornax cluster is a barrel spiral galaxy. In the Hubble Deep Field we can see barreled spiral galaxies that look exactly the same. NGC 1300 is only 69 million light years away and what we see in the Hubble Deep Field is at the very outer edge of the visible universe, which is billions of light years away. A recent creation that fits with the Biblical time frame would support this observation.

In other words, what we see is a fully formed, mature universe that was set in place just as we are told in Genesis. Because the universe is young, galaxies have not had time to fly apart. Therefore, no need exists for all these unobservable, immeasurable and non-testable ad-hoc explanations because the universe is, in fact, young. This knowledge has transformed me to a confident astronomer.

Problems Arise

As president, I was the president of all the members, even the ones who disagreed with my Christian Theism worldview. I never ever kept anyone from giving a program or a talk on how they thought the world came into being, even if it was evolutionary. Being raised in America, the principle that everyone has a right to express his or her perspective was important, and it would be wrong to try to suppress anyone else's viewpoint.

As it would turn out, many CAS members would wonder why the creation position was never presented at the club meetings while I was president. That was about to change. However, an important point needs to be stressed: I would have shown a young universe creation cosmology if a professional presentation was available, *but I never used my position as president to promote my personal viewpoint.*

In October of 1999 a professional astronomy program produced by the Moody Bible Institute of Science became available. The video program, *"Journeys to the Edge of Creation,"* was part of a video collection. This professional program presented the Astronomical Biblical Creation viewpoint without ever mentioning evolutionism or attacking it. The Bible is mentioned, *but evolutionism was not, a very important point.* An official of the CAS called about our showing the video "The Milky Way and Beyond." In February of 1999, I had contacted several CAS officials and told them about the series, and offered to let them preview it before it was shown to the club, but they *never* bothered to follow up on my offer.

The CAS meetings are on the second Monday of each month. On Saturday night before the October 1999 Monday meeting, I received a phone call asking me to present the video because the presenter had canceled the program scheduled for that evening. Here was an opportunity to present my position and honor the Lord's creation without having evolutionism criticized. The video was a very professional outstanding presentation, but several people got up and walked out, and the firestorm that followed even took me by surprise. Two atheists that did not even attend the meeting raised the greatest stench. On the club's website chat room the discussions were scorching.

Because I was not on the Internet at this time, a club member friend sent me a copy of all the emails that went around on the chat room. Not every email was against the film, but emotions were running high. My observation about the emails is the fact that none of the negative emails ever tried to refute any of the evidence presented in the video for creation. All the negative emails attacked me personally; so much for *scientific evidence*. After reading the emails, I made up my mind to invest in a new computer to get on the net, which opened a completely new world for me. I learned there were many creation organizations and websites.

On the Creation Research Society website I asked if anyone knew Dr. Danny Faulkner, the scientist in the video. Dr. Glen Wolfrom responded and gave me Dr. Faulkner's email address. After sending Danny an email and introducing myself, to my joyful astonishment he responded. I told Danny what had happened when the video was shown, and even he was surprised to learn of the nasty reactions. From this experience I learned of a real ministry in the field of amateur astronomy called Creation Evangelism.

Danny Faulkner and I have since then become good friends. Danny even presented an astronomy program for the CAS to a packed room, and no one walked out. Nevertheless, after his presentation someone who I thought was a friend has never called me again and will not return my phone calls, even when I asked his wife to do so. One of the CAS members said he did an investigation on Dr. Faulkner, but could not find anything concerning Dr. Faulkner. Yet, I did not have any trouble finding information about him. The CAS members could not believe that anyone with a Ph.D. in the field of astronomy from a secular university could conclude that the world had been created and the universe is young!

Another club member contacted the CAS leadership to see if it would be permissible to show "The Milky Way and Beyond," the same video I showed in '99. He was informed that he could not use this video for a CAS presentation. After the officer in the CAS was denied the opportunity to present the video, the member contacted me and I explained to him why the CAS officer was censoring the video—namely this was the same presentation I showed that caused the uproar. In my opinion, the reason for the censorship was the pressure exerted by the atheists within the leadership and membership of the CAS. Except for two manuscripts, these videos and related articles have been *blacklisted* by the supposedly *open-minded leadership* of the CAS. Of course, the officials and membership will claim they are *open-minded* and the club officials are no doubt doing what the majority of the supposedly *open-minded* CAS membership wishes.

Once again, here is another example of where evolutionary philosophers have set themselves above reproach and actually believe they are being scientific and open-minded! Bona fide science is based on the premise of point and counterpoint. In addition, without counterpoint, genuine science does not exist, just indoctrination.

Beware of the "one-hand clappers." Evolutionism has reached its sacred cow status, not by scientific evidence, but by how the evolutionary faction has restricted the jargon of the debate to naturalistic explanations. Any other explanations are automatically deemed religious, therefore are not allowed, no matter how factual the information. The evolutionary clique has learned not to tolerate any contradictory data by claiming all counter evidence outside of atheistic naturalism constitutes religion. Moreover, by doing this they have set themselves up as the judge, jury, and executioner *of what they say are relevant scientific evidences.*

I stated evolutionism has no factual scientific evidence because evidence only becomes confirmed when counterpoints are allowed. If the theory of evolutionism could withstand the whole gauntlet of counter evidence, which would include not merely naturalistic counter evidence (and there is great quantity of that) and evidence that is beyond the realm of naturalism, then their scientific evidence would become compelling. The evolutionary camp has even been allowed to manipulate the definition of what constitutes counter evidence. If authentic counter scientific evidence is not allowed to scrutinize evolutionism, the theory of evolutionism becomes nothing more than metaphorical belief, not authentic science!

The CAS has taken *one step beyond* in their stand against anything that would make them appear to have any religious viewpoint. We used to have a *Christmas party* and it was called that for many years. Now it is called a *holiday party*. The creation video truly tweaked the CAS atheists and their cohorts! Since 1999, I have gone into Creation Astronomy Evangelism full-time. I have never found anything so fulfilling than doing Creation Astronomy Evangelism.

A Mathematician finds Order in the Universe

At the age of forty-two, Dr. Herrmann was a transformed from a "fire-breathing" atheist to a Christian after he accepted Jesus Christ as his Lord and Savior, and, at first, theistic evolution. Two years later, the science of mathematical modeling transformed him into a creationist who accepted a literally interpreted Genesis account as historical fact.

My transformation from atheist to creationist is rather unique. The short interval between these two worldviews required an intermediate step. By 1977, I had become a well-known research scientist and educator and was placed in situations where I could indoctrinate the minds of the young. I was then, like many professors, a fire-breathing hater of the concept of an active supernatural God and attempted to destroy the belief of individuals who claimed to have a "personal relationship" with such an "absurdity," as I termed it then.

When not pursuing my scientific endeavors, I attempted to eradicate the "deity" of the man called Jesus of Nazareth. I used various intellectual and insidious devices for this purpose. However, my activities were not confined to intellectual endeavors. I slowly became an extremely vile individual, while being unconcerned about the welfare of my family.

My anger was also directed toward those I loved most, my wife and my children. I leave out the details, but it is enough to mention that my continued behavior would eventually have corrupted their mental wellbeing. But, my wife brought these activities to an end. Without my having any knowledge of her pending actions, during the morning hours of April 6, 1977, she removed herself and our children from my immediate influence.

On the 7th, I recall finding myself sitting in a rocking chair staring blankly out of the front windows of my nearly empty home. I suddenly felt completely alone and lost. I had been forced into a corner with two possible choices. One was complete debasement, and the second choice presented itself in the following manner: as I sat there, I discovered that only one book had been left behind, a book purposely left in the hope that I might read it. When I picked up this volume, it fell open to Matthew 5. While slowly reading the entire chapters 5,

6, 7, it occurred to me that, if I had only attempted to follow the principles outlined by Jesus, then this terrible personal tragedy would have been avoided.

Immediately following this "revelation," something unexpected happened: nearly thirty years of the deepest intellectual reflection and personal deception evaporated. All of my scientific knowledge and experience in such areas as logic, mathematical modeling and the like, led me instantly to one irrefutable conclusion. No ordinary human being could describe these concepts as Jesus did. The descriptions must have come from God.

I said out loud, "Jesus, I believe! The atmosphere about me became heavy, yet tranquil. I felt "something" pressing in on me externally, as well as another, but different, sensation within my lonely spirit—a sensation I had never experienced before. I was being wrapped up—literally—by an indescribable "love" that signified I was not alone and that Jesus was near at hand. I immediately accepted Jesus Christ as my personal savior and the truthfulness of the Bible. I was radically transformed!

God started to use my knowledge, my experiences, my training and abilities for His purposes. He literally changed my mental patterns, and His power has led me to new knowledge and its wise application. The most significant application began a year later, an application that led to my second transformation.

In the spring of 1978, I and some other members of the Naval Academy Mathematics Department were studying C. S. Lewis books, namely *Mere Christianity* and *Miracles*. On October 10, 1978, an idea suddenly occurred to me. I wondered if I could construct a mathematical theory that models (i.e. mimics) mental activities that lead to certain types of perceptions.

As I began my construction, a more significant idea occurred. I conjectured that, if this construction is possible, then I could indirectly verify some of the statements made by Lewis. In particular, Lewis' statement that events in the "remotest part of space appear to obey the laws of rational thought." Then, from *Mere Christianity* the statement "what is behind the universe is more like a mind than it is like anything else we know."

During the 1978-1979 academic years, I began constructing such a model. The basic method uses mathematical statements that model many of God's attributes as they are compared to similar human characteristics. Some statements also model fundamental Christian concepts. For example, it is scientifically rational to state that God's intelligence, wisdom, and love are infinitely greater than any that can be displayed by any life form. Furthermore, there exist rational descriptions that characterize a higher intelligence. Hence, it is scientifically rational to assume the existence of a higher intelligence. I realized that the model destroys this claim that Christians irrationally believe in a higher intelligence.

The mathematical methods used did not exist until 1969. All of the mathematics I used to construct and refine this mathematical model, and some basic physical applications, is contained in articles 9903038, 9909078, 9903081, 9903082, 9903110, 9911204, 0112037, 0306147, 0412562, 0512559, 0603573, 0605120 found at http://arxiv.org/a/herrmann_r_1.

In 1979, I discovered the *American Scientific Affiliation* (ASA), which I joined, and my conclusions were published in the first 1982 issue of their journal. These results at that time were considered very significant by the ASA. I accepted a theistic evolution idea that, although God was active within our universe, He allows organisms to develop by evolutionary means. I presented papers consistent with this idea at various ASA meetings. They welcomed my ideas enthusiastically.

When I was flying from Chicago to Duluth, Minnesota in August 1979, I talked with John A. Wheeler, the Joseph Henry Professor of Physics Emeritus at Princeton. He suggested that I try to develop a consistent scientific theory that unifies all physical laws and accepted theories. It would need to include some truly fundamental entity that produces all of the physical objects that yield a universe governed by these laws and theories. Such a theory does not unify only the "four fundamental physical forces," but it unifies "everything," a scientific unification often termed the "Theory of Everything." It then occurred to me that a modification of the model I developed in 1978-1979 might lead to a solution that would also verify the statements made by Lewis. The approach would not start with the "bottom" of the scientific hierarchy, assumed fundamental particles and processes, but it would begin with the "top," a universe itself, and progress "downward."

To construct a scientific theory, most scientists use physical assumptions. Moreover, I needed some way to construct a universe that is, at least, consistent with the principles of theistic evolution. Shortly after returning home from Duluth, I opened the Bible to Hebrews. I was not aware that Hebrews would help with such a construction, but as I read, I noticed the phrase "sustaining all by his powerful word" in Hebrews 1:3.

I wondered if it actually were possible, using only physical assumptions and mathematical objects that behave like dictionary "words," to model processes that produce all of the physical aspects of the universe in which we dwell. After some effort, I discovered that my mathematical model predicted just such objects that I call "ultrawords." These are the basic mathematical objects that lead to my General Grand Unification (GGU-model) Model. This general theory produces every physical object from a predicted new particle type. It also predicts all the alterations in the behavior of every physical-system, where the term physical-system means a defined combination of physical objects. Further, the GGU-model displays higher intelligence characteristics.

The GGU-model is not based on hypotheses that assume the existence of unobserved physical objects and their behavior. It is based on actual observed behavior that is mathematically modeled. The mathematics then predicts behavior and the existence of specific entities. The GGU-model is a cosmogony that generates different types of universes, one of which is the one in which we dwell.

Shortly after discovering ultrawords, the mathematical model revealed a startling conclusion. Not only will ultrawords yield our universe, but our universe can also abruptly appear in a complex and fully functional form without any evolutionary processes. The mathematical model states that the step-by-step process for the creation of our universe and alterations in its behavior can follow the pattern laid out by a straightforward reading of Genesis 1 – 8. Physical entities can appear in fully functional form and in the exact Biblically stated order. Even a global flood can occur exactly as described in the Bible. The model verifies that it is rational to interpret Genesis 1 - 8 in a literal fashion and the entire physical universe is evidence for such an interpretation.

Although a very literal Genesis 1 – 8 interpretation is scientifically rational, this did not immediately lead to my accepting the Biblical statements as fact. Consequently, I began an extended investigation of the oldest Greek manuscripts from which our Bibles are complied. They are the Sinaiticus, Vaticanus and Alexandrinus. They are written in ancient Greek and were penned around the 4th century AD. The portions of these manuscripts we term as "books" were originally transcribed by many "authors" over a few thousand years.

Analyzing these manuscripts, I realized that it is statistically impossible for logical consistency to be maintained by the Bible scribes without being mentally influenced by the Holy Spirit – the Spirit of Truth. The GGU-model coupled with this linguistic truth is what convinced me to accept a literal Genesis 1 – 8 creationary scenario as historical fact.

I thought I was the only Christian who had discovered that a literal interpretation of Genesis 1 - 8 is scientifically rational and fact. Then I discovered the Institute for Creation Research (ICR) and, in particular, their May/June 1981 Impact article #95/96. On page 2, the article states how ICR members view special creation.

1. The universe and solar system were suddenly created.
2. Life was suddenly created.

Each of the article's seven presented statements matched what I had produced through mathematical reasoning. Actual evidence for special creation, as discussed in that article, contradicts that presented for theistic evolution. The General Grand Unification Model rationally upholds special creation as an alternative to secular and theistic evolution.

It is a remarkable fact that one Biblical phrase from Hebrews 1:3 trans-formed me from a theistic evolutionist into a creationist through the application of the GGU-model and linguistic analysis. My family upholds me in this choice although, after I publicly announced my conclusion, we have been discrimi-nated against in many ways. This personal discrimination is not only fostered by secular science-communities, but also by some liberal Christian organiza-tions. However, under no circumstances will such prejudice cause me to alter my stance. Although I retired in 2004, I continue to do research and to popularize the General Grand Unification Model. In particular, the higher intelligence as-pects of the model, General Intelligent Design (GID), and why special creation, the literal interpretation of Genesis 1 - 8, is not only a viable rational choice, but is a better explanation for the physical evidence.

A Forester Finds Faith

Growing up in the public school system, Tom was inundated with the evolutionary belief that we could explain all life without God. He despised religion and the hypocrisy in his religious and dysfunctional family was palpable. Through high school and into his early years of college he was satisfied, at least on the outside, that no Creator was needed to explain life. However, after a series of amazing circumstances that included sleepless nights, answered prayer, miraculous intervention, and deep soul searching, he gave his life to Jesus Christ. The transformation brought him peace of mind and a purpose to a lost soul. Tom is now an associate professor of biology at Truett-McConnell College.

For 15 years, my public school teachers taught me that macroevolution was a scientific fact. This indoctrination began in the primary grades when I was introduced to dinosaurs, and it was presented as fact throughout the rest of my high school and college years. No one questioned it, neither students nor teachers. In college, I felt comfortable with what I thought was the fact of molecules to man evolution and believed that I was really grasping the "true" history of life. All of my favorite television science programs only reinforced what I was learning in my classes, thus helping to solidify my views.

As I reflect on my life at this time my naturalistic worldview affected me in many ways. I was often angry, rebellious and miserable. My relations with my immediate family were strained. My anger could have metamorphosed into pure rage, and my potential for violence sometimes scared me. I spent a lot of time alone in the woods, learning about the wilderness with the goal of moving as far away from the human race as I could. I was free, the master of my destiny.

I loved animals and absolutely hated those who wantonly killed them; swearing that if I ever observed such behavior, I would take the human beast out myself. My spiritual life was arid and desolate. I thirsted for meaning, but my hunger was never quenched. My time in the woods was lonely and unfulfilled, though at the time I didn't recognize its desolation.

I considered religious people, especially Christians, ignorant lunatics. They occasionally approached me with the "Good News" of Jesus Christ, or invited me to church, but I blew them off as fanatics. Why would anyone bother going to church or believe the Bible when evolution proved that we could explain life and the universe without a god? Little did I realize that my life and worldview were about to drastically change.

The year was 1980 when I was attending a forestry college in Northern New York. We had the unique opportunity to travel to North Carolina and observe southern forestry practices. When that week was finished, all of us looked forward to our spring break. At the end of the week, one night several students got into a discussion about origins. Two Christians in our group then shared the scientific case that a Creator was behind life and the universe, and not natural chance process that occurred over millions of years. These two had invited me to Bible studies before, and I had politely told them to take a hike.

That night was different because they presented the case for Christianity by starting with evidence for a Creator, a perspective I had never heard before. They stressed that scientists were not present at the beginning, and so do not know for certain the initial conditions. They, therefore, must come up with conjectures based on preconceived philosophical assumptions. I had never considered this fact before. I hadn't realized that the presuppositions with which I had been indoctrinated were actually based on the atheistic philosophy of naturalistic materialism. I don't recall everything discussed that night, but I do remember that I could not sleep because my worldview had been shaken, thus unsettling my mind, and I soon would be transformed.

The next morning, the two Christians (Larry and Dave) wanted to go to the airport early so they could get home to enjoy a longer spring break with their families. They wanted to know if any of us wanted to go with them. We bought supersaver tickets, and had to stay an extra day for our confirmed flight, but they wanted to get home early by flying on standby. Against the advice of our professor, two of us decided to join them.

When we arrived at the airport our professor asked us if we wanted him to wait in case we couldn't get a flight. Both Larry and Dave said that they felt the Lord would be with us. Meanwhile, I was fretting, thinking: "Do I really want to be traveling with these fanatics"? I was still in great turmoil from the previous night because I was beginning to question all that I had believed, and now even getting home was questionable.

The standby flight from Charlotte to Atlanta was uneventful. However, when we approached the departure gate for our destination, it was packed. Open seats for the four of us did not look promising. Larry and Dave prayed and I stressed. The two felt at ease and peaceful as they were confident this flight would take us all back home. In fear, I blurted out, "If we all get back on this flight, I'll go to church with you on Sunday" to which they replied, "Fine, and we'll pick you up!"

Fifteen minutes before the flight departed, the person in charge told us that they had three seats left, but because there were four of us, we'd have to draw straws and the loser would need to take the next available flight. As we drew straws, I watched Dave go off by himself, pray, and return with great joy on his face. He proceeded to tell the loser not to worry about having to take the next flight because he was going to be with us. I said, "Are you off your rocker? The lady just told us there were only three seats available!"

Five minutes before departure, the lady huddled us again and whispered, "Guys, I feel real sorry about your situation, so I've put your losing buddy in the first class section so that you can all stay together, no extra charge. Please don't tell anyone!" The rest of our class ended up with a shortened spring break due to a snowstorm that kept them in North Carolina for an extra three days.

Needless to say, I found myself in church on Sunday! As the pastor approached the pulpit to give the sermon he had spent all week preparing, he shared with the congregation that he was going to preach another sermon, since he felt that someone in church that day really needed to know Jesus as his Lord,

Savior and Creator. As he spoke, I thought to myself, "How does he know so much about me?" I was finding it difficult to breathe.

Some would argue that these events were purely coincidental. That would be a logical interpretation, but the fact is the incidents that occurred in those few days brought me to a church where I heard a sermon that forever transformed my life. In my view, the evidence suggests that the God of the universe permanently shook my world! One defining moment was when I realized that the Pastor really didn't know anything about me, but my Creator and Savior knew me intimately.

As I look back, I would normally have had nothing to do with Christ because of my philosophical beliefs in evolution. The stumbling block of my atheistic, evolutionary worldview had to be removed before God could open my eyes to His Word and my need for a Savior. Through Larry, David, the Pastor, and my own study, I learned that His Word was true and reliable. The Bible states that Jesus is alive and shepherding his flocks, and those who know the shepherd will hear His voice. The Great Shepherd was leading those men because they followed and believed His Word, and I watched God answer their prayers! The life I thought I understood faded as I realized that it was empty when compared to the light of knowing Christ. That night I began my walk with Jesus in my favorite place, the forest.

It has been 33 years since I first heard His call, and when I responded my life was transformed. My study of the scientific evidence proved to me that an intelligent Creator, not evolution, was responsible for the creation. My biological research continues to be consistent with the idea that the Bible is God's Word and Jesus is who He says He is. For example, Darwinists believe that random beneficial genetic changes, combined with natural selection, provided the means that produced all of life's diversity. Claimed examples of these types of genetic changes include bacteria; their resistance to antibiotics, their ability to genetically adapt to environmental stresses, and their abilities to obtain energy from materials like nylon.

However, when you study these bacteria closely, new insight has shown that when the beneficial changes occur, there is a loss of pre-existing functions in the original (wild) bacteria. This elimination of existing machinery may provide a temporary survival value to the bacterium in a new environment, but does not explain how the machinery was built in the first place.

The other fascinating discoveries of these and other mutations such as the genes involved with differences in mammal coat color, suggest that many mutations are not random, but directed, a prediction that is consistent with a biblical worldview.[41] For me, this is major evidence that many of these observed genetic changes give every indication of a designed system. This adaptive process does not add any complexity to the already existing system, but subtracts from its

---

41   Anderson K. and G. Purdom. 2009. A creationists perspective of beneficial mutations in bacteria. http://www.answersingenesis.org/articles/aid/v4/n1/beneficial-mutations-in-bacteria Lightner, J.K. 2008. Genetics of coat color 1. *Answers Research Journal* 1: 109-116. www.answersingenesis.org/articles/arj/v1/n1/coat-color

total genetic fitness. Evolution is going in the wrong direction and, therefore, cannot explain how life began.

To make matters more complex, Neo-Darwinists trumpeted "junk DNA" as useless chemistry left over after millions of years of random mutations, and I believed claims like these for years. Today we are finding that the DNA/RNA connections, in the words of Microsoft founder Bill Gates, are "like that of a computer program, but far more advanced than any software ever created."[42] Genetic research is continually shedding light on the complexity of organisms. For example, in order for living things to continue living, they need programmed information that continually reads, proofreads, corrects mistakes, updates, modifies, and builds structures according to the genetic instructions.

What is becoming apparent through genetic research is that genes and proteins are specified, just like meaningful sentences or lines of computer code. Not only so, but genes have multiple codes, like two or more written messages embedded into one another. However, these codes are not "written" but are in a chemical format that is so complex that different messages are produced in multiple layers and different programming instructions are "written" in multiple directions. To put this in perspective, some have used the analogy of comparing the embedded information found on both coding and non-coding (once called "junk") DNA with reading a self-help book about a variety of skills you can learn, depending on where you begin reading. There are multiple instructions embedded within multiple instructions in multiple directions.

For example, if you read the book from front to back, you would learn all about building a car. If you read it from back to front, you would learn how to design the electrical circuitry of a house. Starting in the middle and reading forward then backward you could learn a new language or, alternatively, if you began reading in the middle, reading backward, and then forward, you would learn calculus. The complexity is mind boggling and inconsistent with random natural process. In 1994, evolutionist Kenneth Miller wrote, "If the DNA of a human being or any other organism resembled a carefully constructed computer program, with neatly arranged and logically structured modules, each written to fulfill a specific function, the evidence of intelligent design would be overwhelming."[43]

Though Miller still does not acknowledge the intelligent design of the biological language programmed into all organisms, the research is quite clear that it is a staggeringly complicated chemical language that our best minds in genetics are attempting to decode. This code, more sophisticated than any produced by our best computer minds, is consistent with our common life experiences

---

42   Wells, J. 2011. *The Myth of Junk DNA*. Discovery Institute Press, Seattle WA, p. 104.
43   Wells, J. 2011. *The Myth of Junk DNA*. Discovery Institute Press, Seattle WA. p. 104

that enable us to distinguish design from random accidental processes and convinces me that it took a very intelligent Creator to produce it.

Another piece of evidence that has convinced me of the Creator involves the concept of life and its origins. Biologists are in a unique position of trying to study life, yet they disagree on exactly what life is. Textbooks abound that describe the characteristics of life, but few attempt to define it. Life seems nonphysical. For example, at the death of an organism, there are no measurable physical changes. Mass and volume remain constant one minute before death and one minute after. This is also consistent with Scripture. God is the author of life, yet He is non-physical. In Genesis 2:7, though Adam was molded in the Creator's image from the dust of the ground, life was not given until God breathed the "breath of life" into him. This same soul life was also breathed into the animals (Genesis 1:20-21; 24-25).

Since I was educated only in the naturalistic interpretation of biology, pure naturalists reject the idea of any non-physical life and believe that only physical organisms can be life. Biblical creationists believe that the physical organisms possess life, but are not life itself. Therefore, naturalists posit first life to be the first organism(s) that randomly arose from chemicals over billions of years. Biblical creationists realize that God, the infinite and non-physical Author of life, gave life to all physical organisms, and that our observations about life are consistent with a "non-physical God providing the non-physical cause that one might expect for the origin of life."[44]

Furthermore, observations made over centuries of biological study confirm that life always comes only from previous life, according to the law of biogenesis. When naturalists posit life originating from non-life, they contradict all known biological data. Life generated through random chemistry has never been observed. Therefore, belief in random chemical events presumed to produce life is not only based purely on faith, but is not supported by the scientific data.

Finally, as an ecologist, I am interested in relationships with regard to how creatures interact with each other and their environment. In recent years, ecologists are amazed at the complex relationships all organisms are involved with, most of which are mutualistic where all benefit from the relationship. If all organisms need each other in an ecological balance today, how did any single organism ever survive long enough to establish the required relationships with others in order to survive? Two examples of mutualistic relationships come to mind.

---

44   Wise, K.P. 2012. Devotional Biology: Learning to Worship the Creator of Organisms. (Biology Textbook used at Truett-McConnell College, In Press).

Humans are made up of a community of organisms. There are more bacterial cells on and in you than your own cells. Most are in a mutualistic relationship with you. You provide the needed environment for them and, in return, depending on the types of bacteria, some are helping you to digest food, others are crucial for the health of your immune system, still others may have been involved with organ formation during your embryonic development. Without them we could not survive and vice versa.

In nature exists an important biological process causing nitrogen to be cycled from earth to air to creature. Nitrogen is important for all organisms, and is used for protein building, DNA/RNA production, and other crucial chemicals needed for life. This nitrogen cycle is a highly complex system that requires a minimum number of parts, mostly creatures, in the right place at the right time and with the right equipment. This complexity is compounded when you realize that it is one of many similar chemical cycles, working interdependently in order to ensure the persistence of life on planet earth. Note the following five steps ecologists have listed as involved in the nitrogen cycle process.

1. Nitrogen gas (N_2) makes up 78 percent of the atmosphere, but is in a form that plants can't use. The first step of the cycle requires that N_2 be changed into ammonia (NH_3) a form plants can use that requires bacteria with the right equipment. Since oxygen disrupts this chemical process, this has to take place in an oxygen-less environment. To overcome this problem plants, like clover, provide oxygen-free chambers on their roots called root nodules. A special protein is also needed in order to help carry excess oxygen away, so it will not interfere with the reaction. What is incredible is that the plant and the bacteria cooperatively manufacture this protein and coordinate production rates and amounts by communicating with each other.

2. A different group of bacteria, and sometimes fungi, carry it to the next step and change ammonia into nitrite (NO_2^-) and then nitrate (NO_3^-). Sometimes certain bacteria have only the equipment to change ammonia into nitrite and then the baton is passed to another group of bacteria that can change nitrite into nitrate. Nitrate easily dissolves in water and can be transported to other organisms that also require it.

3. A new group of microbes change nitrate back into nitrogen gas that can be released into the atmosphere. This is an important step because, without these organisms, nitrate could build up in the soil and make it toxic for life.

4. Nitrates made in step 2 are easily absorbed into plants where they convert it back into ammonia in order to make other important compounds, such as those required to make proteins.

5. There exist huge numbers of bacteria, fungi, and others that break down waste products of all life and, in so doing, nitrogen is continually recycled.

As I reflect on the complex relationships required in just one cycle and all the systems and creatures that must come into play simultaneously in order for all life to persist - and then ponder life's complex computer-like programming and origin, these observations are most consistent with an infinite and intelligent designer and make no sense in an evolutionary Darwinian world. If Christ spends that kind of energy in the maintenance and care of His creation, how much more is He willing to be intimately involved with my transformation into His image?

As He transformed my view of this world, He also transformed my personal life. He showed me that, in my desire for independence and freedom from Him, I became a slave and prisoner to selfish desire and materialism. I was never satisfied and it resulted in a meaningless tedium of purposeless living. Belief and trust in the saving work of Jesus produced freedom as His eternal waters washed my moral filth away, sparked new life within, and healed the anger that once consumed me. His eternal flood tide filled a thirsty void in my being that only He could occupy, and this immersion brought forgiveness to a repentant heart, meaning to a meaningless world, and eternal refreshment to a parched and weary soul.

Because of God's love, alcoholism and abusive life cycles that plagued past generations of our family were broken for the first time in memory. Though life remains difficult in this fallen world, as I center my life on Christ and learn how to love and forgive, my family relationships continue to be healed. Before Christ, my life was characterized by self-centeredness and a desire to be in control, but the Holy Spirit of God was critical in my transformation.

Today, the Lord continues to instill an attitude of selflessness in order to make my life count for others and for eternity. Through His Word we are told to love and comfort people with the love and care He has given to us (2 Corinthians 1:3, 4). As followers of Christ we have been given the responsibility to walk in obedience to the Creator and to flesh his care out for others. To the extent that God's people are willingly empowered by God to do this, others will see Christ in us. It is my desire to love and encourage others as Christ has done for me. Ultimately, I rest in the fact that my significance and security are found in God alone.

At one time this self-centeredness and need to be in control also manifested itself in a fear of death. My need to cling to life, thinking it was the only one I had, caused much apprehension, especially when it was threatened by various emergencies faced during my early firefighting career. During times of danger I realized that I was not in control and fear often took over. However, I learned that God created us to be eternal beings and that the life we have now is but a preview and a shadow compared with the eternal life yet to come. This has given me a great peace and confidence as I trust my life into His capable hands. The result is an irrepressible hope and a great freedom from worry, fear of dying and rejection. I am reminded of a great promise from God found in Romans 8; *"I am convinced that neither death nor life, neither angels nor demons, neither the present nor the future, nor any powers neither height nor depth, nor anything else in creation, will be able to separate us from the love of God that is in Christ Jesus our Lord."*

When I enter the woods today it is with renewed joy. Gone is my view of the forest as a product born of time, chance and random events. In its place is the perspective of a beautifully designed ecosystem, the product of an all-loving Savior. Because of these new eyes, I no longer feel alone backpacking in wilderness areas or canoeing in back country lakes, for I know that He is with me and His Presence is near and dear.

From this perspective He has given me a calling to be a science teacher and has provided various life experiences that assist my teaching; from working with rattlesnakes and bats to attending Bible College and exploring the Galápagos. To work with animals that also include wolves, bears, Arctic foxes, and various amphibians has given me a great appreciation for God's creatures. I long for the day that all creation will be restored. As all believers have gifts endowed by their Creator, He continues to instruct me in my use of them for the encouragement and comfort of others.

For example, for two years I had the opportunity to share the case for creation through a local radio program. I have also served as a tour guide at the local zoo, demonstrating how a worldview affects the interpretation of scientific data by comparing the evolutionary story, told by the zoo, and interpreting the data with a creation perspective.

Through the years I have also had many opportunities to share the case for a Creator with secular audiences and various church and youth gatherings. Presently, as Associate Professor of Biology at Truett-McConnell College, I have great opportunities to give glory to the Creator in my biology classes and encourage students in Christ. I also have more time to write articles focused on ecology and biology for various creation magazines and science journals, with the objective of building a creation model of ecology that is more robust than a macro-evolutionary one.

My passion is to teach students how to think about origins, rather than what to think. My prayer is that they will understand the issues, and when the Lord is ready to burst in on their world, evolution won't be a stumbling block. May they avoid the weary, dead-end road of evolutionary humanism and may they be overwhelmed by the love of their Heavenly Father as they travel His road to everlasting life and peace.

From Feminism to Faith

Kitty was a 47-year-old feminist atheist when her beloved Christian mother died. Shattered by her loss, she responded with an intensive, 15-month search for the truth about eternity -- and emerged a radically different person, with radically different priorities, lifestyle, and views of life and death. Her web site is www.EverlastingPlace.com.

Picture this: On the one hand, we have a 47-year-old freelance copywriter, a libertarian feminist atheist, consumed with making money and having a good time. On the other, we have her beloved 87-year-old mother, a God-fearing follower of Jesus Christ, dying of colorectal cancer, overjoyed to be heading Home at last.

If Hollywood were handling this story, the old lady would probably be miraculously cured, and the daughter would have another chance to educate her mother on the finer points of secular humanism.

But that's not how this real-life drama played out. The old lady was not cured. And the daughter was so shattered by her loss that she spent 15 months in a desperate search for the truth about eternity.

Rebellion Meets Grief

It was May of 2000 when these events began to unfold. I was the 47-year-old libertarian feminist atheist copywriter, and it was my mother Ethel Boehm Foth who was so looking forward to seeing her Savior, face to face.

Our journey together had started in Green Bay, Wisconsin, in the 1950s – a decade that we feminists would later scoff at in unison, dismissing those perfect mid-century American families as just one more myth designed to keep women barefoot and pregnant. Pretty hypocritical of me, considering that I was living proof that those perfect American families really did exist, that perfect parents really could love each other till death did them part, that children really could be deliriously happy in an environment of mandatory church attendance and Bible-based discipline and morality.

Alas, those perfect '50s gave way to the "do your own thing" '60s. I was among the millions of teens who discovered that rebellion can be more fun than obedience, especially for accomplished liars whose parents were total innocents.

I *did* receive a horrendous wake-up call a few years into my revolt: On September 1, 1970, three days into my college career at a small liberal arts school in central Wisconsin, my perfect 59-year-old daddy dropped dead of a heart attack, breaking my heart and my mother's. But instead of giving me eternal eyes, his death left me utterly convinced that this God they'd been pushing on me my whole life could not possibly exist, and that this heaven they always talked about was nothing more than a pipe dream.

Returning to college on a Greyhound bus following my dad's funeral, I made a final assessment of my alternatives: Love with abandon and lean on a mythical God who was incapable of protecting me from sure disaster. Or avoid loving anyone too much, living instead for self and pleasure and keeping heartache forever at bay.

It was no contest: the hands-down winners in this sorrowful spiritual battle of mine were self and pleasure.

The Making of a Feminist

It was on a Saturday in late autumn, 1974, that I stumbled across the book that would shape the next quarter century of my life. By then living in an apartment in the big city, studying journalism at UW-Milwaukee simply because my mother and oldest sister had been journalism majors, I had the self and pleasure part of life down pat. But I was pretty fuzzy on the subject of what I wanted to do with my life, having ruled out marriage and family in the wake of my father's death.

I found the answer in a used bookshop on Milwaukee's east side. It was here that I picked up an almost-new copy of *The Feminine Mystique* by Betty Friedan, the self-proclaimed housewife behind the Women's Movement that was transforming our culture. Betty was very persuasive, I soon discovered. She no doubt understood very well the spiritual vacuum many young women were occupying in those days, and she swooped in to fill it.

First she identified our problem: "We can no longer ignore that voice within women that says: 'I want something more than my husband and my children and my home.'"[45] Then she solved it, by pointing us to careers, and incomes, and identities of our own. But she didn't mean any old job: "If a job is to be the way out of the trap for a woman," Betty wrote, "it must be a job that she can take seriously as part of a life plan, work in which she can grow as part of society."[46]

---

45 Betty Friedan, *The Feminine Mystique* (New York: W. W. Norton & Company, 1997), p. 32.
46 Ibid p. 345.

This made sense to me. All I needed to escape the trap that had broken my mother's heart was a profitable career. That would be my purpose in life, and my reward would be a non-stop good time.

And death? Not to worry, I told myself. Either there was no afterlife, or there'd be a heaven along the lines of Lewis Carroll's Wonderland, a never-ending adventure for anyone who'd been a good person in this life. I had no doubt that I'd be welcome there, if it existed. All my friends said I was a *very* good person.

An Education in Evolution

As far as I know, mine was the first generation to be taught that evolution answered every last question one might have about our origins. It was comforting to know that scientists had figured everything out, and fascinating to see the evidence: I remember being especially enchanted with my 9th grade Biology book's photographic-quality pictures of modern horse and its ancestors.

For a kid who'd spent nearly every Sunday morning of her life hearing God-this and God-that in church classrooms, it was also very liberating news. After all, if Darwinism was true, then there was no need for this God of our fathers, *or* his silly rules. He was either dead, as *Time* magazine had proposed in 1966, or, more probably, had never existed at all.

Years later, my professors would augment this conclusion of mine with a number of complementary teachings.

Perhaps most important, I learned to reject Authority – spelled exactly this way in my college papers and blue-book exams, with an upper case "A." I also learned to reject absolute, objective truth; reality is the product of the observed plus the observer, my professors said, and there is no reality apart from this combination.

And there was more. My journalism curriculum included a generous helping of General Semantics – described as a sort of "mental hygiene" to keep language from bringing us to false conclusions about ourselves and others. We were taught never to say anything like "I am a liar" or "he is a thief." Instead, if we had to address such negative thoughts at all, we were instructed to say, "I am a person who lied in this instance," or "he is a person who stole under these circumstances."

Why? Well, we're all basically good people. Which explains why, to many in my generation, the greatest sin was being judgmental; the greatest virtue, tolerance. By which we meant tolerance for all points of view – except for those held by reactionaries such as parents clinging to the status quo.

General Semantics also taught me "the ploggly theory." Developed by a professor of speech pathology – and for some unknown reason thought by our professors to be relevant to journalists-in-training – this theory defined a ploggly as anything we can't see, and therefore a figment of our imaginations. Examples included fairies, demons, devils, and, naturally, gods. That this teaching was a contemptuous dismissal of Christianity and the Bible either did not occur to me, or did not matter.

Such ideas were reinforced by professors in other disciplines. For instance, I spent most of my electives on Modern History courses, including Russian and German history. From them, I learned to venerate the teachings of Karl Marx – including his claim that "religion is the opiate of the masses."

I took Art History, too, learning to embrace impressionism, expressionism, surrealism and fauvism – anything but realism. After all, my professors said, the best art is subjective, and reality is in the eye of the beholder.

I studied philosophy as well, but not the classics. My teachers focused on philosophers like Marxist Herbert Marcuse, existentialist Jean Paul Sartre and feminist existentialist Simone de Beauvoir. I embraced everything they taught me, acing almost every course I took and graduating *summa cum laude*.

Success on All Fronts

For the next 25 years, I pursued my dual goals of a great career and a good time.

After brief stints at PR and ad agencies where I picked up technical writing experience, I hung out my shingle as a freelance writer, turning out copy on high-tech topics, such as nuclear magnetic resonance and positron emission tomography. I was good at my work; referrals accounted for almost all my business.

In my spare time, I dabbled in creative writing, figuring that the best way to gain immortality would be writing the great American novel. That particular goal eluded me, but I did win a contest that resulted in the publication of my first novel, a medical thriller inspired by an interview I conducted in Washington D.C. with a luminary gastroenterologist on behalf of a Philadelphia developer of monoclonal antibodies.

My personal life was equally successful. I had this great boyfriend by the name of Dave, and by the time Bush clobbered Dukakis in the 1988 elections, we were happily living together in a '60s-era ranch house on a wooded suburban street west of Milwaukee. We had two cats and two dogs, a magnificent and ever-expanding flower garden, a huge pool that was perfect for Wisconsin's blistering summers, and a mammoth library of the mysteries and thrillers we both loved. Among the other interests we shared was a fascination with politics, with both of us firmly ensconced on "keeping government out of our wallets and our lives."

My mother remained a huge part of my life over the years. She and I spent many weekends together and even traveled to Europe together several times on magnificent low-budget journeys that made us just about as close as two people can be when they're living in entirely different spiritual realms.

Finally, as she neared 80 in the early 1990s, she moved to Milwaukee, first to a seniors' apartment building, and then into a nearby nursing home. Her health was beginning to fail, but her mind never did, nor did her faith in this imaginary Friend of hers, or her insistence on calling Him to my attention at the most irrelevant times.

The Minister of Defense

It was right about that time that I developed an obsession with pro football and my hometown Green Bay Packers. In fact, Dave and I attended a number of Lambeau Field games that would become legendary – including the Bengals contest in 1992, when Brett Favre stepped onto the field to begin making football history.

But far more significant to me personally was the Packers' January 12, 1997, NFC Championship game against the Carolina Panthers. It was a huge game: With a win, our precious Packers would go on to the Super Bowl for the first time since the Vince Lombardi era. And it turned out to be a magical game as well, with the Packers in control from the opening kickoff. By the 3rd quarter, we fans could smell victory, and we were cheering ourselves hoarse.

But then, during a timeout, something unusual happened. Suddenly there appeared on the Jumbotron the Packers' Reggie White, perhaps the greatest defensive end ever to play the game and an outspoken Christian.

Reggie was not wearing football gear. And he wasn't hanging around a football field. Instead, he was standing in street clothes in some idyllic outdoor scene, singing a song I'm not sure I'd ever heard before.

"Amazing grace," he sang, in what I remember as being the most beautiful male voice I'd ever heard. "How sweet the sound."

The crowd fell silent.

"That saved a wretch like me."

The crowd disappeared. Or so it seemed to me.

"I once was lost, but now am found."

I was told later that 60,000-plus people joined Reggie, forming what may have been the largest choir to ever sing that song.

"Was blind but now I see."

But I didn't hear them. For perhaps 60 seconds, I was alone in that stadium, listening to Reggie White deliver the most magnificent song I'd ever heard.

A Change of Heart

The song ended and the moment passed. The Packers went on to win that game and, two weeks later, to win the Super Bowl, bringing the title back to Titletown and joy to the hearts of Packer backers everywhere. But except for being instantly transformed into fans of the world champions, not much had changed, except, apparently, what I thought of in those days as my "value system."

Take abortion, for instance. As a feminist, I'd been pro-choice ever since the Supreme Court had discovered a right to privacy buried in the Constitution, to make abortion legal in this country. My thinking went like this: Death isn't hard on the dead; it's only hard on those left behind to grieve. Abortion could therefore be sad only for the one who aborts, and since she didn't want the baby, there was nothing tragic about aborting him or her. End of discussion.

But in the months following Reggie's transcendent rendition of "Amazing Grace," I found myself strangely drawn to debates over the issue. In particular, I started reading pro-lifer columnists like Phyllis Schlafly, and found myself secretly agreeing with them.

Horrified by my betrayal of women everywhere, I didn't breathe a word of my treachery to anyone except my mother, who seemed to be inordinately pleased by it.

Then there was the subject of marriage. To put it bluntly, I was against it.

Not that I ruled it out completely. Every April, I dutifully checked the tax tables to see if Dave and I would be better off financially if we got hitched. And every April I discovered, much to my relief, that Uncle Sam didn't seem to like marriage any better than I did.

But apparently my heart was changing on that score, too. At first, it simply crossed my mind now and then that maybe marriage wasn't the worst thing in the world, at least for other people. Then it started sounding like "the right thing to do," whatever that meant. And finally, it became a moral imperative, even for Dave and me: After 17 years together, we were going to have to get married.

And so in early 1999, we did just that. We went to the courthouse, took our vows, and celebrated with lots and lots of champagne in a local bar.

My friends were uniformly horrified. I honestly couldn't explain why we'd done it, except to guess that maybe we were taking a stand against Bill Clinton's moral failures – an explanation that satisfied no one.

The only one who never questioned our motivation was my mother. She was so happy about our marriage that you'd think she'd just received an answer to prayer.

A Sorrowful Search Begins

A little over a year later, my mother was lying in a morphine-induced coma in her bed at the nursing home, on her way to the eternity that she'd been longing for ever since my dad died 30 years earlier.

It had all happened so suddenly that I was still in shock. She had been hospitalized for weeks with pneumonia, supposedly, when a surgeon – a surgeon!

– asked to see me in a conference room down the hall from her room. Here, he told me that my mother had inoperable cancer and two years to live, max.

He was woefully wrong on the timing. Just 11 days later, on May 30, 2000, she was lying comatose in her bed at the nursing home and I was kneeling next to her, whispering in her ear so that the others in the room couldn't hear me making an incredible promise.

"I'll see you there, Mom."

It was an incredible promise because I hadn't believed in "there" since I was a kid. And I had no idea what "there" could possibly mean. But suddenly, I was determined to find out.

Less than 12 hours later, my mother was dead and I had set out on a desperate quest to find out if she might still exist somewhere where I could find her again.

It would take me 15 months of intense study to be sure. Interestingly, my copywriting business practically dried up during that period, but I didn't care. It gave me all the time I needed to seek the truth about eternity.

The Ultimate Whodunit

When I started my research, I still doubted that a god of any kind existed. Yet it seemed clear to me that the answer to the "is there a god?" question would be the key to my quest. Does that seem a bit bizarre? In retrospect, it does to me. What led me to look first for a Person named God rather than a Place called Heaven? Divine guidance, perhaps? Or something He'd written on my heart before I was even born?

Whatever the reason, I floundered at first, looking in vain for hard evidence that this theoretical Person existed – or did not exist. It's true that I wanted the answer to be "yes, there *is* a God and in fact your mom is with Him right now." But wishful thinking wasn't going to do it for me. I had to be sure, one way or the other.

Then I stumbled across a claim that there are only two choices: Either this universe had been born out of time plus blind chance – or it was created by an Intelligent Designer. There are apparently no other possibilities.

I thought long and hard about this idea, and could find no flaw in the logic. Even the idea of space aliens planting us simply moved the problem to a new location; where had the aliens come from?

Now I just needed to figure out which one was responsible, time plus chance, or an Intelligent Designer. It was a *whodunit* that would take this mystery lover the whole summer to solve.

A Surprise Ending

Oddly, it was an atheist friend who pointed me to the key: a book she'd bought for herself, called *God the Evidence*. I raced to the bookstore to buy my own copy – and was amazed to find myself, just a few hours later, reading a scientific argument for the existence of God.

It was startling enough to witness someone using science to demonstrate His existence. But I was even more blown away by the evidences that author Patrick Glynn presented. Chief among them was the anthropic principle, which says that "all the seemingly arbitrary and unrelated constants in physics have one strange thing in common – these are precisely the values you need if you want to have a universe capable of producing life."[47]

Glynn rolled out fantastic and yet indisputable proofs for the anthropic principle – proofs involving everything from gravity and magnetism to the nuclear weak force. I was amazed not only with his facts but also with his claim that this principle was an open secret among scientists in the late 20th century.

How could that be? Why had my science teachers never even hinted at these eerily perfect constants? Why had journalists – even the science writers whose work I'd been reading for years – totally ignored them? Why had all the experts conspired to give us the impression that there's nothing unique about our universe or earth's position in it, that it's all just a happy cosmic accident?

I devoured Glynn's book, looked for more like it, and soon found myself immersed in the Intelligent Design debate.

Over the course of that first summer, I learned a great deal about the claims of God-free evolution, and why it couldn't possibly have happened – and watched in amazement as my long-held atheistic views tumbled down in the wake of such findings as these:

- Natural selection is a Quality Control process, not a creative process. It can account only for conservation of traits, never for their original appearance.

- In order for new traits to evolve, evolution needs additive mutations to augment a critter's genetic information. And these additive mutations simply do not seem to occur very often, if at all.

- Irreducible complexity shows us that every living thing, down to individual cells and probably beyond, consists of mutually interdependent parts that could not possibly have evolved.

47   Patrick Glynn, *God the Evidence: The Reconciliation of Faith and Reason in a Postsecular World* Rocklin, CA: Prima Publishing, 1997, p. 22.

- Biogenesis says that life only comes from life – period. It does not say "life only comes from life except for when it first emerged from that primordial soup."

- Those famous missing links are still missing.

Bottom line: evolution theory's essential mechanisms and evidences are myth. And evolution is far from the "fact" that the modern scientific establishment claims it to be.

By the autumn of 2000, the only logical conclusion had become obvious to me: There is an Intelligent Designer – AKA God. Just one more question to answer, and I'd be home free.

Which God Is the Real Deal?

"Which God?" turned out to be a tough question. I didn't even know where to begin.

But then I fell across another pivotal book – *The Universe Next Door* by James Sire. It provided me with an excellent overview of worldviews from deism, Christianity and Islam to Hinduism, Buddhism and the New Age, with solid detours into existentialism and nihilism. I studied it carefully and came to two important conclusions:

- First, these worldviews contradict each other in key doctrines. For instance, some say there's no god, some say there's one, some say there's a mess of them, and some say you are God. Given such fundamental contradictions, only one of these worldviews could be entirely true.

- Second, with one exception, the worldviews allowing for some sort of god and heaven say that what gets you there is being a good person in this life – the exception being Christianity, which says that what matters is Jesus.

These two facts made it logical to divide my investigation into two distinct and somewhat manageable groups: Christianity, and everything else.

"Everything Else" Sounds Good

I started with "everything else."

The truth was, I didn't want to be a Christian. Except for my mom, serious Christians seemed to be boring, rigid, judgmental, and not much fun to be with. Besides, "everything else" said that what gets you into paradise is being a good person. My mother had certainly been one, and I was determined to be the absolute best from that point on. So if one of the "everything else" religions turned out to be true, we'd be in fine shape.

I began by setting up a gaggle of mental buckets, each labeled with the name of a major religion. Hinduism stood on the left, the New Age on the right, with religions from the Baha'i faith to Islam in between. My thinking was that I'd just start investigating them all, and as I came across proof for each one, I'd drop it in the appropriately labeled bucket. Then, at some as-yet unspecified time in the future, I'd sift through the contents of each bucket and decide which religion looked to be closest to truth. It seemed like such a sensible plan.

There was just one problem: I couldn't find a single piece of proof to drop into any of my buckets.

"Because we have a sacred book" did not constitute proof in my mind. Who doesn't, after all?

"Because it works" didn't do it, either. That's pragmatism, not proof. Besides, they all claimed to work.

"Because there are so many of us" was equally unconvincing. Not only could most religions make this claim; it has always been abundantly clear to me that the majority can be dead wrong.

After a year, every last mental bucket stood empty, and only one worldview was left standing.

It was, of course, Christianity — to be specific, Biblical Christianity. My investigations into "everything else" had shown me that you can't really gauge truth unless you have an unchanging set of propositions and standards to evaluate, and that those unchanging propositions and standards are most easily and reliably found in sacred books.

By this time, I'd almost given up hope of finding a concrete answer to the "which God?" question. I figured that if I came up empty with Christianity, too, I might spend a little time investigating some of the weirder worldviews – Chinese Taoism or Anglo Saxon paganism, perhaps – before throwing in the towel and making up my own God.

As it turned out, that never became necessary.

My first big step was finding out what's actually in the Bible. I didn't have a clue, even though I'd spent my entire childhood attending Congregational Sunday School classes. Apparently I hadn't been paying attention.

It turned out to be a fascinating exercise. I learned that the Bible purports to be the God-breathed history of man from first day to last, and His revelation of Himself to His creation. I also learned that it seems to be 100 percent historically reliable; archeologists are constantly unearthing evidence confirming the Bible's accounts of everything from the fates of cities and nations to the identities and reigns of the ancient world's power brokers. So far, its advocates say, not one piece of contradictory evidence has been found.

There's Just One Explanation

I was impressed, but not yet convinced. After all, there's nothing particularly supernatural about getting your history right, is there?

Early on in my research, I'd come across nutcases claiming that the Bible boasted "stunning scientific accuracy" on the origins and operations of the universe.

Huh? I'd seen *Inherit the Wind*; I knew that scientists wielding Bibles were at least deluded and quite possibly dangerous!

Imagine my surprise to discover that I was wrong – that while the Bible is not a science book, its references to science reveal things that "real" scientists did not discover for hundreds or thousands of years. A few examples:

- Far from teaching that the earth is flat, the Bible clearly says that it is round. For instance, Isaiah 40:22 tells us that God "sits above the circle of the earth." Isaiah wrote around 700 B.C.; I could find no earlier references to this claim.

- In books written hundreds of years before Christ, the Bible talks about the water cycle (Ecclesiastes 1:7 and Job 26:8), the springs of the sea and recesses of the deep (Job 38:16), and the mountains of the ocean floor (Jonah 2:5-6) – the latter features "discovered" by scientists only in recent centuries.

- Who or what is holding up the earth in space? Rather than simply sidestepping the issue, the Bible explains it neatly in Job 26:7: "He hangs the earth on nothing."

- Does the sun orbit anything? Until late in the 20th century, scientists said "no way." But then they discovered that our sun *does* cruise through the Milky Way – just as King David noted in Psalm 19:6 back in about 1000 B.C.: "[The sun's] rising is from one end of heaven, and its circuit to the other end; and there is nothing hidden from its heat."

Then there's all this great stuff about the stars. For example, we presume today that no two stars are alike. But how in the world did the apostle Paul know this in the 1st century, when he wrote in 1 Corinthians 15:41, "One star differs from another star in glory"?

How did the 7th century B.C. prophet Jeremiah know that "the host of heaven cannot be numbered," equating the stars' ranks to the incalculable grains of sands in the sea (Jeremiah 33:22)? The unaided human eye cannot see more than 8000 or so stars on even clear nights; and telescopes weren't invented until the 17th century A.D.

And that was just the beginning. Scripture also told the children of Israel to leave their fields fallow every seventh year, a fertility-boosting practice that was apparently unknown in the rest of the ancient world. It told them to bury their waste outside of their camp, and warned pregnant women against drinking alcohol. And it commanded circumcision on the eighth day after birth – the day on which our blood's ability to clot just happens to peak, medical science now knows.

If that had been the extent of it, I might have simply played the coincidence card and sought out a book on Taoism. But there was so much more that this study took my breath away – because these comments, claims and commands were made by men who had no business knowing any of these things.

It began to seem plausible that the Bible's writers had indeed received supernatural inspiration from the only One who knows everything about this world, because He made it Himself.

And if that is true – and if such ancient observations about our physical world can be trusted – is it reasonable to trust what the Bible says *metaphysically* about where we came from, what we're doing here and where we're going?

It was beginning to look very reasonable to me.

Red Herrings and Research

It will come as no surprise to anyone who has researched these things that atheists in particular have come up with some red herrings to lead seekers away from the Bible. My favorite is the idea of parallel universes, about which we can know nothing now and will never know anything.

I took the bait initially, but didn't waste much time on this whopper. Why would you bet your eternity on a fantasy that can't be confirmed?

Instead, I focused my investigation on things that could be evaluated – including attacks on the Bible's credibility. I read a ton of them, as well as Biblicists' responses. Any seeds of doubt planted by the attacks were quickly washed away.

The Future Before It Happens

I was about 90 percent of the way to total confidence in the Bible when I came across Isaiah 42:9, in which the prophet quoted God Himself: "Behold, the former things have come to pass, and new things I declare; before they spring forth I tell you of them." In more modern terms: "I'm going to tell you the future before it happens."

And that is just what He did.

I am not a sucker for this sort of thing. I'd grown up in the heyday of "psychics" like Jeane Dixon, and knew enough not to believe a word they said. I'd also lived through years marked by intense interest in the very vague and very creepy Nostradamus. I wasn't buying any of it without some solid evidence.

But that's just what I found in the Bible, thanks to tour guides like Hal Lindsey and his eye-opening 1970 book *The Late Great Planet Earth*. It didn't take much research to find out that roughly 80 percent of the 2500 or so detailed and specific prophecies of the Bible have already been fulfilled with 100 percent accuracy, with the rest concerning earth's last days and still pending fulfillment.

Lindsey focused on the events surrounding the most amazing fact of modern history – Israel's rebirth as a nation in 1948, which played out just as the Bible predicted in numerous Old and New Testament passages. But there are also many other prophetic statements in Scripture, including hundreds of highly specific Old Testament prophecies about the Messiah's birth, life, death and resurrection.

Each of these prophecies had been fulfilled to the smallest detail in Jesus Christ. As I studied, it became abundantly clear that He is God incarnate, who paid for the sins of the world on the cross, so that whoever is willing to repent and trust in Him will live with Him forevermore.

This leg of my investigation brought my quest to a jubilant end: I had become one of millions who would call Jesus my Lord and my God.

Fifteen months earlier, I had whispered a wild promise, not having a clue whether I'd ever be able to keep it: "I'll see you there, Mom."

At long last, I knew I'd be keeping that promise after all.

A Promise To Keep

Ethel Boehm Foth went home to her Lord and Savior on May 31, 2000.

She hadn't been under any illusions that I was heaven-bound. In fact, she'd kept a journal in her later years. And when I finally had the courage to read it in 2005, I was saddened to find this entry from March 5, 1993:

> "I look forward to death, except for one reason only. How can I possibly live in a world, no matter how heavenly it may be, if my little agnostic Kitty is not there?"

How heartbreaking, I thought, that she died unsure that she'd ever see me again, knowing instead that if I remained unrepentant, I'd be headed for eternal punishment rather than eternal joy.

But then I thought back to some of the events of her last few years. Maybe she had found herself with some reason to hope.

There was the whole abortion issue, for instance. In 1997, I'd confided my inexplicable change of heart to her, making her promise not to breathe a word to anyone that I was no longer pro-choice.

Then there was my sudden decision, in late 1998, that getting married was a moral imperative, for reasons that I could not put into words.

And then there was a luncheon at one of our favorite restaurants just months before her death. Various relatives were with us, sitting at a big round table in the sunroom, when my very-Christian niece Jenny gave me a belated wedding gift — a beautiful framed cross-stitch that she'd made herself, bearing these words above Dave's and my names and our wedding date:

"Whither thou goest, I will go; and where thou lodgest, I will lodge: thy people shall be my people, and thy God my God." —Ruth 1:16

Whether I'd ever read those words before, I don't know, but I knew instinctively that they were from the Bible. And I burst into tears.

When I'd finally dried my eyes and regained my composure, I noticed that my mother was beaming. Perhaps she realized then that these were not the tears of an atheist or even an agnostic.

And perhaps she now knows that I'll be keeping my last promise to her.

A Transformed Life

Have I been transformed by the evidence for the Lord Jesus Christ and His word?

I don't think you can enter through the narrow gate to life without being radically changed. So it's no surprise that once I placed my trust in Him, coarse language immediately vanished from my vocabulary through no effort of my own. The Bible promptly replaced my once-steady-diet of mysteries and political non-fiction. And a few months later, through the power of the Holy Spirit and frankly against my will, I quit drinking alcohol and ditched a decades-old, three-pack-a-day smoking habit – cold turkey, with nary a prescription drug or support group.

There have been other changes, too, many described in my memoir *Heaven Without Her: A Desperate Daughter's Search for the Heart of Her Mother's Faith* (Thomas Nelson, 2008). For instance, earning big bucks is no longer at the top of my priority list; instead of maxing out my billable time, I now spend about 40 hours a month volunteering at nursing homes. I now feel compelled to share the gospel with all who will listen (including healthcare professionals who ask if I smoke, and then get to hear how the Lord freed me from that particular vice).

But perhaps the most remarkable change is in my vision – for He has given me eternal eyes.

In 1961, my parents decided to spend much of the summer in Europe visiting family and friends while my daddy conducted some business. I was only eight, too young to appreciate such a trip. So my parents left me with dear friends Arlene and George in Madison, 150 miles southwest of our home in Green Bay.

It was in many ways a magical summer, filled with a warm and wonderful cast of characters who did their best to make me feel happy, secure, and loved. So it turned out to be one of the best summers of a truly idyllic childhood.

But I also ached with longing for my parents and our home. So it was also the only truly unhappy summer of my childhood.

As Dickens said, "It was the best of times; it was the worst of times." But the good outweighed the bad, because I had no doubt that my parents would one day come to pick me up and take me home. And when I pictured them pulling up in front of Arlene and George's house, my heart would almost burst with joy.

It's the way I feel all the time these days, knowing that I'll one day head Home to join my folks, to live forever in the presence of our Savior.

Life is good. I'm surrounded by loved ones from a fine husband to an amazing church family. We have a nice house and big garden and all the cats and dogs we can handle. The commute to my office is about 10 steps from the kitchen. And as a freelancer I get to spend all the time I can spare with my elderly friends.

And yet this life is a long way from perfect – especially because my mom and dad are no longer here. So I'm sometimes consumed with a new sort of homesickness, a longing to be with the Lord in a joy-filled land that's free from heartache and pain, hunger and thirst, and every trace of sorrow.

The first time I read Philippians 3:20-21, I rejoiced to know that I was not alone in this longing: "For our citizenship is in heaven," the apostle Paul wrote, "from which we also eagerly wait for the Savior, the Lord Jesus Christ, who will transform our lowly body that it may be conformed to His glorious body."

So yes, life is good. But it's going to be exponentially better one day soon. And for many of us, it may well happen as Paul said in 1 Corinthians 15:52, "in the twinkling of an eye."

My Experiences as a Creationist Graduate Student

Many arguments trumpeted during the latter part of the 19th and early 20th Century that were used to support large scale evolution (macroevolution) have been refuted. These include embryological recapitulation, similarity of blood and sea water, structure and function of vertebrate hearts, and homology. Small modifications (microevolution) can be caused by environmental conditions, but these adaptions do not lead to macroevolution. When Professor Frair realized this, his thinking was transformed.

My home was in Melrose, Massachusetts and so, after my discharge from the U.S. Navy, I entered the University of Massachusetts. My first course in biology was taught by a brilliant professor, Ray Ethan Torrey. The course had been advertised as General Botany but, it turned out to be primarily a consideration of how the flowering plants demonstrated evolution. Plant embryology was presented as a shortened summary of their entire evolutionary history. During the second semester, I studied general zoology under a relatively new Harvard Ph.D., Gilbert L. Woodside, an embryologist who was convinced that the stages in embryological development displayed a summary of the ancient evolutionary past.

One professor in my general zoology course presented data indicating that animals had evolved from a marine environment because their blood fluid had the same constituents as seawater. An evolution argument that was well illustrated in our textbook was the claim that the hearts of fish, amphibians, reptiles, mammals and birds showed a beautiful evolutionary progression. The two-chambered heart of fish evolved to the three chambered heart of amphibians, followed by the intermediate type of four chambers in reptiles, and then avian and mammalian four-chambered hearts.

I also learned about homology as illustrated by the similar limb bone arrangements of amphibians, reptiles, birds and mammals, likenesses that were interpreted as the result of common ancestry. Later, I was taught that Rutgers University scientists had been involved within blood serum studies (a field called *serology*), which was believed to be evidence for evolution.

I was a new Christian then, believing the Bible for what it claims to be and never doubting my salvation, but was somewhat uncertain just what to believe about the subject of origins. Many evolutionary arguments seemed very convincing. I recognized that the book of Genesis was inspired by God, and it appeared to be presenting factual historical information, thus producing a conflict. The conflict became so great that in my junior year I transferred to a leading Christian college (Houghton), majoring in zoology with minors in chemistry and Bible. After graduation, I spent an additional year and summer at another Christian College (Wheaton) taking a full load of science, theology and apologetics courses. I was somewhat concerned during those Houghton and Wheaton years because professors were not able to answer, at least to my satisfaction, some of the questions I had regarding evolution. But I received enough good answers to keep me going in a science career.

I taught middle and high school science, biology, physics, and health before returning to the University of Massachusetts for graduate school. To my surprise, I found myself in an experimental embryology class with Dr. Woodside, my former freshman zoology professor. He was a great teacher, and I chose him as my advisor for a Master's Degree in embryology. I also worked in his laboratory, and we coauthored a paper on effects of the first-discovered anti-cancer drug, 8-azaguanine.

A big surprise was the discovery that Dr. Woodside completely had changed his view about embryology and evolution! He had been transformed by the evidence, and so was I. Embryology had been Darwin's main "proof" for evolution, but another scientist, Ernst Haeckel, had distorted the evidence that had led Darwin to this conclusion. Dr. Woodside groaned that, "There has been only one Nobel prize given to an embryologist (Hans Spemann) because good embryologists came to one dead end after another trying to fit their data into an evolutionary pattern." This effort had not worked because there were far too many exceptions, and, therefore, many good embryologists had become disillusioned and moved into other fields.

After receiving my MA degree for a thesis on chick embryology I completed more graduate zoology and biochemistry courses at Brown University in Rhode Island, and then accepted a position as Biology Instructor at The King's College (TKC) in New York. I commenced further graduate studies in the Biology Department at nearby New York University (NYU) while continuing to teach biology courses at TKC.

On the topic of creation and evolution, I read a variety of books, including Byron C. Nelson's *After its Kind* that dealt with Genesis kinds. I also read literature distributed by the *Evolution Protest Movement* in England and met men who were Christians and scientists belonging to the *American Scientific Affiliation* that had been founded in the early 1940s to oppose evolution. The

Taylor University biologist, Dr. William Tinkle, and other scientists strongly encouraged me to hold to a creation view. I also studied a book titled *Evolution, Creation and Science* by Professor Frank Lewis Marsh.

He argued, very convincingly, that scientific evidence favored the concept of separate kinds that had diversified to produce all the varieties existing among fossil and living forms. Material in that book was a very important reason why I accepted the "kinds" concept as my own working view. Also, geneticist and theologian, Dr. John W. Klotz, by his writings and personal talks helped to transform my thinking to a solid creationist position.

An NYU summer school course I took was taught by the Biology Department Chairman, Dr. Harry A. Charipper, who, at the beginning, gave us a slide-making assignment for the entire course lab time. I decided to show the professor how fast that work could be done, and I worked furiously, completing it in three days! Dr. Charipper was amazed at the quality of my work completed in such a short time, and he gave me a good grade. Professor Charipper knew I had an interest in embryology, and so he wrote an excellent letter to the department's vertebrate embryologist, Dr. H. Clark Dalton, highly recommending me as a potential Ph.D. student.

Before my appointment in the office of Dr. Dalton, I had known him only by his apparently good reputation. He soon learned that I had some questions about evolution and asked if I happened to be a Christian, to which I replied in the affirmative. He reacted with a caustic verbal attack on my faith and beliefs, "How do you expect to be a Christian and a scientist? he queried me angrily. Later he wrote a scathing letter about me to the Department Chairman.

Some days after my interview with Dr. Dalton, I was in the Biology Office to obtain a copy of my transcript. The secretary handed me my whole folder and in the folder on top was the letter from Dr. Dalton to Professor Charipper. I could hardly believe how he literally "tore me apart." I was stunned! I also saw the prior very favorable memo from the Dept. Chairman, Dr. Charipper. However, it was clear that my future in embryology at New York University had been terminated!

Shortly after this, I was accepted as a graduate student in the Zoology Department at Rutgers University in New Jersey—which was like a breath of fresh air! Faculty members there were friendly and anxious to help and encourage students! Many professors in the department attended local churches. I was a laboratory instructor and took graduate courses the first year, had an NSF grant covering all expenses (especially research) the next year. My transcript was replete with graduate credits, and so after just the one-year of courses at Rutgers, mostly on turtle research, I wrote my dissertation, and received a Ph.D. in serology.

My advisor, Dr. Alan A. Boyden, was the Zoology Department Chairman and the senior professor in that department. During the 1930s Professor Boyden had initiated blood-serum-protein studies in the United States. I was the last of his many Ph.D. students, and Dr. B (as he affectionately was known) had a genuine respect for those like me who were serious about their Christian commitment. Because of his research and that of his many previous students, Dr. Boyden had become recognized as the "father of biochemical taxonomy." Most scientists tried to use the results of these studies to support evolution, but they were greatly ill-informed.

During the spring semester of my first year at Rutgers, I had entered a "bombshell" graduate course titled "History of Zoology," taught by the master, Dr. Boyden. This was an origins course, and all we studied was evolution. But, to the amazement of all of us graduate students it actually was an anti-evolution course, at least as most of us understood the word evolution. Defining evolution as change the professor distinguished between microevolution (small change) and macroevolution (large change), and emphasized that it was bad science to extrapolate from small changes (for which there was plenty of evidence) to large changes, all which were imaginary. Those in the class were stunned at first, but as the weeks went on nobody could doubt the force of his arguments. Most evolutionists think that small changes eventually lead to large changes, and so this whole process simply is termed evolution, even today, by a majority of the scientific community. Dr. B, however, called these evolutionists ancestor worshipers or people with a backward look.

Professor Boyden later published some anti-evolution thoughts in a book titled *History of Zoology* (Pergamon Press). Dr. Boyden considered this book to be the sequel to a 1960 publication, *Implications of Evolution* (Pergamon-Elsevier) by Dr. G. A. Kerkut. In that book, Professor Kerkut, a well-known British invertebrate authority, distinguished the special theory of evolution (microevolution) from the general theory of evolution (macroevolution), arguing that the latter is conjectural. Kerkut himself had his own thinking transformed by evidence discovered during his studies of invertebrates.

My research at Rutgers involved reptiles with an emphasis on turtles. In my investigations I focused on classifying the close to 300 different types of living turtles and unraveling their diversification from the time they first appeared on the earth. Authorities on the fossil history of turtles do not agree on their evolutionary origin. The picture is exactly as Dr. Kerkut had found exists for the invertebrates, and it is generally true for other groups—that is, it is difficult to fit the facts into an evolutionary pattern.

The various evolutionary arguments that seemed so convincing during my early months of studying biology consistently have yielded to contrary data.

The similarity of blood fluid to seawater does not indicate evolutionary relationship. Careful studies have showed that the various constituents that were being compared are not in the same *proportions* in blood as in seawater. When I pointed this out to one professor he simplistically proclaimed that only the *proportions* would have been the same for sea water and blood fluid in the first fish when leaving the water and later continuing evolution on land. When I asked what these figures were, he dogmatically declared that we would have to know proportions in the seawater and in the fish *at that time* which, of course, we do not know, and cannot know, with any degree of certainty.

Clearly, this whole scenario is vacuous because there is no evidence for it! However, it is true that some fish today can propel themselves on land by using their *fins*, but these creatures are without question fish and not intermediates between fish and terrestrial vertebrates. But why do we even have similar constituents in both blood and sea water if not because of an evolutionary connection?

The simple answer is that our bodies (and bodies of animals generally) have the same substances that are found in the soil (dust of the ground) because we obtain these from the soil. Animals eat plant tissues produced from chemicals in the soil; or they consume tissues from other animals that are linked in a short or long series of a food chain back to plants. Wherever an animal (or person) is in a food web, the source of its body chemicals (including blood) is terrestrial. The oceans contain these substances because they have washed down in the rivers and were deposited in the oceans. For this reason we would expect some similarities between blood and seawater.

Many studies have revealed that all living things have highly integrated parts similar to a well-functioning automobile motor. Did cars evolve from wagons, rickshaws, bicycles, roller skates or something else because they have similar parts (wheels, for instance)? Of course, one type of car often precedes another, but they both are the products of intelligent design—not the evolution of one into another by some naturalistic process. Does the fact that we can compare the hearts of various animals point to a naturalistic evolutionary series? The two-chambered fish heart functions perfectly well in the fish with the blood cell types and other aspects of the hemodynamic physiological characteristics of fish. This is consistent with a design perspective without regard to origins.

Why would there be change in a fish heart, and many concomitant changes in other body parts, that would allow the fish to convert into a well-integrated amphibian? Since there still are plenty of fish in a great variety of environments, it appears very unlikely that the integration of fish body parts could be modified in ways that would disrupt the integration and still have improved survival value. The three-chambered heart works well in an amphibian, but it wouldn't work well in a fish. A certain motor works well in a car but not on a wagon. *All* parts of both machinery and living things must be designed to function together as a unit.

When the heart of the reptile is drawn in evolutionary diagrams, the septum usually is portrayed as vertical so that it only partially divides the ventricle into two compartments. Thus, it looks like an evolutionary intermediate between the three-chambered amphibian hearts and the four-chambered avian or mammalian hearts. However, a researcher named Holmes reported[48] careful studies of these so-called partial septums that found these elevations of tissue in the large chambers (ventricles) of the hearts characteristically were *horizontal* and *not vertical.* This orientation functions best in directing blood flow through the ventricle. Here again, we recognize aspects of dynamic design and not an evolutionary intermediate condition.

But doesn't the concept of homology point to evolutionary relationships, as I was taught when I was a university freshman? Professor Owen, who coined the term in the 1800s, was not thinking in evolutionary terms. My Rutgers advisor studied the whole issue in depth and concluded that most evolutionists are misusing the term homology. Doesn't embological similarity mean common descent, as most evolutionists claim? I learned that the answer is *no* except when discussing small variations or microevolution—those small changes that occurred, for example, when plants or animals (such as turtles) diversified.

More than a half century ago the English scientist Gavin de Beer recognized the currently well-known fact that similar structures often do not have similar developmental patterns and that similar embryological pathways can lead to *different* types of structures. Modern biochemical genetics (including of Hox genes) has shed much light on many of these issues. The problems are not all solved from either a limited-change or unlimited-change perspective but, as I continue to examine the issues, I am more and more convinced that the facts fit best into an abrupt appearance, limited change (kinds) model. Understanding of the collected facts continues to be perfectly consistent with belief in *intelligent design by the Creator.*

In my own laboratory we examined the red blood cells of the largest turtles in the world today, the sea turtles. An interesting result emerged! The larger the sea turtle, the *larger* the red blood cells. This does not appear to be true for other turtles, but for marine turtles we believe that this observation is connected with their physiology and behavior. While studying these animals I surveyed the red

---

blood cells literature among all the vertebrates (amphibians, birds, fish, mammals, and reptiles). Evolutionists postulated that, as organisms climbed branches of the evolutionary tree, their red blood cells became smaller, and thus more efficient at loading and unloading oxygen. But I found many exceptions to this general concept.

Fish would be expected to have the largest red blood cells and birds and mammals the smallest. But the largest ones are found in certain tailed amphibians, not fish. Birds and mammals would be expected to have small cells because they are warm-blooded and need to load and unload oxygen more rapidly to maintain their relatively constant body (especially high) temperatures. This is generally true, but some birds have even larger red blood cells than some fish. It seems that many scientists endeavor to present their observations in an evolutionary context, not because the evidence is compelling, but for other reasons, which are consistent with their atheistic philosophy.

The position that I feel is most consistent with Scriptural and scientific data today is that God created certain basic kinds or types which, over time since the creation, have varied to a limited extent, producing the many varieties presently found as fossils and living forms. As a result, my own thinking has been solidly transformed from acceptance of large-scale evolutionary changes to the recognition that only very limited modifications have occurred in history within the basic types created by God.

My transformation has resulted in a very active involvement with the Creation Research Society since its inception in the early 1960s. For several decades I served on the Board (Secretary, Vice President, and President), various committees, author of many articles and book reviews as well as promoting the sale of books and audio-visual materials. It has been my continuing concern that the Society should conduct, promote and publish high quality empirical research so that many others would recognize the validity of a creationist model and, consequently, have their own thinking and activities transformed.

Origin of Life Experiments

Doug Sharp and Rich Geer are brothers-in-law and convinced creationists, but their faith was severely challenged when Doug's sister, Rich's wife, was afflicted with brain damage in a hospital accident. The answers they received while investigating God's creation prepared them with answers that dealt with this challenging situation.

Molecular biology and the chemistry of life were the key sources of evidence that caused me to consider God as the creator of life. I remember being enthralled in eighth grade as we studied the periodic chart of the elements and discovering that each of the elements had individual personalities because of their weight, number of electrons, protons and neutrons, and how easily they shared electrons with each other to form bonds with other elements. Later, I read Linus Pauling's *The Nature of the Chemical Bond* and learned how specific orbits of electrons, especially of carbon, could be shared by other elements in forming complex organic compounds. Furthermore, I learned that there were many other bonding types that normally would not be significant, but in complex biochemical situations are essential for the function of proteins.

My interest in the creation-evolution question began with the Miller-Urey experiment, which was an exhibit at a science fair I participated in during high school. My exhibit was a Van DeGraaff generator I had constructed that produced six-foot long sparks. But the Miller-Urey experiment caught my interest because it used the Van DeGraaff generator to create lightning, causing chemical reactions that produced the precursors of life, amino acids. I reasoned that the next step in the formation of life was to assemble amino acids into proteins; so I set up an experiment where I applied additional electrical sparks to the amino acids.

My experiment was flawed, though, because it was done in the presence of both oxygen and water, and I later found out that oxygen was deleterious to the required reaction. In order to form peptide bonds, water molecules needed to be removed. In fact, if the Miller-Urey experiment were set up properly to account for the formation of both amino acids and nucleotides, both necessary for life and co-dependent, the reagents would interact, harmfully and neither one would be produced. Therefore, one would have to postulate two different atmospheric chemical environments, one that produced amino acids and the other nucleotides. That scenario seemed very unlikely to me and I concluded that origin of life from non-life required a creator God.

Some skeptics asked me, "Why did you stop there? You can't give up, for there may be hundreds of chemical reaction possibilities to investigate. Given enough time, experimentation and research, scientists should ultimately be able to discover the right conditions that would have produced life!"

My response was that it triggered a search in a different direction for answers that were much more satisfying. As a youngster, I did not encounter a major negative experience with church, and I had parents who modeled the Christian life. When I compared what I had with that against the lives of skeptics I met in college, it was an easy choice.

At college, my search for answers began when I met Dr. John N. Moore, one of the founders of the Creation Research Society (and then managing editor of CRSQ). He introduced me to the writings of Dr. A. E. Wilder-Smith and Dr. James F. Coppedge. Both of these scientists reinforced my belief that evolution could not work at the biochemical level. Coppedge 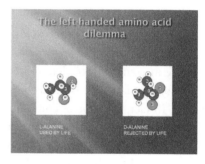 pointed out the amino acids that are produced in these experiments consist of equal mixtures of two different isomeric forms called left and right handed. Because life only uses the left-handed variety, a dilemma materializes for evolutionists. According to Coppedge[49], the odds that an average length protein could form by chance with all left-handed amino acids is one chance out of 10^{123}, an impossibility that can be quantified by comparing it to a race combining amino acids to form proteins at a rate of 400 tons per second, and a snail whose job it is to move the entire earth to the other side of the known universe and back one molecule at a time. To make it tougher, assume that the snail moves at a rate of one millimeter in a million years! By the time you form one protein usable for life, the snail will have won the race, and the volume of proteins you have produced will far exceed the bounds of the solar system! Then, once you have produced that single protein, you would have to find more than 100 more to build the first living cell, all with left-handed amino acids, out of the vast ocean

---

49   Coppedge, James F. *Evolution: Possible or Impossible?* Zondervan, Grand Rapids Michigan, 1973. p. 71-77.

of amino acids produced. Then DNA, RNA and the rest of the chemistry required for life must be produced before you have life.

The left-handed amino acid dilemma is only the beginning of the problems. The next issue is to consider the order in which the amino acids are assembled, which is determined much like a language forms words, or a computer program forms instructions. I marveled as I learned how the DNA molecule codes for a sequence of amino acids that formed proteins. The DNA double helix unravels one section at a time until a string of nucleotides are formed, creating a RNA strand called messenger RNA. Messenger RNA acts much like a computer program whose code manufactures proteins. An assembly line is created where a machine called a ribosome travels down the messenger RNA sequence and provides the mechanism for forming new proteins.

Another type of RNA, called transfer RNA, carries an amino acid to the point of assembly; the ribosome forms the peptide bond and attaches it to the growing sequence of amino acids. A sequence of three nucleotides provides the coding to connect the correct amino acids together, and the nucleotide sequence in the messenger RNA determines the amino acid sequence in the new protein. This system far exceeds the technology found in computers.

In fact, the type of computer program in DNA resembles a modern programming technique called object-oriented programming that creates reusable sections of code for specific purposes. One difference is that the code in living systems is three-dimensional. Each so-called object has properties that can be turned on or off, and "events" or behaviors that occur when something happens to it. In life, these common sections of reusable code are mistaken as homological structures from evolutionary descent. Instead, I believe that these are the mark of a super-intelligent creator who reused the same design structures when creating each species of animal or plant.

Each of the 20 amino acids have side chains whose chemical characteristics cause proteins to fold up into unique three-dimensional shapes, and the shape determines the protein's functionality, much like a three-dimensional computer program. The side chains might be ionic in nature, hydrophilic or hydrophobic (attracts or repels water), to produce covalent or hydrogen bonds.

All of these bonds are not strong enough to be very permanent, but their protein structure becomes strong enough for their purpose. This is achieved by producing a "lock and key" bonding with the other molecules that determines their activity. These proteins fold into their optimal formation only in water, and become active only when they achieve this formation. Enzymes are special complex proteins that catalyze reactions in the cell to allow the reaction to occur more rapidly.

An amazing process involved in this system is called induction and repression. When an enzyme produces enough substrate (end product of a reaction) sufficient for the needs of the cell, the substrate binds to the enzyme and forces it out of the normal conformation, cutting off the further production of the substrate. This, in effect, acts as a servomechanism. The opposite of this also occurs when a co-enzyme is produced that bends the protein into the proper conformation to produce the required reaction.

Enzymes are responsible for most of the energy production required for life's activities, and, ultimately, many enzymes are involved in the formation of DNA. The activity of DNA polymerase is critical because it catalyzes the formation of DNA, has an error-correction mechanism to reduce mistakes, and prevents the double helix system from kinking as new nucleotides are added. In order to explain the origin of life from non-life, a scientist must explain the origin of both DNA and proteins, and the incredible dance of reactions that runs like a complicated series of three-dimensional computer programs. This mind-boggling set of activities speaks of a Creator whose mind far exceeds ours.

Before I started considering these issues, for me church life was more of a social club where I went out of habit. With the help of Dr. Moore and a zoology student I met at Michigan State University, Barry Moeckel, I was transformed to realize the significance of the creator God, and made my decision to live my life for Him. I saw that he wrote his signature on His creation everywhere. Understanding the gospel of Jesus Christ, his death on the cross, and the suffering he did for me for the forgiveness of sins, transformed my life.

I realized that when God created us, he built within all of us this same sophisticated computer code along with the mechanisms, and engineering that went into the creation far exceeded my ability to comprehend it. God places tremendous value on life and the care and detail He applied to design a living organism is beyond even what a team of thousands of scientists working on the problem for hundreds of years could not duplicate, much less improve. The biochemical processes required to turn hay into milk in the laboratory are still too sophisticated for scientists, yet cows do it every day naturally.

As I was working out many of these issues, I shared them with my next-door neighbor, Rich Geer, who had just returned for the summer from the University of Wyoming where he had taken a course in Biblical Archaeology. This evidence, and what he had learned from his class, also caused him to consider the claims of Jesus Christ. He realized that there were two choices: either Jesus Christ was Lord and Savior, or he was not whom he claimed to be and, ultimately, you are dust. Rich invited Jesus into his life and a radical transformation also came over him. His formerly foul speech cleaned up immediately, and he spent days searching the scriptures.

Rich and I were good friends, but after Christ transformed him, we realized that God wanted us to share what we had learned through science and Biblical archaeology study with other people. I remember the two of us attempting to assemble a short movie based on a Christian tract we thought was very significant. That foreshadowed what God wanted us ultimately to do.

Later, Dr. John N. Moore introduced me to the Creation Research Society and books by Drs. Henry M. Morris, Duane Gish, Richard Bliss, and Erich von Fange. Their writings caused me to gain an interest in geology, and I decided to change my college major from chemistry to physical science so that I could tackle many of the broader questions concerning evolution. I knew that evolution didn't work at the chemical level; I needed to know if what I was being taught concerning biology, geology, paleontology and anthropology was correct.

Rocks are not clocks. Dr. Moore set up an independent study class for me on radioisotope dating. It was there that I had the rather unpleasant experience of having my grade held in jeopardy until I rewrote my thesis to be favorable toward the evolutionary model. It wasn't until the 2000 RATE (Radioisotopes And the Age of The Earth) study under the direction of the Institute for Creation Research that many of the speculations I made during that class were confirmed).[50] In order for a clock to accurately register time, it must be sensitive, calibrated correctly, run at a constant rate, and be wound up. There exist too many assumptions in this process for the radioisotope method to be called absolute, yet it is the foundation for justifying millions of years.

The year I graduated from college, I married and went into the military service. During that time, Rich fell in love with my sister and they started a Christian band called Charis at the Master's House, the coffeehouse ministry where Rich came to know the Lord. Just before I was discharged from the Navy four years later, Rich and Carol married.

The Navy stationed me in San Diego where the Institute for Creation Research had just been formed. I had the opportunity there to meet several of the people who wrote for the Creation Research Society, and worked with Robert Kofahl and Kelly Seagraves of the Creation-Science Research Center.

In the meantime, Rich and Carol's Charis group influenced hundreds of people to come to the Lord. When I was discharged from the Navy, the Master's

50   Vardiman, Larry, Snelling, Andrew A. and Chaffin, Eugene F. *Radioisotopes and the Age of the Earth,* Institute for Creation Research and Creation Research Society, 2000.

House was revived at a new location, and for several years I was able to do presentations on the creation-evolution issue to the Charis group.

My pastor encouraged me to write about my passion for the creation-evolution issue and set up a Bible Training Institute course. This book was titled *Revolution Against Evolution*, and after several years Rich and I decided to teach the class on public access television. That opened up an opportunity for us to interview many prominent creationists and also write about their discoveries. The advent of the World Wide Web, allowed us to expand even further.

In 1999 we arranged our first Revolution Against Evolution adventure, a trip to the Grand Canyon, Monument Valley, Canyonlands National Park, Arches National Park, Capitol Reef National Park, Bryce Canyon and Zion National Park. In successive years, we set up trips to the Smoky Mountains, the Colorado Plateau, Hawaii, Glacier National Park and Red Rock Canyon. We also participated in an excavation of dinosaur tracks at the Paluxy River in Texas.

Each year, we held a Charis reunion in July that attracted over 100 people for a picnic, swimming, and fellowship. But one of our greatest experiences was in 2005 when creationist Joshua Gilbert invited us to South Africa. We had the opportunity to interview many different creationists in that country, tour Kruger National Park, and were honored with 25 speaking engagements.

The end of that summer (2005) we had planned another trip to Grand Canyon. This time my sister Carol was going to accompany our group. She had always wanted to see the Canyon. But she was experiencing some physical problems and was scheduled for surgery to take place that July. It was to be a routine colon resection to repair some of the bowel problems she was having. That day caused the greatest test of our faith ever because, while the anesthetic was being administered, she had a reaction that caused her heart to stop beating. By the time the doctors noticed that there was a critical problem, almost 20 minutes had passed without oxygen to her brain. The doctors furiously worked to revive her, and for the next few weeks, she was in a coma on life support. The prognosis was dire and grim: massive brain damage.

The doctors managed to save her life, but they did not expect her to live very long. Our family and friends undertook a prayer vigil that went on for hours, days, and weeks, almost around the clock. She remained in that coma for several weeks with a respirator keeping her alive. All of a sudden our outreach and ministry was confronted with the same issues that surrounded the debate concerning Terri Schaivo.[51] We set our minds to preserve life for Carol and give

---

51   See http://www.terrisfight.org/.

her a chance for recovery. We had seen prayer heal many people, and had people literally on every continent except Antarctica praying for her.

The Charis and Friends group, and the new coffeehouse ministry called Visions, held a fund-raising benefit for Carol where many of those who participated in Charis had formed their own Christian bands. This musical benefit helped carry Rich and our family through this difficult time.

While researching Carol's condition, which was termed *global ischemic anoxia*, we discovered that positive results were seen with hyperbaric oxygen treatment. This caught our interest, since several creationists we know have experimented with hyperbaric oxygen when attempting to simulate the earth's atmosphere before Noah's flood, and achieved some interesting results. One of our friends, Lawrence Tisdall of the Creation Science Association Quebec, had set up an experiment involving growing raspberry plants in hyperbaric oxygen environment, and had produced large-leafed plants very different from those grown under normal conditions. Dr. Carl Baugh at the Creation Evidence Museum also conducted similar experiments. Rich decided to contact Dr. Neubauer in Florida, and eventually took Carol there for treatment.

Because of Carol's comatose condition, many people expected that she would not come back alive. When the accident occurred, the director of the department at the hospital sat down with her family and told us that the prognosis was very bad, and that Carol would tell us when she had enough. But we had many people praying for us, and we found a pilot's volunteer service that would fly her down to Florida for free.

Rich spent a month with Carol in Florida, and she responded to the hyperbaric oxygen treatment. He subsequently found a service in Michigan that would treat her, and continues to do so. Though Carol is out of the coma and alert and aware, she remains severely handicapped and cannot communicate except by answering yes and no through blinking. But we believe that the life God granted her in the beginning is precious, and Rich continues to involve her by taking her to Visions, and caring for her as much as he can.

Carol's condition has challenged the foundation of everything we stand for. Why did God allow this to happen? Carol had just started a part-time position as the worship leader for her church. About a year prior to this, she had been healed of fibromyalgia, which cleared up after Rich had prayed for her. All we know is, though we do not have the answers, our choice is that we will serve God with all of our heart in good times and in bad. We realize that hundreds of people have come to know Christ through Rich's enthusiastic teaching, and the friends we have cultivated over thirty years have observed our response to difficult times.

We have only one choice, and that is to continue ministering to others with the source of our strength, the fountain of living water that God continues to give us. Our prayer is that someday we will be able to fulfill Carol's dream to see the Grand Canyon. She has survived in this condition far longer than what the doctors expected, and outside of her brain-damaged condition, she remains quite healthy. We credit the creation-based hyperbaric oxygen treatments for this. Recently, the Lord has made it possible for Rich to bring Carol home and has arranged for her to have in-home care. With these new developments he can continue with new treatments that are not available at the nursing home.

God has given Rich Geer and me enough answers to make up for the questions we cannot answer now. Science is insufficient as a life-sustaining all-encompassing paradigm because answering one question often raises six more. We are imperfect, sinful, limited human beings with a short life span, and we have no business challenging God and telling Him how to run his universe. We do know that, though our challenges are tough, God has given us ample resources through our church family, friends and even strangers who have helped us during our time of need. Because God gave us enough evidence to trust and rely on Him, transforming our lives, we were able to respond to difficulty without compromising our faith in Him.

Founder of the Creation Science Information Service, Durban, South Africa

Joshua is the founder of the Creation Science Information Service in South Africa, that supplies creation programs for radio broadcasts. His wife, Indira, was deliver from oppression when their family was ministered to by a Christian neighbor.

I was born into a Christian home in South Africa and was brought up to believe that the Bible was the Word of God. While still at high school, I came into contact with a radio preacher, Garner Ted Armstrong, whose writings introduced me for the first time to scientific evidence for creation. As a result, I became casually interested in the topic.

When I committed my life to Jesus Christ around 1968 I became interested in evangelism, but had no specific interest in the creation message. In 1976, my brother Christopher and I founded Grace Tape Library, a free cassette lending library. Our main goal was to provide a resource center for those who desired to study God's word and to have a Christian perspective on contemporary issues and problems.

I wrote to several Christian organizations in the USA requesting permission to use their cassettes in our tape library. One of the organizations I wrote to was the Voice of Truth Tape Library based in Seattle, Washington. I was amazed at the number of cassettes in its catalogue dealing with creation from organizations like the Institute for Creation Research and the Bible Science Association. The speakers were highly qualified committed Christian scientists who believed the Bible to be the Word of God from the very first verse.

This exposure was the beginning of my interest in the creation ministry. For the first time in my life, I realized the importance of the creation message and the need to make people aware of the lie of evolution. I also realized the Gap Theory that I had believed in as a result of my contact with Garner Ted Armstrong and the Schofield Reference Bible was both unbiblical and unscientific. I wrote to several creation scientists in the USA and concentrated on getting as much information on creation as possible. I started sharing this information with others.

In 1978, I married a wonderful Christian woman, Indira. She greatly encouraged me in the ministry, even though I spent most of my "free time" in the tape library, building up the creation resources. Our first child was born on 17 October 1980. I eagerly watched her progress by ultrasound and was fascinated. When I watched my daughter being born, I knew that we were indeed created, fearfully and wonderfully made as Psalm 139:14 records. The births of our other children, Esteleen, Quinlin and Arlton, served to reinforce my belief in our creator God.

After I was married, some friends took over the tape library, and I was free to concentrate my efforts on the creation ministry. In 1986, we founded the Creation Science Study Center to promote Biblical and Scientific creationism in our country. I did this without having any formal scientific qualifications, and working my full-time job on a part-time basis. I was soon in touch with organizations, such as the *Institute for Creation Research, Creation Research Society, Biblical Creation Society, Creation Science Research Centre* and the *Creation Science Movement*, whose resources we used with complete confidence. In 1988 we changed the name from *Creation Science Study Center* to *Creation Science Information Service*.

In September 1990 we passed a major milestone in our ministry. We had the special privilege of helping to co-ordinate the lecture tour of Dr. Duane Gish at locations in and around Durban (KZN, South Africa) where we lived. It was a special privilege to have him and his wife living with us for a most unforgettable week. He impressed us greatly with his tremendous knowledge of creation and evolution, as well as his simple humility. Although he knew that I had no formal scientific background, he encouraged me, and at no time did he make me feel inferior. Meeting with this outstanding servant of God spurred us on to do greater things for our Lord.

In 1991, we worked to get books on creation science into the libraries of all the universities in Southern Africa. The lecturers and students in these institutions needed to be exposed to the creation viewpoint in addition to the evolutionary one in which they were being indoctrinated. We had no funds to undertake such a huge task, so I wrote to several creation organizations and individuals to assist in this project. Dr. A. E. Wilder-Smith wrote in a letter of May of 1991 concluding "to ask university libraries to carry creationist literature is like having Hitler preach a John Wesley sermon!"

In 1992, with the help of Dr. Wayne Frair, we were able to place, not one or two books on creation science as we had hoped, but more than a dozen books in each South African university. Only two universities turned down our offer. We were able to put such books in the university libraries of neighboring countries as well. This project gave us much encouragement, and we looked for other avenues to spread the creation message in our country.

Dr. Wayne Frair continues to faithfully send creation books for us to distribute free of charge to public libraries and educational institutions on a regular basis. We receive many "thank you" letters from institutions and individuals for the books donated to them by us. It is a joy to go to our local public libraries and see our donations being read.

The Lord opened many other doors to spread the creation message, and each time gave us the desire to do more. In 1992, with the encouragement of Dr. Carl Wieland of the Creation Science Foundation (*Answers in Genesis*) in Australia, I became its official representative in South Africa and helped to market their outstanding publications—*Creation Magazine* and *Technical Journal* - in our country. It was a great joy to hear from people all over South Africa who had been blessed and edified by these magazines and the creation books that I imported from Australia and the USA.

In 1997 my family and I had the special privilege of helping to co-ordinate the visit of Dr. Andrew Snelling, to Durban and the surrounding areas. He greatly encouraged us in the ministry and helped us to spread the truth of Genesis creation throughout South Africa. The ministry grew tremendously and, in 2002, *Answers in Genesis* officially opened a branch in South Africa. Although I serve on the board of *Answers in Genesis* - South Africa, I continue working with the Creation Science Information Service.

Perhaps the most important milestone in our South African creation ministry was realized in 1997. The Lord impressed on us to become involved in the radio ministry, even though we had no resources or experience in this field. For several years I had tried to introduce the ICR radio program "Science, Scripture and Salvation" to our local Christian radio stations, but without success. In that year, the Lord opened doors in some of these radio stations for airing the ICR radio programs *Science, Scripture and Salvation* and *Back to Genesis* as well as, the *Answers in Genesis* radio program, *Answers with Ken Ham.*

For the first time, the creation message was reaching many thousands of people in South Africa and the neighboring countries of Zambia, Malawi, Zimbabwe, and Swaziland. The responses from listeners is a tremendous source of joy that spurs us on to continue our work. We have since introduced more creation radio programs to South Africa, viz. *Creation Moments* from Creation Moments Inc., *Jonathan Park* from the ICR and *The Stones Cry Out* from *The Associates for Biblical Research*. We are praying that more radio stations will air our radio programs. It is sad that some of them were not willing to because they are either theistic evolutionists, or they do not see the relevance of the creation message to the Gospel.

In spite of the wonderful way the Lord is using our radio ministry, we realize that we were reaching the "intellectuals" and not the majority of people in our country because our programs are too technical for them. While thanking God for allowing us to reach the "intellectuals," we started praying that God would give us a non-technical creation science radio program that could reach the layman and people whose first language was not English. *We need non-technical creation science radio programs to reach these people. We* are also praying that *the Lord will eventually make it possible for us to reach the whole of Africa with the creation message in the languages spoken by the different peoples.*

Thus far we have reprinted two creation books in English, and translated and printed two creation books in Afrikaans, one of the languages spoken widely in South Africa. We are still faced with the reality that the creation books are also too technical for the ordinary layman and those whose first language is not English, but are praying that our Lord will help us to overcome this problem.

I praise God for enabling me to do all this on a part time basis with the help of my family since 1986. He has faithfully provided the necessary resources, expertise and strength to do the work. In September 2002, I took early retirement from the teaching profession after 32 years of service, and now carry on in the ministry full time.

The Lord continues to open doors, and each time, we marvel at His leading and thank Him for using us in His service. I thank God for the encouragement and support of my wife, Indira and our children Emmeleen, Esteleen, Quinlin and Arlton. Without their patience and encouragement I would not have been able to do the work the Lord has given us.

President of Crying Rocks Ministry

Guy was raised by a pantheist mother. His father was a Christian, but never spoke to Guy about Christ before he died when Guy was ten. Though he never heard either parent speak directly about religion, by the time Guy was in college, he was a committed new age pantheist. After he married a Christian woman, Guy was convicted of his need for Christ while studying the book of Romans in the Bible. Challenged by a church deacon to investigate the first chapter of Genesis, Guy quickly realized that scientific data actually points away from naturalistic causes and toward creation. 30 years of creation science study later, Guy has a creation science ministry and is on offense in proclaiming the creative power of God, who, in the person of Christ Jesus, is the creator of the universe and all that is in it. His web site is http://www.cryingrocks.org.

"I'm a pantheist." When those words came from my mother's mouth, I understood her well and knew this was going to be tough. There I was, 47 years old and I am hearing my mother summarize her belief in three words. I had explained creation science to my mother several times and she had decided she needed to know what to call her belief; so she did the research. Stubborn, she had often called herself. Stiff-necked, the Bible would describe her. Ten years later, stiff-necked she remains. She has lost much of her memory, but remembers that she is a pantheist.

In my late teens I was a searching, philosophical kind of teenager. Into my early twenties, I remained philosophical and searching, but I knew the word to describe my beliefs: pantheist. Being a pantheist was the greatest thing in the world. The reason is pantheism gives you the freedom to create your own religion based on just a few basic concepts. We get to keep trying until we have finally created a perfect religion for ourselves. Reincarnation is the methodology that gives us unlimited chances to get it right. The idea is that we are 100 percent god, all part of the cosmic supernatural force that some call god. Since we are all born good, and only want the best for ourselves and everyone else, our religion also has to be good.

By my mid-twenties, I found there was something deeply lacking in pantheism. It wasn't spiritually or intellectually satisfying. It didn't work when applied to the real world. If everyone is part of an all-loving god, where did evil come from? Evil should not exist, but it is all around us. I had been a practitioner of the religion in my early twenties, but became a non-committed pantheist in my mid-twenties. Life was good, and why mess with a good thing? Just ignore the obvious and all is well.

Then Cindy entered my life. A fabulous woman with all the characteristics I was looking for in a wife. But, good grief, she was a Christian. Worse yet, she was a Bible-believing Christian. But, we got married only six months after our first meeting. I had agreed I would go to church with her every Sunday, and I kept my promise. Little did I know that it would transform me. In a Sunday school class for young-married couples we studied the book of Romans and I discovered why pantheism had left me philosophically and intellectually dissatisfied. The basic assumptions of pantheism were simply wrong. Practical experience backed Paul's straightforward explanation of our sin nature. I was hooked by Paul's intellect… and by the Spirit of God, which entered my heart and mind.

I wasn't a bad person in the world's eye, but was generally kind and soft-spoken. I hadn't committed any major "sin" as I understood the term then. But I realized I wasn't really seeking God. My life was good. Why would I want to mess up a good thing? Though I had thought of myself as one who was seeking truth and God, I realized that what I was actually seeking was self-approval. I wanted to be my own God and create my own truth, yet I had always known there was something greater, MUCH greater, than myself.

Next came a verse that was the second passage of a one-two punch. James 2:10… For whoever keeps the whole law and yet stumbles in one (point), he has become guilty of all." Together, these two verses made it clear that I was a sinner who had rejected God in the face of knowing He is there. He is a holy and righteous God who is pure. Being a technologist, the idea of purity was an easy concept for me to grasp. When microchips are manufactured, the materials must be pure. The slightest impurity nullifies the material. It cannot be 99 percent pure. The material must be 100 percent pure. Just one speck of impurity and microchip material is worthless scrap.

I readily understood that I was impure because I had failed God's command. I knew that just one impurity in my life was grounds for rejection by God. Many claim that they could not accept a God who was so judgmental. However, could God be God if His standard is less than perfect? That was when I made sense of John 3:16… For God so loved the world, that He gave His only begotten Son, that whosoever believes in Him should not perish, but have eternal life. I could not approach God, so God invited me to approach Him.

When these verses were tied together, a perfect plan created by a perfect loving, holy God shines forth. I am lacking in holiness and love so God had to do it all through Jesus. Though I still resisted, the resistance lasted only a few days and, in 1979, on a November Friday afternoon, after work, sitting along the railroad tracks, I asked Jesus to give me salvation. I became a free man in Christ that day. Shortly thereafter, a fellow teacher told me I had suddenly changed for the better. I told her why. How ironic that her daughter had recently accepted Christ and was witnessing to her mother in deed and word, but Sue just couldn't accept it for herself. Sue's reaction reminds me that we must always remember how we are sinful, and that those I witness to are still blinded and in chains. We must always witness in compassion for lost souls.

It was time to join a church. Deacon Randy asked me the simple question that was the challenge of a lifetime. Genesis explains that the world was created in six days and the rest of the Bible confirms that it was about 6000 years ago. What in the world was I going to do with that fact? And that is what Randy asked, though in a kinder manner than my thought had confronted me. Didn't he and I both know that evolution is a fact of science and history? Apparently, I thought, Randy missed that part of his science classes. Next, he spoke those words that always mean trouble, "Guy, I want you to read a book and let me know what you think."

The book was Scientific Creationism by Henry Morris. By page 50 I was mad. I wasn't ready for the idea that evolution or an old earth was wrong. The evolution I was taught as fact was really an interpretation. Morris showed that creation cannot be proven as gravity can. (Duh, doesn't everybody already know that?) and that evolution cannot be proved either; they are both beliefs. But surely there must be more circumstantial evidence for evolution. It was now impossible to set the book down until I reached the last page.

Along the way to the last page came many convincing arguments. The universe had a beginning, so it had to be created. The Second Law of Thermodynamics allows no other possibility. Endlessly progressive upward evolution was a contradiction to the Second Law of Thermodynamics. Then he discussed probabilities as the key to evolutionary dogma. I had heard the story that a million monkeys typing on a million typewriters would eventually produce Shakespeare by random accidents. Then I read that just putting 300 amino acids in correct order by random chances has just one chance in 10^{600}. Why, 300 letters is less than half a page of Shakespeare. And there are only 10^{80} electrons in the entire universe. I wasn't a wizard at math, but the monkey logic was obviously totally irrational. In fact, it was deceptive. Shakespeare isn't going to result, ever.

But didn't geology demonstrate evolution? Morris had it covered. What about radiometric dating? The book had all of the answers I needed. There were things I'd never considered or heard of before, such as the amount of salt in the ocean shows that it is young. It was not so much that the evidence was absolutely compelling to me, it was the obvious implication that the science I was taught was completely deceptive. No science teacher in high school or college had ever presented anything but old ages and evolution as absolute fact, supposedly proven time and again.

Their assumption had been taught as truth. That made me angry! And it showed that science, in the end, was all about countering Christianity. John 18:37... Therefore Pilate said to Him, "So You are a king?" Jesus answered, "You say (correctly) that I am a king. For this I have been born, and for this I have come into the world, to testify to the truth. Everyone who is of the truth hears My voice."

By the end of the book, I started to doubt evolution, but still was not convinced of a young earth and special creation. But I was on a quest for truth and would soon be transformed again. My philosophical side would settle for nothing less, and my spiritual side demanded it. I realized that the eternal fate of every person rested on the truth of the matter. I immediately purchased The Genesis Flood, also by Morris. This book wasn't only showing the weakness of the evolutionary/old-earth argument. Morris was an expert on the evidence for a young earth. Chapter one gave the geological evidence for Noah's flood. I was struck by the very basic concept that gradual erosion results in sloped banks and rapid

erosion results in vertical banks. That jibed with what I knew to make realistic scenery for my model railroad setup. Any fill material will settle and erode to a 2 to 1 slope no matter how steep you make it to begin with.

The fact that hit me the hardest, and still does to this day, is the fact that fossils do not form if the creature is not buried immediately in mud or other material such as amber. One can immediately see the dramatic implication of this simple fact. What is the difference between strata with fossils and strata without fossils? Nothing at all, except for the fossils. So we now know that virtually all strata containing fossils were deposited rapidly as a mudflow. The rest of the strata may just as well have been deposited as mudflows. There is no evidence it was deposited slowly. But the implication is that it may well have been deposited rapidly, just with no

Figure 1: Guy's geological research attempting to explain the processes that caused soft sediment deformation (folding of strata) in the Sedona, AZ region. We have included several photographs of a few of the folds Guy has discovered.

dead creatures to fossilize. The assumptions of long ages in many cases appears to not even make scientific sense.

If the earth is young, evolution is scientifically bankrupt. The unfortunate fact is that in 1980, the two books I had read, comprised a good percentage of all the books on creation science. I wanted to read more, lots more, and things are different now. Hundreds of books on creation are now available. With the Internet, we all have a huge library of articles describing scientific research and the implications of new discoveries. Where, during the 1980s, much of the argument was against the assumptions made by the naturalists, today creation science is on the offense. The evidence is mounting daily that the universe, and you and I, are special creations by God.

My favorite argument today is the magnetic field of the earth and other bodies in our solar system. When a materialist starts talking about the big bang, I bring that person back to our solar system. The nebular theory of solar system formation requires a very specific mechanism for maintaining a magnetic field over billions of years. Years ago it was discovered that the earth's magnetic field is decaying at nearly three percent per century. If you extrapolate backwards, the amount of electrical current required to create the field would also create so much heat that the earth's crust would melt. Naturalists were quick to point out that the field was possibly breaking up, but the total strength was unchanging, an unlikely but possible solution. Launching a satellite to measure those small fields that had supposedly broken away from the main field tested that theory.

It turns out those fields are there, but are not nearly strong enough to account for the loss. The naturalists gain about 10,000 years but need 4,000,000,000 years. Russ Humphreys came up with a model that explains the creation of the magnetic field within a young-earth creation. Not only does he get it right for earth, he gets it right for all the planets. In 1975 the magnetic field of Mercury was measured for the first time. The first problem was, according to the naturalists, Mercury wasn't supposed to have a magnetic field. Humphrey's model fit the data perfectly. Humphreys made a prediction of the rate of decay of Mercury's magnetic field in 1984. In 2008, the Messenger spacecraft made a measurement of Mercury's magnetic field, proving Humphreys' prediction correct.

Today, when confronted by an evolutionist, I am on the offense, not the defense. All of their arguments are so easy to attack, and it is easy to present good, solid evidence that young-earth creation is true. The magnetic fields of the planets in our solar system are a classic example. When the naturalists made predictions, they got it wrong. When they try to model the actual measurements, the models become complex and full of conjecture. Humphreys' young solar system model is simple and does not need to be modified to fit each planet. It is accurate and makes accurate predictions in advance of measurements taken. Naturalists are always claiming that creationist theories never make predictions, and this is one of the best examples we can use to show them that their claim is false.

In 2001, just two years before my retirement from teaching in Ohio, Cindy and I made the plunge. We asked God to direct us to a place where we could have an evangelical ministry. A small town would be good; small enough that we could have an impact, large enough where my city-girl wife would not feel completely stifled. We spent two years searching and praying. Two weeks after retiring, we were in our new home, 1,950 miles from where we had lived up until then, in Sedona, Arizona. Everyone has an impression of Sedona. Some regard it as the new age Mecca. Most don't realize it, but it is also an atheist haven.

When we first decided we would have a creation-science based ministry, Cindy demanded, "Are you absolutely sure you are right?" "Absolutely," I responded, a strong position on an important question. When we began writing and sending Creation News Update to all 10,000 homes in the Sedona area I was challenged time and time again by readers. Even just a few years ago my response was too often that research has shown that evolution is incorrect. The past few years have been remarkable in science research and publication. I ask, "Explain how a dinosaur fossil can have blood vessels, blood cells and soft tissue? We know the half-life decay of organic chemicals that make up life, and that means those fossils must be only a few thousand years old." The opponents demand, "Cite your source!" So, I do. Now I demand, "Cite your source." They have none. The evidence has transformed me.

In the 1990s, homosexuals began wearing tee shirts that read, "I'm queer. I'm here. Get used to it." Their strategy was brilliant. And it worked on the general population. My new motto is "I'm here. I'm a Bible-believing young earth creationist. Get used to it." This is no time to be timid. The atheists are on the attack because they know that only blustery behavior has any hope of covering the truth. We must all pounce on the evidence and take it for our firepower. There is no question now. Scientific research has made it clear that naturalism is intellectually bankrupt.

"I don't label my beliefs or belong to any organized religion," a friend, Dan, said as he explained his beliefs. Frank and I were almost to the summit of Bear Mountain. Dan had just started back down toward the bottom. Dan is a pantheist and everything he said described Hindu-based pantheism. Of course, his was creative in some details because that is the beauty of pantheism. You can tailor the religion to your own beliefs. "But Dan, how would you explain that to sex-slaves in Darfur? How could you have lived a thousand lives, there hasn't been enough time? How could there be so many evil deeds committed, even by reasonably good people, if we are born good, all divine, and god is pure love and goodness? How could any evil exist?" Dan had no answers and didn't care. He has no desire to be philosophically and intellectually satisfied in a rational manner. He didn't even come across as spiritually satisfied. Dan just wanted to be his own god, to define "good" as that which he does. I understand. I have been there myself.

But that was 35 years ago. Today, having been transformed by the evidence, instead of being my own god, I am a philosophically, intellectually and spiritually satisfied messenger to the world about the battle for eternity that is occurring in the world.

Today, I work to transform others by the evidence. Sedona, Arizona is the new age Mecca of the western world. Millions visit our little city each year to experience the supposed energy vortexes and enjoy one of the most beautiful

places on earth. Many residents are of the new age persuasion, but we have discovered there are also a lot of atheists in town. Our newsletter is crafted to grab the attention of both of these groups.

Reactions to the newsletter are often interesting. New age advocates that contact us are many times angry. They are being confronted with the same thing I was confronted with in my 20s. In the end, new age philosophy just doesn't make sense, but they don't want their world messed up with truth. The atheists are generally more rational. Those who really understand what they believe carry on intelligent discussion with me personally and via email. Most email includes some new scientific discovery that supposedly falsifies creation. I write back with what the study actually found, and why it does not support their cause. I then add some discoveries that contradict naturalism. The usual response is that is the end of the email exchange. They cannot support their position, so they fade away, sometimes to reappear with another attempt at a later date.

As I go about my business around town, a person will often say, "I know you from somewhere." I tell them they saw me on the cover of our newsletter. Surprisingly, the most common response I get is, "Oh yeah, that's where I've seen you. You have some really interesting information in that newsletter and I enjoy reading it." They are still a long way from accepting our Lord as their savior, which is our end goal, but at least they are reading about creation and the truth of the Bible, many times for the first time ever. Hopefully, many of those readers will be persuaded by the evidence to look more deeply into the matters of creation, and the meaning of their life and the universe. The tag line on many of our articles is… Jesus is the Creator of the universe, you and me. And that is the truth that lies at the end of the trail of evidence.

Journey from Murderer to Creationist

Michael Bailey is an inmate in a correctional facility in Ohio serving a life sentence. In his story he recounts in some detail his journey from being a murderer to a convinced creationist.

Why did I murder someone? Why do people harm each other? What makes me who I am? I will try to answer these questions in this chapter. As an adopted child, I have many questions about my origins that have persisted throughout my life. The quest for knowledge of my past, and the answers that I entertained over the years, has had important implications in my life. These are questions that face everyone, not just me.

Roger and Carole adopted me when I was only three months old. "Your real parents didn't want you, we shouldn't have picked you either!" is how Roger explained my history to me. He was a violent and perverse alcoholic, and my brother (adopted from a different family) and I never knew what to expect from him. Any failure on our part invited rage that resulted in beatings and destruction of furniture and other things. I vividly remember the snake-like nature of his sexual advances toward me as a child. Carole, while not a part of this, turned the other way when it occurred. When she attempted to leave him, she believed his lies, and would take him back. She was not evil or perverse, merely weak and afraid. Roger died when I was twelve; his body poisoned from alcohol. His passing brought me great relief, but also much grief and guilt.

God was not any part of our home life. Roger openly mocked people of faith; even discussions of God were not allowed. My mother and grandmother believed in God, but their faith did not impact me as a child. School was no different. God showed up for the pledge of allegiance, but was nowhere to be found during the rest of the day. Evolution and its principles were taught to us from elementary through high school. I learned that people were not special, but were the result of eons of aimless evolutionary progression, and I thought that applied to me. I believed what I was taught – and had nothing else to grasp for guidance.

After Roger's death, Carole married Bill. He was also an alcoholic and, while drunk, his behavior was from smarmy to ugly; yet was different from Roger. I believed that he loved my brother and me as best he could. Even so, his words and actions added to my already damaged soul. Bill was a churchgoer and we began going to the local Episcopal Church. The people there were open and loving, and their unfeigned love drew me to Christ. Yet there were parts of my life that I wrongly then believed were too ugly for even God to accept, so I did not surrender my life to Him. Despite this, I was active as an acolyte (altar boy) and a peer counselor in the diocese. I even started a prayer and study group at the local public high school. During this time I also did many ugly things that I would later regret. In retrospect, many of my activities were just attempts to find meaning in life.

In high school, my education on the evolutionary origins of mankind continued. Haeckel's diagrams, peppered moths, and the "ascent of man" chart all pointed to Darwinism. Millions of years rested securely on the geologic column. It all made sense to me but, as is true of most young people, I was not a critical thinker. Evolution was all that was presented and, although I had some reservations, I accepted it. My faith did not challenge evolution: I believed that God had merely overseen the process. This did not offer much comfort, though, and was soon challenged.

"'Free will' does not exist," a buddy claimed, "Everything from the Big Bang on is part of a predictable chain of cause and effect events. Consciousness does not exist either; everything that occurs in our mind is the result of chemical and electrical reactions to stimuli. We have no more control over our thoughts and actions than does a pot of soup on a stove. With heat and stirring it ends up ok, with too much heat, it overflows."

I protested against this line of thinking, but what he said seemed to make sense. Everything—quarks, muons, molecules, motes of dust and neurons, amoebas and men—obeyed the unalterable laws of the universe. What we call consciousness and choice is the result of a set of causes, often unknown to us, that go back to the Big Bang.

These events are part of the chain of causes leading to an unavoidable future. Free will and all that goes with it, including our seeming ability to ponder our existence, are all illusory. I was unprepared for this assault on my incipient faith. Although I thought he was mistaken, I could not debate him. I tried to use the Bible and my rudimentary understanding of science, but I could barely convince myself, much less anyone else. It shook my faith, and I settled into the deep-seated opinion that I was garbage, and that who I was could not be changed.

My home church, although conservative and somewhat evangelical, did not offer much help. They loved and supported me, but offered me no insight as to who I was or what made me do the things I did. There was no alternative to Roger's verbalizations (or my own). Much as my mother had silently enabled Roger's words and deeds to warp my opinions of the world—and of myself—the church enabled the schools (and society) to teach me that my ultimate value rested in the few dollars' worth of chemicals that made up my body.

Throughout this time I was filled with the pain and a sense of betrayal. I had tried many things (good and bad) to end this pain, and was about to try something new: after high school, I spent three years in the Army trying to be all that I could be. The same problems I had in school stayed with me in the Army. Away from home, I indulged my dark side even more. Roger had used violence to get his way, and so did the Army. The Army is full of good, brave, dedicated people, but war operates on the premise that violence is a natural and effective means of solving problems. I picked up discipline and respect while in the military, but like my life situation before this, I found nothing to answer my basic questions about who I was or why I existed.

When my time in the Army was completed, I returned home. Like many victims of abuse, I was drawn there (and kept there) by an inexplicable gravity. To try to live my life, I worked and went to college, but the pressure within me continued to build and I did not think there was any way to safely release it, so I did not try. Not much had changed at home and the longer I was there, the more fragile and unstable I became. In February of 1990 in a fit of rage and pain that was building up for years, I shot and killed both Carole and Bill.

Returning to the question posed earlier: what made me a murderer? Were my actions the inevitable results of electrical and chemical reactions reaching back to the dawn of the universe? Was I but a hairless ape acting out in an atavistic rage? Was I fated, by blind processes, to stay in this state of continued confusion and pain? Or was there another option? Perhaps I was someone who had been through unbearable situations and had made one bad decision after another, resulting in one really terrible one. Could the course of my life be changed and was there even anything worth salvaging at this point in my life?

I had suppressed the knowledge of the crime and, convinced of my innocence, I fought the charges and told everyone I did not do it. Nevertheless, in November of 1990 I was convicted. Before my conviction my grandmother arranged for a friend, George, to counsel me and help me get through the grieving process. George continued to visit me after my conviction. He was able to see through my lies, and helped me to admit my guilt. "You have to tell your grandmother" were his words.

Doing so was the hardest thing I have ever done. I had killed her only child, my mother. She could have done anything, from hang up the phone to curse me. Yet, her first words were "I love you and I forgive you." She did not excuse what I did, nor did she give me a free pass, but she forgave me. She stood by me and insisted that not only could I, but that I *must* change. More than the many loving words of my mom, or the people at church, it was her unnatural love that touched me. God used her to get through to me, and He began to show me that I really am a child of God. Until her death in 2004 she continued to support me and urged me to become a better person.

Prison provides a great deal of free time. For me it has been a time of struggle and growth. In searching out the causes for my crime, I had to find out who I was and what made me that way. While getting counseling to overcome my emotional damage, I had to study to overcome the intellectual damage done to me by Darwinism. George and my grandmother challenged me, as did my fellow inmates. Many kinds of people are in prison including atheists, agnostics, nominal Christians, Jehovah's Witnesses, Muslims, Nation of Islam, Wicca, New Ager's and people with a wide variety of personal beliefs. We live nearly on top of each other.

Many in here hold to some kind of Darwinism evolutionary Naturalism, pre-Adamic humans, cycles of death and renewal and billions of years of struggle and destruction. Many also share the fatalism of my high school friend. Often this worldview was used to excuse (or justify) their actions.

I became a critical thinker, questioning what I had been taught and read in school and in *National Geographic* and in *Scientific American*. I sought materials about the Bible and its reliability. I began with archaeology and recorded history. As I became convinced that the Bible was true, I began to study the topic of origins in depth. In this study I was helped greatly by *Answers in Genesis*. Although I was in prison, they treated me with great respect, and this watered the seeds that my grandmother had sown. They were always happy to send materials.

Reading Dr. Henry Morris' *The Genesis Flood* and *The World that Perished* was also very influential, as was *The Waters Above*, even though much of the theory in it is no longer held by many creationists. Other books provided solid reasons to support the biblical record and the view that the scriptures were reliable and reasonable. Writings of people like Dr. Jerry Bergman spelled out the far-reaching implications of an evolutionary worldview. This helped me to see how I had been damaged as a child, and to change the way I viewed myself.

As I discovered the frailty of the factual support for Darwinism, I shared this with others. I passed around my magazines, books, and articles and discussed them with believers and non-believers alike. I came to realize that no firm empirical evidence for the Darwinian worldview exists. Indeed, the vast array of evidence—both physical and societal—is clearly against it. It surprised me how many Christians held to Darwinism and how obstinate some of them were in holding to this worldview. They defended theistic evolution and various gap theories as though their lives depended on these ideas. Even after all of our discussions, many of the people I spoke with either could not understand or did not care about the implications of their beliefs.

What are those implications, and what do they say about who I am and why I became a murderer? Does this have anything to say about humanity's future or my own? The theory of evolution did not kill my parents; yet, its incessant message echoes throughout the pain of my life. It led me to believe that I am an accident of natural forces, the product of long years of God-absent or, worse, God-sanctioned death, bloodshed, and perversion. It supports everything from the casual lie, to the Holocaust, and the murder of my parents. It says that all of these things are natural and, in some sense, is a "good" called natural selection. It tells me that there is no hope for change in my own life, much less the life of the world. We will always be red in tooth and claw, and the fittest survive.

The message of the gospel, beginning with creation, sends a very different message. It allows for the unnatural and, at times, demands that the chain of cause and effect be broken. It says that I, like my first parents, bear the image of my Creator and that I am no accident. The creator Himself can enter creation and break the chain. It allows for the unconditional love of my grandmother. It says that people like me, who have made terrible choices, can accept the forgiveness offered by Christ and that will transform their life, as it did mine.

It is true that terrible things were done to me, including teaching the lie of evolution, but I chose to believe these lies. I chose to nurture the hatred and rage that Roger had sown in my life. I was the one who stored everything away until the fragile container that was my soul snapped. Yet, the break was not inevitable. It always rested with me to continue in that cycle or to be freed by my Creator. It was my choice to believe the lie that people are mere pieces of the evolutionary machine, rather than of a loving Creator who has crafted each of us. Whether I am in prison or out, I choose to share the message of hope found in the creation and redemption of humanity by Christ that transformed me from murderer to follower of Christ.

Wonders of Creation

Jean was astounded when her evolutionist professor told her that the fossil record did not support the concept of the gradual evolution of life. It was at this point that she realized that belief in evolution had nothing to do with the evidence. Jean's research has contributed much to the understanding of the differences that have arisen within created kinds since the time of the Flood.

I was raised in a nominal Christian home. For several years we attended the same church as my aunt and uncle. There I encountered the gospel and was impressed at how the teaching I received made so much sense in light of everyday life. I knew that I had been selfish and unkind to my siblings; I knew it was wrong and I didn't want to be a selfish person. I recognized that I needed forgiveness and the power to overcome my selfishness. So during this time, around the age of 10, I accepted Christ as my Savior. I also found God's world amazing. I developed a strong interest in science, loved nature shows, and dreamed of being a veterinarian someday. Seeing the wonders in creation further deepened my admiration for God and my desire to please Him.

Sometimes there were evolutionary claims in the science materials that I came across. A family member pointed out to me that the theory of evolution contradicted the biblical teaching of creation. When I took high school biology, I wondered what evidence for evolution would be presented in class. We studied homology, which I considered fairly weak circumstantial evidence. Anatomy could be similar because two creatures were related, but it could also be similar because they were intentionally created that way. I remember pondering briefly the idea that life was not created. After lying on my belly in the grass and staring at the detail in a dandelion, I concluded that was a silly notion. The flower was too incredibly intricate in its design; I knew someone far wiser than I must have created dandelions.

In college I took biology, zoology, genetics, biochemistry, and microbiology to prepare for veterinary school. I continued to be in awe of the amazing complexity of life. At the same time, I was surrounded by professors and other students who openly mocked the Bible and Christian beliefs. There were several times when I experienced strong doubts. Once, when I knew the Bible commanded me to do something I found difficult, I was assailed by doubts. It was as if a voice inside told me that doing that difficult thing was stupid: there was no God; after all I had never seen Him. Despite this inner turmoil, I chose to do the difficult thing. I reasoned that, even though in that moment I felt like God probably didn't exist, I was still going to do what was right because if He really did exist, I wanted to please Him. Fortunately, these times of intense doubt didn't last very long. I could look at the teachings of the Bible, such as on forgiveness or honesty, and see that these were important. If evolution is true, there is no point in forgiving others or being honest when it seems inconvenient. I also could look back at what I learned in class about the incredible complexity in the design of life and know that God must have created it. The study of nature quieted my doubts and enabled me to trust the Bible, which transformed my life.

Throughout my undergraduate studies I read my Bible regularly and grew in my faith. I was very interested in knowing the truth. Professors would make comments about the overwhelming evidence for evolution; yet I had never learned anything in class that was convincing to me. Since I didn't want to believe a lie, I figured the best course of action was to investigate and find out what they were talking about. I attended several elective classes on evolution. One class that was supposed to show examples of evidence for evolution discussed extensively shifts in the genetics of populations. These were not examples of change supporting the idea of onward, upward evolution; no new body parts were being evolved.

I was in for a big shock when I sat in on a graduate level class on evolution. The professor, an evolutionist, told us that the fossil record didn't really support the concept of gradual evolution of life on earth. As a result, some scientists had proposed ideas about how evolution occurred in large jumps. He said the problem with that was that most biologists didn't feel this view was consistent with what they saw in the world around them. So it had been suggested that life evolved on another planet and was skyrocketed to earth after major developments had taken place.

At this point I felt like rolling on the ground in laughter. I couldn't believe I had heard this from science professor at the Ohio State University. Why was this science fiction scenario taken seriously? I chose not to laugh, but sat politely in my chair. It was at that point I realized that belief in evolution had nothing to do with the evidence.

One thing I did find very puzzling during my undergraduate years was the differences in chromosome numbers between horses, donkeys, and zebras. It seemed to me that chromosome numbers shouldn't be able to change without causing serious problems. In genetics class we learned that chromosomes line up in pairs at meiosis. If one part of a chromosome moved to another chromosome, the homologous (matching) regions would bend or twist so that each gene would line up with its mate. Such rearrangements should naturally lead to difficulties in meiosis (cell division that results in gametes, that is egg cell or sperm). So these chromosome changes should make it very difficult for the animal to reproduce. Yet creationists considered all equines to belong to the same created kind, in spite of differing chromosome numbers. It would be years before I had the opportunity to examine the evidence in more detail and come to a satisfying conclusion.

I enjoyed veterinary school and continued to be astounded by the extraordinary design in animals as I studied anatomy, physiology, and embryology. I had intended to go into practice after vet school, but when I graduated I was halfway through a surprise pregnancy. This meant my dream of being a large animal veterinarian was interrupted. I ended up taking a job as a research assistant where I was paid to earn my master's degree. I enjoyed this research position very much. In one class, we were required to read research papers from various journals and decide if the authors' conclusions were supported by the research they had completed. This was a real eye opener for me.

I had always assumed scientists were relatively unbiased and that peer review would weed out excessive conjecture. I was astounded by how much opinion was presented in a dogmatic way in a number of papers we read from reputable scientific journals. It seemed that the more bold and sweeping the conclusions, the less those conclusions were supported by actual research. I didn't realize it at the time, but this graduate level course was very important in preparing me for what I was to do in the future.

After graduate school, I worked for the U.S. Department of Agriculture for just over three years. Then I resigned to stay home and home school my four young children. Nearly 15 years later, when my children were more independent and scientific literature had become readily available through the Internet, I went back to digging through the scientific literature. I also began writing for several Christian apologetics organizations. This turned out to be a very rewarding opportunity for me. I had been reading and studying my Bible regularly since late high school; I had found it immensely practical in many areas of life. My new research required that I dig in the Bible for relevant information along with digging into the scientific literature. Since the Bible gives important history that is ignored or rejected by secular scientists, creationists have a source of critical information that can help our understanding of natural history. For example, the Bible clearly states that animals were created by God according to their kinds. Since most kinds of land animals were represented on the Ark by only a single pair, we know that the diversity within these kinds was very limited immediately after that point in history. Using this information, we can get a fairly accurate estimate of the amount of variability that has arisen within various kinds since the Flood.

It was during this time when it became much more obvious how well my graduate work had prepared me for understanding the creation/evolution debate. Evolutionists were commonly claiming one thing or another was evidence for evolution. In reality, the evidence was just explained within an evolutionary framework. The same evidence could be understood within a creationary model just as easily. This is why the evidence had never seemed compelling to me. But my graduate studies took me beyond this point to where I could see underlying assumptions. When I came across evidence that did not make sense to me, I learned to identify my assumptions and question them.

Eventually I got back to the issue of differing chromosome numbers within created kinds. I was astounded to find out that chromosome numbers within certain species could vary considerably. Even more surprising was that, in many cases, no detectable loss of fertility resulted in these animals. These variations in chromosome number were not from an extra chromosome showing up (as in Down's syndrome) or one being lost. Instead, they resulted from one chromosome becoming attached to another or a previously existing chromosome dividing in two.

It didn't make any sense to me that accidental rearrangements could occur so frequently and not adversely affect the animal. After all, chromosomes carry the code necessary for the animal to survive and function; random chopping and rearranging couldn't be a good thing! Finally, I realized that I was thinking like an evolutionist; I was using their assumption that all changes to chromosomes were chance errors. Nothing in the Bible suggests chromosome rearrangements can only result from accidents, a haphazard chopping and pasting back together. The fact that some are harmful had made it easy to assume that all were just accidents. However, when I dug into the scientific literature, the data I found implied that numerous mechanisms must be in place to allow for successful rearrangements. [52] This means there was design involved! Also, since it is common for different chromosome numbers to be characteristic of different species within a Genesis kind, it appears likely that these rearrangements serve some useful purpose.

I also became interested in mutations in various genes. As a vet, I had assumed that mutations were always accidents since I knew many of them caused disease. Yet, as I dug into the scientific literature and considered that animals from unclean kinds, such as horses or dogs,[53] would have had a maximum of four alleles (different versions of a gene) between them in the pair preserved on the Ark, I realized that

52 A semi-technical article summarizing my early findings is Lightner, J.K. 2006. Changing chromosome numbers. *Journal of Creation* 20(3):14-15. http://creation.com/changing-chromosome-numbers. A later more technical article looking at patterns in cattle is Lightner, J.K. 2008. Karyotype variability within the cattle monobaramin. *Answers Research Journal* 1:77-88. http://www.answersingenesis.org/articles/arj/v1/n1/karyotype-variability-cattle. It is known that the cell has enzymes that cut DNA as well as ones to repair cuts. These are used during homologous recombination, when corresponding chromosomes pair up during meiosis and swap segments.
53 Lightner, J.K. 2009. Karyotypic and allelic diversity within the canid baramin (Canidae). *Journal of Creation* 23(1): 94-98. http://creation.com/images/pdfs/tj/j23_1/j23_1_94-98.pdf.

a lot of genetic change had occurred in some genes since that time. I noticed that sometimes researchers would use statistical methods to show that the mutation patterns were not random. Many just assumed that underlying mutations were random and concluded that the statistics implied selection had occurred.

The problem was that often there would be no obvious reason why selection would be strong enough to account for these changes. So, the statistics could just as easily have been evidence for non-random mutations.[54] A considerable amount of data suggests that many mutations (changes in the nucleotide sequence of DNA) in animals may be directed. In other words, the DNA sequence was not created to be static and unchangeable; in some cases God had provided a means for it to change.

This brings out the point that even the ideas of creationists are not always as biblically based as we might like. At creation and again after the Flood, God told his creatures to reproduce and fill the earth (Genesis 1:22, 28; 8:17; 9:1). So certainly He has enabled them to adapt as they do so. Unfortunately, the evolutionary ideas of random mutation and natural selection, which I had accepted as an explanation for all genetic changes since creation, had obscured what is really happening in the world around us. In reality God, in His infinite wisdom, designed animals to be able to undergo certain genetic changes that would enable them to adapt to a wide range of environmental challenges while minimizing risk. This brought an added excitement back into biology as I saw God's provision in a new way.

I recognize that changes can and do occur over time. I also recognize that they are not necessarily accidents. All life was designed to be able to adapt. However, evolutionists need more than just change to support the idea that life shares common ancestry. A particular pattern of change is necessary: mutations must be building complexity or they cannot explain where complexity comes from. This is not what we see when we look at mutations. Instead, mutations that are adaptive tend to erode complexity.[55] The adaptations we see going on today require that the complexity already be in place and designed to allow for useful changes.

The evidence, both in the Bible and in nature, has clearly transformed my life. It played an important role in drawing me to salvation and inspiring a love for science in my youth; it was important in maintaining and nurturing my faith during college; it continues to provide new insight and direction in my research. The evidence from the intricacies of design in a dandelion to the genetic complexities in mammals all points to a wise and powerful Creator who cares for His creation. I was transformed from a nominal Christian to a committed active, Bible believing Christian.

---

54   Lightner, J.K. 2008. Genetics of coat color I: The melanocortin 1 receptor (MC1R). *Answers Research Journal* 1:109-116. http://www.answersingenesis.org/contents/379/Genetics_of_Coat_Color_I.pdf.
55   See previous reference. Also, Anderson, K.L. 2005. Is bacterial resistance to antibiotics an appropriate example of evolutionary change? *Creation Research Society Quarterly* 41(4):318-326.

Sorting Through Compromise Theories

Coming from a Christian home where the Bible was taught as truth, Jaap tried to reconcile scientific statements that he learned in college with the Genesis record. At the University of Stellenbosch he majored in geology, mathematics and physics, and was taught to believe that the earth was at least 2 billion years old. Though he had settled on the gap theory compromise as taught by Harry Rimmer, his mind was changed during a series of meetings that took place on the campus of the University of the Western Cape where the young earth flood geology model was explained.

Having grown up in a Christian family, I believed the Bible fully. Nonetheless, for many years, from high school on, I tried to reconcile scientific statements with the Genesis record. In about my last year at school (1946), in a pamphlet entitled, *Die Bybel en wetenskap* ("The Bible and science"), an uncle of mine (D.Sc. in geology) expressed doubts about "all those millions of years" proclaimed by other scientists. I do not remember which view he advocated, but he did not conclude that the earth was young, only that one should be skeptical about scientific pronouncements.

At the University of Stellenbosch I majored in geology, mathematics, and physics, and was taught to believe that the earth was at least two billion years old. I still haven't really forgiven my geology professors who gave absolutely no indication of any other possibility! Even though the works of George Mac-Cready Price were available at that time, he was not mentioned at all. Eventually I settled for the "Gap Theory" as expounded by Harry Rimmer; I still have some of his books, which I bought in Stellenbosch.

For thirty years I treasured Rimmer's books, and even wrote one or two articles in the same vein for the *Vereniging vir Christelike Wetenskap* (Society for a Christian View of Science), explaining, for example, how God's breath could have made a couple of apes human. During all those years I really did not believe that biological evolution ever took place, and tried to resolve the conflict by advocating the "gap theory".

Approximately twenty years ago, a series of student meetings was held on the campus of the University of the Western Cape where I was teaching computer science. The topic was "Creation." The first talk was by Duane Gish. That was the very first time I had heard about flood geology. It was like a bright light illuminating and ending my years of frustration. Suddenly, everything seemed to fall into place as I visualized the main South African geological sequences being formed during and after the flood year.

When created, the earth was "without form and void". Gap theorists like Rimmer told us that it BECAME formless and empty, but it struck me that if it had become formless, no structures could have survived — no sedimentary layers, no fossils. The fossils could not have survived the supposed upheaval, and there is no way that the entire geological time scale could fit into a supposed gap.

In 1982, I took up the gauntlet by responding to newspaper articles with stories about millions of years. From time to time quite lively debates ensued, but the establishment always had the last word. One noteworthy member of the evolutionary establishment is Jurie van den Heever, a paleontologist from Stellenbosch University. His specialty is the "mammal-like" reptiles, fossils that are plentiful in the Karoo sediments. He often discusses the middle ear bones that supposedly migrated from the lower jaw to the ear. However, he had no examples of the many required transitions.

From time to time, emphatic stories about hominids purporting to be ancestors of man appear in local newspapers with lots of diagrams, pictures and evolutionary rhetoric. But it is quite useless to point out the shortcomings of these theories because some years ago the top Afrikaans daily in Cape Town (*Die Burger*) and other papers started to censor all contributions that opposed evolution. I have had similar experiences with other newspapers and magazines.

Liberal theologians have caused a lot of confusion and turmoil in South Africa. Ordinary church members do not know what to believe any more. They are told "ex cathedra" that chapters 1 to 11 of Genesis should not be regarded as history, only allegorically, a poetic description. These theologians like to say that the Bible only tells us THAT God created everything; not HOW or WHEN the earth was created. Recently, the Western Cape Synod of the Dutch Reformed Church sought to settle the minds of ordinary church members by allowing them to accept Genesis chapters 4 to 11 as actual history; now only chapters 1 to 3 are supposed to be allegorical. Could the reason for accepting the account of the Flood (Genesis 6 to 8) as historical, be that some geologists have seen "signs of a flood" in the Black Sea? I would like to follow up on this possibility.

The official newsletter of the Dutch Reformed Church has also been ignoring contributions that oppose evolution. The theologians who edit and publish this newsletter emphatically believe that Genesis was written during or after the Babylonian exile by some priests who based their stories on Babylonian myths, especially that of Gilgamesh. From time to time I have "crossed swords" with some of these theologians, but to no avail.

In any case, people who believe the biblical accounts of creation and the flood are regarded as a fanatical unscientific fringe that labor under the delusion that the entire Bible is historically true. It is a sad and tragic state of affairs that one's own church denomination rejects the early chapters of Genesis and actually commands the ordinary members to follow suit. The burning question is: Should one stay inside and fight the good fight, or should one look for and join a creation-wise more congenial congregation/denomination?

I joined "Deus Dixit", a South African creation society, and also contributed to the journal. When visiting Pretoria, I was privileged to address one or two of the meetings. Walter Lang of Bible-Science fame attended at least one geological hiking "expedition" in which my wife and I also participated. The focus was on the Drakensberg escarpment separating the *highveld* from the *lowveld*. I remember Walter's remark when we looked over the impressive canyon below the Berlin falls: "I see only catastrophe."

Werner Gitt, one of Europe's leading creationists, has also visited South Africa several times. We have become well acquainted. He is a prolific author, and Rudolf Steinberg, one of his German friends living in South Africa, urged me to translate his book *Schuf Gott durch Evolution?* from German into English. It was published in Germany in 1993 with the title, *Did God use Evolution?* This was followed by three more of Werner's books that I translated: *Stars and their Purpose — signposts in space* (1996), *In the Beginning was Information* (1997), and *The Wonder of Man* (1999).

I have also prepared an Afrikaans version of the latter, and have translated Hennie Mouton's *Evolusie: die onwetenskaplike leuen* from Afrikaans into English: *Evolution: the Unscientific Lie* (2001). I have compiled a brief overview of the geological history of South Africa in which I totally ignored the traditional "eras", referring to them only to locate certain familiar formations. With the aid of some official geological publications I have been able to pinpoint the transition from Flood sedimentation to post-Flood formations.[56] In conclusion, what I learned about creation has transformed my life from a nominal Christian to an actively involved believer.

---

56   During the initial stages of the Flood, there could have been no sedimentation because unimaginably violent and voluminous tidal flows "circumnavigated" the earth. The first sediments collected in so-called "geo-synclines". The gold-bearing Witwatersrand formations seem to be deltaic beds in a water-filled depression. Together with the Table Mountain quartzites they comprise the base of the main flood sequence. Then follows a volcanic interlude (the Ventersdorp lavas). Subsequently, the Transvaal and the Bokkeveld/Witteberg sediments consisting of alternating layers of shale and quartzite/sandstone, were conformably covered by the Dwyka turbidites and the Ecca shales. The latter contain large coal deposits, indicating that the raging flood waters started to subside to such an extent that the floating "mats" of vegetation could settle (mostly Glossopteris). The Ecca formations were laid down in the open ocean, but the subsequent conformable Beaufort Series in an inland sea. There is no coal in the Beaufort formations, but there are numerous indications of temporary settlement by migrating reptiles.

Information Theory Convinced Me

Rudolf was an engineering officer in the German navy during World War II. The Nazi ideology was based upon Darwinism, and he was fully aware of the contradictions between what he knew about what the Bible said about the origin of the world, and what he learned in school about the evolution of man, culture and the universe. In time the writings of professors A. E. Wilder-Smith and Werner Gitt convinced him to abandon theistic evolution.

I was born in February 1924 in Hanover, Germany and being raised up in a Christian Brethren family, I was familiar with Bible teaching from childhood. When I was only 7 years old I realized my position before God and surrendered my life to Jesus Christ. The truth of His reality and the knowledge that He can answer prayers has not left me since then.

The National-Socialist German Workers Party came to power in Germany in 1933. Their ideology was, among other things, based on Darwinism and penetrated all areas of education. At the time I wrote my "Abitur" (Matric) I was fully aware of the contradictions between what I knew from the Bible about the origin of the world and what I learned in school about the evolution of man, culture and the universe. As I tried to uphold the truth of God's Word, the tension between these worldviews within me increased and I started searching for a solution.

Early in 1942, during World War II, the German Navy drafted me to become an engineering officer. In the many discussions I had with my mates, especially with those trained on the "National Political Education Institutions", I found that I had very few rational answers to their often-penetrating questions about God and creation. They just took for granted long periods of the existence of the universe and rejected Biblical answers.

Shortly after I completed the submarine Chief Engineers' training, the war ended. After being released from the navy, I started studying Electrical Engineering at the Technical University in Hanover. Although I was actively involved in Christian student work, the question of creation was not an issue then because I held to the theistic evolution worldview that was generally accepted in many conservative evangelical circles at that time.

Upon completion of my studies, I obtained a degree equal to a Masters of Engineering. Siemens employed me as Electrical Engineer and sent me to South Africa in 1958. There, I kept abreast of the German evangelical literature in which Prof. Dr. A. E. Wilder Smith was the lone voice that openly propagated the worldview based on a six-day creation. This worldview appealed to me, but I was not fully convinced, and still had many unanswered questions. Then, in the mid- to end eighties I read the book of Prof. Werner Gitt entitled 'Logos or Chaos'. I was fascinated with the alternative he offered for biological evolution. From this time onwards, the books written by Werner Gitt influenced my thinking.

After I had retired from Siemens in 1988 I spent three months in Germany. This period was crucial for my thinking regarding theistic evolution and special creation. First, my wife and I visited Werner Gitt in Brunswick. His information theory convinced me that a substantial part of life consists of the non-material entity "Information" that needs an intelligent source at the beginning. To me, as an engineer, it was clear that the highest possible density of information, as found in the DNA molecules, could not have evolved by chance. His publication, *Did God Use Evolution?*" gave me an insight into the basic assumptions of Evolution, Creationism and Theistic Evolution.

Dr. Gitt advised us to call on Dr. Joachim Scheven to visit his museum "Lebendige Vorwelt". There we saw the fossils of stems, barks, stigmarias and other elements of the "carbon vegetation". In the past, these had formed huge floating mats of forests on which ferns, horsetails and cordites had settled. Dr. Scheven's theory states that these floating mats were deposited in a short period of time after Noah's flood. His theory is contrary to the view that it took 40 million years to grow the vegetation that is deposited in the 300 seams of coal lying one upon another in the Ruhr area in Germany. Dr. Scheven explained his geological time scale in terms of biblical revelation and answered many (but not all) my biological and geological questions. His theory proved more acceptable to me and opened up a way for me to understand how the rock strata could have been deposited within a short period of time.

I was then introduced to the German Creation Association *Wort und Wissen* (Word and Knowledge) that operates quite independently from other international Creation Societies. The literature of *Wort und Wissen* is also unique. Since then, my studies of Creation have had a firm basis. As I study the issue in more detail, it leads to more questions. But I have arrived at satisfactory answers to many of these questions. Many are still unanswered, but are no longer threatening. I have been transformed by the scientific evidence. I find it interesting to observe that the major scientific discoveries in our time point more and more towards "Special Creation" and little by little, they reveal the brittleness of evolution theory.

Since then I have been able to assist Prof. Dr. Gitt in his three visits to South Africa. He presented more than 28 lectures at universities and training institutions on his "Natural-Law Theory of Information", which is a scientific refutation of the general idea of evolution.

I am very thankful to my Creator for opening up this wide field of research for me after my retirement. In these studies I experience His love and see His wisdom and greatness day by day.

My Faith Remains Intact

Mark Stewart's two older brothers both believed in evolution and instilled in him the desire to pursue science and truth, but these truths led him to believe not evolution, but a recent creation. Though Mark quit attending church, he never doubted the Lord's existence, and felt sure that the Bible meant what it said when taken in its entirety and proper context. Although he didn't always have the answers to the questions he was challenged with by his older brothers, his faith remained intact.

Several creationist publications and radio programs transformed his thinking. He discusses briefly what some of the evidences were that helped to transform his life. From that point onward to this day, Mark reads, writes, and continues to do background research for creation science. He maintains a database of Darwin Doubters along with their educational background, their academic experience, honors and awards they have achieved, the professional organizations they are members of, a list of their publications, contact information, and a data base of evolution/creation articles and the periodicals they appear in.

I was raised in a small rural community of some five thousand people in southwestern Ohio. My father and mother raised my brothers, sister and myself in a small Baptist church in our hometown. We learned the basics of Christianity there, though we did not fully understand much of what we were taught. Nevertheless, the seeds were being planted.

After a number of years my older brothers quit attending church. They had always been much smarter than I was in school, and I had always looked up to them. I followed their example and I stopped going to church, too. Our parents left that decision to us. It didn't end there, though. I recall in the mid-1960s one of my brothers regularly listening to a radio program at night. The speakers happened to be Herbert W. Armstrong and Garner Ted Armstrong of The Plain Truth magazine and The Worldwide Church of God. We also received their magazine, and I recall a number of radio programs and articles that taught about evolution and creation. This was the beginning of my interest in this subject.

Sometime later (in 1969) after we had moved a couple of times, when I was in the ninth grade, I remember someone knocking on our door. I answered it and it happened to be a Jehovah's Witness. I purchased a small blue book titled "Did Man Get Here by Evolution or Creation?" It made quite an impression on me.

Much of what I learned from these early influences began to answer some of the questions I had, and set the foundation for what I knew to be true, even at this early age. I still had a lot of questions and didn't always have answers, but I knew there were legitimate answers to the questions that were deep in my soul about the purpose of life. Regarding some of the other issues that were presented to me by these influences, I was able to sort through those issues later in life as well.

My brothers and I often discussed these issues and had many debates as we were growing up, but they both felt, as I believe they do to this day, that we had evolved to our present condition as a result of natural law, mutations, natural selection, and time. They presented their case and asked questions that I could not answer. One brother asked me to read some good evolution books. He felt sure that I would "see the light" after reading them. It didn't work. I maintained my belief that we were created, that we did not evolve.

When a friend of mine came back from a Christian camp in 1977, he gave me a small pamphlet by Duane Gish titled *Have you been Brainwashed?* This booklet began to shape my belief as a young-earth creationist. From the back page of this pamphlet, I ordered the book *The Genesis Flood* by John Whitcomb and Henry Morris. It was this book that began giving me the rock solid answers I had been looking for. I now had the evidence to demonstrate that my faith in God, the Bible, and Creation, was reasonable.

For example, arguments were presented for a reasonable solution to many of the geological features we see about us today, such as how mountains are formed, why we find fossils where they are located and a means of their transport, why we generally do not find fossils forming today, and what it takes to form a fossil, methods for resolving contradictions in the geological strata, why fossil graveyards exist, an excellent explanation for "living fossils" and much, much more. By this time I had already read Charles Darwin's *The Origin of Species* and had also read the Bible straight through twice. I would have to thank my older brothers for inspiring me to look into this matter in more detail. It has now become a huge part of my life. I began buying and devouring books on creation and evolution. The books that influenced me the most are *The Genesis Flood*, Duane Gish's *The Fossils say No!* and *Physics of the Future* by Thomas Barnes. I have been researching, reading, and writing on creation and creation science for over 30 years since.

I was never an atheist, theistic evolutionist, or even a progressive creationist. I have always believed in creation and I have always taken the Bible at its face value. When I was growing up, though, I did not always have the answers to some questions that I have now or were posed to me by my brothers. Until I had the answers, I had to hold the truth of God's word in faith. A part of my thinking was: "If the Creator of the universe did not convey to us what He was really trying to say, then what purpose could Genesis serve? There are some things God did not choose to reveal to us, but what He did choose for us to have as His written word must mean what it says." In some cases the wording might be poetic, symbolic, or metaphorical, but the context makes it clear when the Bible, in its original language, is taken as a whole.

Some of the subjects I can recall being brought up as evidence of evolution included the Big Bang theory, the speed of light and the time required for transit based on the distances of stars from us, the fossil record of man, radiometric dating, and the claim that no human fossils were ever found with dinosaur fossils.

Time and space precludes my going into details about these so-called faith-challenging arguments but, after reading and learning about all these subjects, I have answered them to my satisfaction and my faith has remained intact. Many of these questions and answers can be found in any of a number of books. I personally recommend for the layperson, *A Case for Creation* by Wayne Frair and Percival Davis, *The Collapse of Evolution* by Scott M. Huse, *The Case Against Darwin* by James Perloff, and *The Evidence for Creation* by Glen McLean, Roger Oakland and Larry McLean.

In the Bible, seven is the numerical symbol for completeness. Seven lines of evidence have persuaded me through the years that the creation model is true. These include: 1) the law of biogenesis, 2) the first and second laws of thermodynamics, 3) the law of cause and effect, 4) design in nature, 5) limitations in variation in organisms, 6) instinct, and 7) the fossil record.

To take it a step further, seven lines of evidence have persuaded me through the years that the young-earth creation model is true: 1) decay of the earth's magnetic field, 2) geocentric pleochroic polonium halos in Precambrian granite and coalified wood, 3) polystrate fossils, 4) "living" fossils, 5) the formation of geological features in a short period of time, 6) the amount of helium in the earth's atmosphere, and 7) the amount of salt/minerals deposited into the oceans.

I wish to briefly focus on one of these lines of evidence because, among many others, it convinced me of the merit of the creation worldview. They transformed me into who I am today, with glasses that act like filters viewing everything in life through the lens of that paradigm. This line of evidence is the decay of the earth's magnetic field.

Creation scientists have studied this phenomenon since at least 1971. Dr. Thomas Barnes pioneered the initial research. Our planet is surrounded by a magnetic field that protects life from solar radiation. Without this magnetic field living things could not exist. Scientists were surprised to find out how quickly the earth's magnetic field was decreasing. The energy stored in the earth's magnetic field has steadily decayed by a factor of 2.7 over the last millennium. At its current rate, the earth and its magnetic field could not be older than 10,000 years, or an absolute maximum of 20,000 years.

A number of measurements have confirmed this decrease of the earth's magnetic field. Ever since measurements first began in 1845, the earth's magnetic field has been decreasing at a rate of five percent per century. Archaeological measurements that have been taken demonstrate that the field was forty percent stronger in 1000 AD. A net energy loss of 1.4 percent from 1970 to 2000 has been shown by the IGRF (the International Geomagnetic Reference Field) records, the most precise measurements ever taken. What this means is that the earth's magnetic field has halved about every 1,465 years.

Conventional evolutionary theories attempting to explain this rapid decrease, including how the earth could have maintained its magnetic field for billions of years, are very inadequate and extremely complex. Evolutionists accept the current rate of decrease but believe it somehow must be self-sustaining. A theoretical process more commonly known as the dynamo model is proposed. This model, however, contradicting some very basic laws of physics, fails to explain the measured electric current in the sea floor today, among other things.

These conventional evolutionary theorists also suggest that the earth's magnetic field decrease is linear, rather than exponential. This is in spite of historical measurements and decades of experiments that have confirmed exponential decay. Still others believe that the strength of some components increase to make up for others that decrease. This conclusion is based on confusion regarding the difference between magnetic field energy and its intensity. This claim has been categorically refuted by creation scientists.

Creation scientists, beginning with pioneer physicist Dr. Thomas Barnes, have developed a much better theory based on geophysical science and offer explanations for key features based on sound physics that explain the origin of the earth's magnetic field, surface intensity fluctuations over time, followed by a steady decrease in time. This theory matches historical and current paleomagnetic data, with the main result that the field's energy, not its local intensity, has always decreased by the minimum as fast as it is currently decreasing.

This theory proposes that the earth's magnetic field is caused by a freely-decreasing electric current in the earth's core. This means that the electric current naturally decreases, losing energy as it flows through the earth's metallic core. Although this theory differs from the accepted conventional model, it is consistent with everything we know of what constitutes the earth's core. In addition, based on our knowledge of the conductive properties of liquid iron, this freely decaying current would have begun when the earth's outer core was first being formed. This young-earth model of a freely-decaying electric current in the outer core generating earth's magnetic field has been confirmed, based on the published accurate and reliable geological field data.

Through the years I have proposed and defended these lines of evidence in publications, including in the letters section of newspapers. For example, I published a letter on August 15, 1989 in the *Record Herald* where I wrote

> there is the argument of geocentric pleochroic polonium halos in Precambrian granite. These microscopic radiohalos of Polonium exist by themselves without any uranium parent in thousands of the biotite or mica that has been examined. Polonium isotopes all have short half-lives (^{218}Po has a half-life of three minutes. ^{214}Po a half-life of 164 microseconds and ^{210}Po has a half-life of 138.4 days. To summarize the empirical data that has been published in journals including *Science, Nature, Applied Physics Letters* and others, these polonium halos indicate an almost instantaneous creation!"

The newspaper published several very encouraging responses. One gentleman wrote to tell me what he had learned from my letter to the editor had changed his life. Another gentleman came to my house, wanting to meet me and express his appreciation for the letters I had written.

I have been working on a book for several years now titled *Darwin Doubters of the 20th and 21st Century*. I have met with great encouragement from the creationist community, and I look forward to the day when I can demonstrate, through this work, the extent in numbers and talent of the Darwin Doubter science movement. Here are just three examples among thousands: Dr. Vij Sodera became a Fellow of the Royal College of Surgeons of Edinburgh in 1981. He graduated from Sheffield University Medical School in 1975 with distinction in Chemistry. Dr. Sodera is a surgeon, artist and author of three surgical textbooks. He is also the author of the book *One Small Speck to Man*, the result of fourteen years of research. Together with his wife Margaret (a qualified nurse), he runs a private minor surgery clinic. Sodera was born in India and has lived in Britain since the age of four.

Dr. Isaac Manly is a retired surgeon and Medical Doctor from an active medical and surgical practice with Raleigh Surgical Associates, Raleigh, North Carolina. He earned his Bachelor of Science Degree in Medicine from the University of North Carolina and his M.D. from Harvard Medical School. Manly is certified with the American Board of Surgery and the American Board of Thoracic Surgery. He has also been an Instructor in Surgery at the University of North Carolina Medical School.

Dr. John McEwan majored in Chemistry at the University of Canterbury in Christchurch, New Zealand. He gained a scholarship and moved to Sydney University for his Ph.D. that involved making natural products. Dr. McEwan is now Senior Chemist at Access Pharmaceuticals, Australia, researching more effective anti-cancer drugs against tumors, making them more specific and lengthening their time in the body to do work. He has published many papers in secular scientific journals.

I thank my older brothers for instilling in me an earnest desire to seek the truth regarding these matters, though things did not quite turn out as they expected. I have learned that being smart does not necessarily mean being wise because, "ever since the creation of the world His invisible nature, namely, his eternal power and deity, has been clearly perceived in the things that have been made. So they are without excuse…" (Romans 1:20). Some of the articles that were critical in my transformation include:

1. "Decay of the earth's magnetic moment and the geochronological implications" *Creation Research Society Quarterly* 8(1): 24 – 29 (June, 1971) by Thomas G. Barnes.
2. "Young age vs. geologic age for the earth's magnetic field" *Creation Research Society Quarterly* 9(1): 47 – 50 (June, 1972) by Thomas G. Barnes.
3. "Electromagnetics of the earth's magnetic field and evaluation of electric conductivity, current, and Joule heating in the earth's core" *Creation Research Society Quarterly* 9(4): 222 – 230 (March, 1973) by Thomas G. Barnes.
4. "Earth's magnetic energy provides confirmation of its young age" *Creation Research Society Quarterly* 12(1): 11 – 13 (June, 1975) by Thomas G. Barnes.
5. "Satellite observations confirm the decline of the earth's magnetic field" *Creation Research Society Quarterly* 18(1): 39 – 41 (June, 1981) by Thomas G. Barnes.
6. "The creation of the earth's magnetic field" *Creation Research Society Quarterly* 20(2): 89 -94 (September, 1983) by D. Russell Humphreys.

7. "Earth's young magnetic field age: An answer to Dalrymple" *Creation Research Society Quarterly* 21(3): 109 – 113 (December, 1984) by Thomas G. Barnes.

8. "Earth's young magnetic field confirmed" *Creation Research Society Quarterly* 23(1): 30 – 33 (June, 1986).

9. "Dwindling resource evidence of a young earth" *Creation Research Society Quarterly* 25(4): 170, 171 (March, 1989) by Thomas G. Barnes.

10. "The earth's magnetic field is young" *Impact* # 242 (August 1993) by D. Russell Humphreys.

11. "The earth's magnetic field is still losing energy" *Creation Research Society Quarterly* 39(1): 3 – 13 (June, 2002) by D. Russell Humphreys.

12. "Earth's magnetic field is decaying steadily – with a little rhythm" *Creation Research Society Quarterly* 47(3): 193 – 201 (Winter, 2011) by D. Russell Humphreys.

13. Reasons to Affirm a Young Earth (CR Ministries, 2007) Paul G. Humber, Editor.

14. "10 best evidences from science that confirm a young earth: # 5 Rapidly decaying magnetic field" *Answers* 7(4): 52, 53 (October – December 2012) by Andrew A. Snelling

The Astronomer with the Bible Study

Larry's high school biology teacher told him that he did not need to believe in God because we evolved, were only animals related to monkeys, and were not created. The next year in his chemistry class, the teacher taught him that life had been created in the laboratory. A classmate of his even won a National Merit scholarship for duplicating part of the Miller-Urey experiment. This indoctrination continued into college, planting seeds of doubt about his Christian faith. Then he had a meeting Dr. Wehrner Von Braun, whose testimony of Christ caused Larry to begin a search for truth which transformed his life.

Like a grubby caterpillar that transforms into a beautiful Monarch butterfly, I was transformed from a lost sinner into a precious Child of the Creator God. A key element that led to my transformation over the years was the realization that the actual observable scientific data in astronomy, physics, chemistry, biology, archeology, paleontology, and logical reasoning refutes the unobservable claims of molecules to man evolution, and supports rather than negates the Biblical account of creation in Genesis, and throughout the Bible. I will in this chapter review a small part of this evidence.

When I was a young child of about five I received a children's Bible from my Grandmother who raised me. I am very thankful for her godly influence on my life, and she continues to influence me as she approaches her 105th birthday. As a precocious reader, I read all about the life of Jesus, and believed that He was real. I wanted very much to be a good boy; I cleaned up my room and tried to help my Grandma with her chores. This was the beginning of my transformation, but I had a long way to go.

I was brought up and confirmed in the Evangelical Lutheran church and, having studied the Bible intensely, I had a strong faith. In my first year of high school I took biology and was introduced to evolution. The teacher told us we did not need to believe in God because we evolved, were only animals related to monkeys, and were not created. I knew in my heart that she was wrong, but the Haeckel embryo drawings in my text book seemed to show that all the embryos of the various life forms looked the same when young.

Years later, I learned that these drawings were faked! The next year in my chemistry class, the teacher taught us that life had been created in the laboratory. A classmate of mine even won a National Merit scholarship for duplicating part of the Miller-Urey experiment. He sparked some methane and got some purple goo, but it was obvious that he didn't create anything close to life. Events such as these did not do much to help me believe that evolution was true, and in those "happy days" we could still pray and read our Bibles in school. We also had spirited debates with our biology teacher - he was in the minority - most of the biology students believed in God.

How things changed when I started college in 1960 at Indiana State University in Terre Haute, majoring in mathematics and physics. My mathematics, physics, chemistry, English, debate, sociology, and biology teachers not only believed in Darwinism, they preached evolution in their classes. I was shocked when my English and math professors ridiculed the Bible, and my sociology teacher claimed that humans created god. As I went deeper into physics, the atheistic, naturalistic worldview, along with wild claims about the origin of the universe, were heavily integrated into my education. Everything, they taught us, could be explained by naturalistic causes.

Eventually seeds of doubt about God were planted in my mind, and the freedom of being away from home for the first time in my life led me into a typical carefree college lifestyle of studying and parties. God was now on the back burner. Then, in my junior year, I studied astrophysics, and my professor announced he was holding a Bible study on Wednesday nights. This was a turning point for me to come back to the Scriptures.

Although my professor believed in God, he embraced the millions of years needed to explain light travel from the distant stars, and the geological strata. This was my introduction to theistic evolution. On a humorous note, when I attended college, the universe was believed to be about 2 million years old and, amazingly, 45 years later, the universe has aged to about 16 billion years! Although my old astrophysics textbook is sorrowfully obsolete, I still have the Bible that I used in college, and it has not changed one iota.

In my senior year in college, I was privileged to meet Dr. Wernher von Braun, the world's leading rocket scientist, when he came to Indiana State University. He told us he firmly believed in God. Dr. von Braun wrote:

"It is so obvious that we live in a world in which a fantastic amount of logic, of rational lawfulness, is at work. We are aware of a large number of laws of physics and chemistry and biology which, by their mutual interdependence, make nature work as if it were following a grandiose plan from its earliest beginnings to the farthest reaches of its future destiny. To me, it would be incomprehensible that there should be such a gigantic master plan without a master planner behind it. This master planner is He whom we

call the Creator of the Universe . . . One cannot be exposed to the law and order of the universe without concluding that there must be a Divine intent behind it all."[57]

This was another turning point for me; if this great rocket scientist believed in God, so could I. I went on to graduate with a B.S. in both Physics and Mathematics, and also received my M.S. in Physics and started working as a Research Engineer for General Motors. Fast-forwarding to January 10, 1973, I was driving home on a Wednesday evening, and I spotted a bus with a sign saying, "CH__CH, what's missing – UR." The church I grew up in had services only on Sunday morning, and so I decided I would go to this Baptist church that night. The sermon was on Isaiah 1:18 which said "Come now, let us reason together, says the Lord…" As a scientist and man of reason, this hit me not only over the head, but also in my heart. When the sermon ended, I ran down the aisle, repented of my sins, and received Jesus as my Lord and Savior. My transformation became a metamorphosis!

I was so excited that I read the entire New Testament in two days, then went back to Genesis and read the entire Bible in two weeks. Unfortunately, I had to work full-time during this time, which is why it took me so long! Everything in the Bible was true; even the science claims made sense to me, even if I could not perfectly understand it all. I was reading the Schofield Study Bible, and the notes explained the fossil record proved a primitive creation millions of years ago, a problem that could be resolved by adding a gap between Genesis 1:1 and 1:2. I was saved, but did not yet understand the inconsistencies of my creation view.

When General Motors brought in Dr. William Sears of Cornell as an aero thermodynamic consultant, I became his technical interpreter for the Director of Research. Dr. Sears liked my work and recommended to the Director that I attend Cornell for my PhD in aerodynamics, specializing in aeroacoustics. Instead GM decided to send me to Purdue for a PhD in Mechanical Engineering specializing in aero acoustics, allowing me to commute from Indianapolis, spending three days a week at school, and working three days a week at GM. I received full salary while going to school, and completed all of my course work.

My PhD advisor landed a NASA contract involving the acoustics of supersonic flow that became the area of study for my PhD thesis. I completed my research on the theoretical shock-wave generation of sound from a supersonic NASA research turbofan engine, conducted experimental verification of the code on the engine at NASA, and published my research in a NASA Contractor's Report. However, as I was completing my formal PhD thesis at Purdue, GM suddenly decided they were not going to allow me to continue my studies. I would have to quit my job in order to finish my PhD at Purdue, and there was no guar-

---

57   Stuhlinger and Ordway, *Wernher von Braun: Crusader for Space,* page 270.

antee that I would have a job at GM when I returned. They added, we are already paying you a PhD level salary and we need you here. I was transferred to another, more critical, product assurance department, where they had lost their star PhD mathematician to another company, and I was selected to replace that person.

Just as this was unfolding, Saigon fell. My wife, a Vietnamese I had met at a science award banquet, was an outstanding State Department Scholar in chemistry and I was selected to receive a Graduate Fellowship in physics. My wife and I suddenly had 13 refugees, including her brothers and sisters and their children that were able to escape Viet Nam, all living in our 3-bedroom ranch home. It was an easy decision between getting my PhD and keeping my job; I stayed at work and helped support our extended family. A man I knew at work, a PhD from Georgia Tech, said he was amazed at how peacefully I handled my situation, and asked me "I want to know your faith; will you take me to your church this Sunday"? I did, and he also accepted Christ as his savior. Also, all of my wife's family went forward in one service, and seven were baptized at my church. It was well worth it.

A few years later, I moved to Arizona after receiving a job offer to work in my field of acoustics, as an engineering scientist, and was blessed to be able to travel around the world. One experience was very memorable. I went to Taiwan to help their military design a more maneuverable supersonic fighter aircraft. When there, I attended a Christian convention in Taipei with over 25,000 men and women from every continent and over 100 countries, and was given the opportunity at the convention to share my faith.

Late in my career I became a member of the Gideon's International, an association of Christian business and professional men who distribute Bibles all over the world. I became Chaplain of my local chapter, and then was appointed to the State Cabinet as Memorial Bible Chairman. In 1991, the Gideon's International had their convention in Phoenix. I was privileged to meet and embrace the President of the Gideon's International in Russia as he arrived at Sky Harbor Airport. Even though we had been bitter Cold War enemies, we were brothers in Christ. One of the keynote speakers at the convention, Dr. Hugh Ross, gave me a copy of his book, *The Fingerprint of God.*

Many Christians were enthralled with his Progressive Creationism view, but many things in his book disturbed me, starting with the contradiction of the creation days in Genesis. Ross claimed the sun had to be created before the earth, but the Bible said the earth was created on day 1, and the sun on day 4. He believed billions of years of stellar evolution existed rather than 6 days of creation; and that a day did not mean a literal 24-hour period. He also believed in a local flood rather than a global flood, and a race of spiritless men were created before Adam and Eve.

I later discovered the excellent book, *Creation and Time,* by Mark Van Bebber and Paul S. Taylor. This work provided an excellent rebuttal of the progressive creationism view expounded by Dr. Hugh Ross. I was also introduced to the work of the Institute for Creation Research (ICR), and the ministries of Kent Hovind and Ken Ham of *Answers in Genesis*. After studying as much material as I could get my hands on, I was transformed by the evidence and the Biblical account of creation into a full-fledged young earth creationist (YEC).

When I was 50 I was forced to retire, but this turned out to be a real blessing because I went into the ministry. At a Gideon meeting, I met a Calvary Chapel pastor who was saved after reading a Gideon Bible in his hotel room. He invited me to speak at his church. I decided to bring my ministry to Calvary Chapel, and was given the opportunity to lead worship and, later, became an assistant pastor there, teaching the Bible and creation science classes.

Testimonies from My Class

One evening at Calvary Chapel a PhD computer engineer named Werner came to my class when I was teaching about the complexity of the "simple" cell compared to the most advanced computer chip. I also covered the difference between changes over time in a species and macroevolution. After class he said he was impressed with the computer/cell comparison, and when I explained micro vs. macroevolution, a light went on; he knew macroevolution was impossible. He asked me to pray for him, and he accepted Christ as his Savior that night!

Another man, who was a truck driver attended my creation class. One Sunday he came up to me and handed me a check for a donation to the creation ministry. He said my teaching had helped him restore his faith in God and save his marriage. This man was literally transformed by the evidence.

The teaching on the Laws of Thermodynamics and the Origin of the Universe had convicted him and, when he got home, he begged his wife to forgive him, restoring his marriage. I told him that God uses the evidence for creation to transform the lives of hurting people in all areas of their lives, regardless of their circumstances. In this man's case, even though the message was not about marriage, his marriage was restored.

In 1996, I founded World View Outreach, a creation science ministry. I am thankful to God for all of the opportunities that He has given me to present the creation message through this ministry to schools, universities, professional societies, home-school groups, Bible College, and elsewhere. In addition to my teaching ministry at World View Outreach Church, I am a member of the Creation Research Society that allows me to keep up with what is going on in the creation vs. evolution arena, and I am an officer and board member of the Arizona Origins Science Association (AzOSA).

I also had the opportunity to speak to a philosophy class at South Mountain Community College in Phoenix. I had just attended a private screening of Ben Stein's *Expelled the Movie*, and was given a leader resource DVD with theatrical trailers and selected video clips from the movie. I was able to use this material to present evidence in the class for Intelligent Design in cosmology, biology, and paleontology. During the question and answer period, the students asked, "Who are you? What do you believe and why?" I asked the professor if I could give my testimony, and she said "Yes" (this was a secular college).

I attended the class before my presentation, and they were studying about Aristotle, so I shared with them Acts 17 about Paul talking to the Greeks about their "unknown god" who is the only true God, the Creator of the universe. Then I explained to them how I was personally transformed by the evidence. After class I was able to share Jesus with several students and the professor.

My mission and vision is that many men, women, and children will be able to hear the creation message. I pray that they all would be, as I was, transformed by the evidence. My prayer was answered in a powerful way in the summer of 2011. I had the opportunity to present a paper at the Faith & Science conference at Evangel University, and I realized the importance of integrating creation science into the college education of our nation's future scientists and theologians. Theistic evolution has become the dominant worldview taught, even in many of our most conservative Christian universities. This evolutionary indoctrination plants seeds of doubt in many of our young people, resulting in many putting their faith in evolutionary science and losing their faith in our Creator God.

I asked myself "What can I do to help turn the tide in this battle waged against our precious children? Then, God opened the door for me to become an adjunct professor of physics at Arizona Christian University. I will also be teaching physical science and have the opportunity to integrate creation science into my classes in astronomy, physics, chemistry, and geology. I pray that I have wisdom and discernment to present the evidence to my students, and that they would also be transformed by the evidence.

Evidence That Transformed Me

There are basically two types of evidence that changed my worldview. First, there is strong evidence against evolution, and secondly, there is even stronger evidence for the Biblical account of creation. Through a process of continuous study I keep discovering that all of the so-called evidence for evolution is not really scientific evidence, but is based on the presupposition that evolution is true; in other words a logical fallacy of circular reasoning or faulty interpretation of the actual evidence is being employed.

My transformation is not a onetime occurrence, but is a continuous ongoing process of growth, much like the experience of salvation and sanctification. I know by faith that God exists, and the Bible is His Holy Word. Therefore, God is the Creator of the universe and all life was created by Him. In my case, one could say I have always been a creationist since that moment I believed in God and accepted Jesus Christ as my Lord and Savior.

I would like to briefly discuss the second type of evidence first, evidence that the Bible is the Word of God. When I was a young Christian I read *Evidence That Demands a Verdict* by Josh McDowell. The historical evidence for the Bible is unprecedented, and is continually being verified by archeological evidence. The New Testament affirming the eye-witness account of the resurrection of Jesus is the most reliably verified and preserved document in history. Jesus is alive! Jesus affirmed creation, so I am a creationist.

As a scientist, I should be able to trust what the Bible says about science. Unlike ancient myths that taught the earth was flat, in Isaiah 40:22 the Bible refers to the circle of the earth, indicating the earth is round, not flat. In Job 26:17 God tells Job that He hangs the earth on nothing, indicating the earth is in outer space, not being supported on some mythical elephant. The rotation of the earth on its axis explains day and night on different parts of the earth at the same time according to Luke 17:36-37.

The Bible even alludes to atomic physics in Hebrews 11:3 (ESV): *By faith we understand that the universe was created by the word of God, so that what is seen was not made out of things that are visible.* Also, in Colossians 1:16-17 we read that Jesus created all things and He holds all things together, and this gives insight into the existence of the nuclear force that is stronger than the electromagnetic force and holds the nucleus of the atom together.

In summary, evidence that the Bible is God's Word is overwhelming. Only God, through His Word, gives us satisfactory answers to the origin and purpose of life, and offers hope of eternal life through faith in our Creator God.

The atheistic, naturalistic, evolutionary paradigm permeates and dominates all of our education systems, news media, and popular culture. Sadly, this paradigm, which states that "overwhelming scientific evidence for evolution exists", is gaining a foothold in our Bible colleges, seminaries and mainstream churches as well, compromising the faith of many. In addition, evolutionary dogma instills in the minds of our youth that creationism, or creation science, is not real science but religion. This so-called scientific evidence transforms in a negative way. By contrast, scientific evidence that refutes evolution has the power to transform, as it has in my life.

Through the years, my faith has been challenged by so-called scientific evidence for naturalistic processes that explain the origin of life and, hence, make creation of life by God unnecessary. When my biology teacher taught us that life on earth evolved from the primordial ocean, and that all modern life forms came from a common ancestor, she showed the Haeckel drawings of various embryos including a fish, pig, monkey and human and offered this as evidence of evolution. This "evidence" for evolution is now known to be false. The initial stages of embryonic development follow very different patterns of cell division and become very different structures in the mature organisms.

The following year my chemistry teacher presented evidence that showed us the results of an experiment by Stanley Miller, where he produced amino acids by sparking a mixture of water, methane, ammonia, and hydrogen but no oxygen. Further examination of the evidence revealed serious flaws in Miller's results. First, without oxygen, life cannot form and survive, but with oxygen, the amino acids cannot form at all. The amino acids were roughly equal proportions of left and right handed molecules, whereas all amino acids necessary for life are left handed molecules. This affects the probability that life could form from non-life. The evidence today is overwhelming that life cannot form from non-life by random chance. In the movie *Expelled*, when Ben Stein asked Richard Dawkins how life could have originated on earth, after a long pause he muttered his answer... "Aliens?"

As scientific research delves deeper into molecular biology and genetics, the new evidence continually reveals more and more complexity of living organisms. The more we understand the complexity of life, the greater the probability against the chance formation of life. This ever growing discovery of irreducible complexity is strong evidence against evolution. The "simple" cell is far more complex than the most advanced super computer. The remarkable advances we are making in understanding the complexity, memory capabilities and computer chips processing speed, pales in comparison to the information we are uncovering about the enormous complexity of the genetic code.

On the other hand, when we look at the many prophesies about the Messiah given in the Old Testament Scriptures, the probability that anyone other than Jesus could have fulfilled just 49 of these prophesies; born in Bethlehem, house of David, hands and feet pierced, betrayed for 30 pieces of silver, rode into Jerusalem on a donkey, etc., is astronomical: one chance in 10^{151} (that is 1 followed by 151 zeroes). In probability theory any number less than 1 in 10^{50} is considered zero. So the probability that anyone other than Jesus could be the Messiah is zero! And, essentially the same degree of probability has been estimated for the chance formation of amino acids into proteins that form DNA. Therefore, the probability that life formed by random chance is zero! The bottom line is, the evidence that transformed me shows with certainty that Jesus is Lord, and that evolution is false; thus my transformation can never be undone.

Evolution was a Sinking Ship

At one time, Lee was faced with a very tough decision. Does he trust the preacher who seems to have no evidence? Or, will he trust the scientists who have lots of evidence? He made the obvious choice: he trusted what he thought was fact over faith. He removed God from his life and embraced the godless theory of evolution. This appealed to him as a prideful and independent teenager. But it was the laws of physics, in particular thermodynamics, convinced him that evolution could not be true.

On August 12th 1994, a four-year-old Irish boy knelt beside his bed and asked Jesus to come into his heart. After he had said his final amen, he clambered into bed and soon fell asleep, his mind far away from the words just uttered.

That little boy was me. I was reared in a Christian home, went to church regularly and, to many, I seemed like a contented, normal 'Christian' boy. Inside however, I was anything but a normal Christian boy. I was confused, despairing and turning my back on everything I had ever believed was true. What caused me to feel this way? I have often wondered this myself. The answer is complicated and cannot be traced to any one person or event.

Most of my primary school years were spent at a local public school. I worked hard and did well. I was twice awarded the best pupil of the year and in my last year, I achieved my dream: I gained an 'A' grade in my 11+ tests. Only five percent of all candidates achieved this level. I was in the top five percent of all the students in my country, boosting my self-confidence to a level I had never reached before. These results allowed me to enter any school I chose. Eventually, I went to one of the country's most respectable academic schools, The Belfast Royal Academy.

While I attended this school I worked hard. I spent day and night doing my schoolwork, and once again, I came out on top. At fourteen I was studying four languages. English, French, German and Latin and, was also offered the chance to study Greek. People looked up to me. Teachers praised me, and I now knew that my destiny was in my own hands. I was now reaching for the stars and felt I could succeed in almost any career I chose. But I was in no rush to choose. I considered politics, medicine, literature, and science and eventually I chose medicine. I felt that with a medical background I would be able to move into any area I wanted. With that in mind I chose my GCSE subjects.

At this point I became even more big-headed than ever: I was accepted into the top science class for that year. I was now studying science at the highest level available for my age. I won the prize for physics and history, and was chosen to study advanced level mathematics. Approximately three percent of the nation's students are offered this honor. I was placed in the top mathematics class of my year and, was placed in the top foreign language class in that year. I really felt that I was in charge and was determined not to let anything stand in my way.

You may ask why I was so confident in my abilities. The answer can be found in one word: evolution. At one time, I was faced with a very tough decision. Do I trust the preacher who seems to have no evidence? Or, do I trust scientists who have lots of evidence? I made the obvious choice: I would trust what I thought was fact over my faith.

And so by the time I was a teenager, I no longer felt that I could trust God's word. Instead, I accepted what my teachers taught me. The world was not created, and the idea of God was dead. So I removed God from my life and embraced the godless theory of evolution. This decision caused major changes in the way I thought. Without a higher authority, morality is only imaginary. Therefore, it must be chosen by the individual. I took this idea to the limit.

I concluded that Christians could choose to be subject to a God if they wanted to, but it was not for me. I was convinced that, if God did exist, and if I did stand before him on judgment day, He would understand. Why should I accept what God said if he couldn't even get his story on earth's history straight? My morals slid steadily downhill. But I took evolution one step further than many. I was determined to apply it to everyday life.

Let me pause in my story for a moment and review what evolution teaches. Basically, evolution demands circumstances that put the creature in a disadvantageous position. Then those who are able to adapt survive, and those who cannot die. Therefore, the key to survival and success was simply, 'rely on yourself, and use anything you can to your own advantage.'

This philosophy became the foundation for my entire thought pattern - I became an arrogant, prideful and independent teenager. Because it wouldn't be advantageous for others to find out about the new 'me', I was careful to keep my true thoughts to myself. I was also determined to get rich as quickly as possible - after all, what was there to hold me back now? In a Christian worldview, riches need to be earned and used wisely. In an evolutionary worldview the wisest way to use money is to use it to make more money.

That is the reason why I was so confident. I had a plan that could fit any situation and woe betide to anyone who would stand in my way. So, you may be thinking, how on earth would I ever come back to belief in God? The answer is very simple: I never did. God came to me.

The Bible states, 'Be sure your sin will find you out' (Num. 32:23). What truth there is in those few words: My sin was finding me out, and I was brought to the end of myself. I was beginning to consider myself one of life's evolutionary failures. My foolproof plans turned out to be like the Titanic, the ship built in my own city of Belfast. It only took one accident for the magnificent ship to sink to the bottom of the ocean. My boat was sinking and I knew it. At the lowest point in my life, I remembered something I believed as a child: 'Though your sins be as scarlet they shall be as white as snow' (Isaiah 1:18). Surely no mature person could believe such fantasy?

I struggled for days with my pride, and finally prayed a prayer to the God that I still didn't believe in. "If you're real then you'll have to prove it to me. I can't accept something that I can't trust." It may have been a very disrespectful prayer, but God knew that it came from a searching heart. And, as a beautiful verse in scripture says, 'Seek and ye shall find'. God answered my prayer, and set out to prove Himself to me.

The proof initially came in a most unusual way - through a set of DVDs of a seminar by Dr. Kent Hovind. When I watched these DVDs I was in absolute amazement. I had seen creation videos, but had only watched them as an observer. Now I was watching as a seeker and I saw it from a whole new perspective. Not only was I amazed but I was shocked by my lack of knowledge. I was hearing things that were so simple and so obvious that I had NEVER considered before. It answered the questions that I had never been able to answer satisfactorily from my evolutionary perspective.

However, I was still a long way from accepting God. It took at least six months of reading, searching and deep thinking before I eventually accepted Christ. Although the reasons that I returned to a belief in God were numerous, I will only share one example that left a very strong impression on me: it was the testimony of physics.

As I mentioned, I won the prize for physics in school. Physics was one of my strongest areas. Many of my classmates found the many and varied formulas and equations monotonous, but I found them fascinating. The fact that the entire universe was controlled by many immutable laws amazed me, but the two laws that controlled our universe that helped to convince me that there must be a God are the first and second laws of thermodynamics.

The first law of thermodynamics is known as the law of energy/mass conservation. It states that while energy/mass may be changed from one form to another, it cannot be created or destroyed. This presents an insurmountable hurdle for the evolutionist. When it comes to the first law of thermodynamics, evolution must somehow account for the fact that the universe consists of various forms of energy and matter. The universe is made of matter and the energy needed to make it run. Even the Big Bang theory requires the existence of energy and matter. However, this law very defiantly states that the universe is not self-created and the energy and matter had to come from somewhere else. And this 'somewhere else' can only be accounted for in the person of God.

The second law of thermodynamics, also known as the law of energy decay or increasing entropy, states that the universe is disintegrating - everything tends towards disorder. This fact is a death blow to evolutionary theory. Evolution teaches us that life is evolving, getting better—we started out as the result of a mindless random "explosion", then life somehow managed to arise from non-living material. These first single cells evolved into multi-cellular organisms which then evolved into all life that we see today entailing a continual, consistent, progression over billions of years. Yet the law of energy decay defies evolution at every turn.

As the British Astronomer Arthur Eddington said, "If your theory is found to be against the second law of thermodynamics I can give you no hope; there is nothing for it but to collapse in deepest humiliation."[58] If the universe is like a giant cosmic clock, that is running down, if everything is unwinding, at one point it must have been wound up. But who wound it up?

Yet another obstacle to my atheism was the very substance that creates the page you are reading. Everything is made up of atoms: it was atoms that caused me to have a subconscious thought that there was some 'power' in charge of universe. Allow me to explain why. There has been, and probably will continue to be, several theories about the atom, but let us set aside 'theories' for a moment, and deal with what we know.

We know that electrons whirl around the nucleus millions of billions of times every second and that the nucleus is composed of neutrons and protons. Neutrons, as the name suggests, are electrically neutral while protons have a positive charge. One of the laws that rule the universe is that 'like charges repel, and opposite charges attract.' I had observed this law in class many times and yet here was an exception! I must admit that, as I looked at my diagram of the atom, my brain was starting to race! I knew that the laws of physics could not be set aside! If all the protons were positively charged then they should scatter into space. After looking at the page for a while, I cautiously put my hand up and

58 *The Nature of the Physical World,* Macmillan, New York, 1930, p.74.

asked the teacher. 'Miss, why don't the protons repel each other?' I was surprised by her honest answer, 'Lee, I don't know.'

In fact, the protons do repel each other. However, they are held together in the nucleus by the strong nuclear force. The problem is, we do not understand why or how this law works.

I believe this particular event did something to me. First, it left me with a question that no one seemed to be able to answer. Every time I was with a teacher who brought up the atom, I was acutely aware that, although they talked with authority, they didn't know the answer to one of the most fundamental questions. 'Why does the atom exist?' Secondly, it kept me searching for the answer because I didn't like to be left without an answer. I wasn't prepared to accept a 'We don't know, and don't care' answer. It may have been unusual for a twelve year old to be so interested, but that question bothered me until I came back to a belief in God.

I now know that the Bible answers this question. It says that Christ, the Creator, "Is before all things, and by him all things exist." Col 1:17. This is only one example of literally thousands. But let's get back to the title of this book, 'Transformed by the Evidence'.

Some readers may want to read an exciting story about a drug pusher or a murderer, someone who lived a wicked life and then got saved. After their enjoyable read they can say 'Wasn't it great that such a wicked person got straightened out. This is not that sort of story. Not because I couldn't relate some evil things I've done, but because I want you to connect with what you read, so will discuss how I have been changed so that you can relate to it. In the Bible we are told that when someone accepts Christ as their Savior He will make them a new person ('If any man be in Christ he is a new creation, old things are passed away, behold all things are made new' 2 Corinthians 5:17) Here is a few examples.

First, I no longer fear death. Everyone will eventually die and, if we're honest, we aren't looking forward to it. What is it that makes us cringe when we hear that someone has died? Or what about the terror that grips us when we think it might be our turn? I believe that it is the fact that we know there is something more – we know we have to face God. The Scriptures tell us 'It is appointed unto men once to die, but after this the judgment.' (Hebrews 9:27). We fear the judgment of a righteous and holy God. However, as a Christian, I no longer have a fear of death.

Not that I want to die, but I no longer *fear* it. I believe God's word that 'whosoever shall call upon the name of the LORD shall be saved.' (Romans 10:13). I know that when I die I will spend an eternity in heaven with my savior, an assurance every believer has. In our Hymn Book we actually SING about the peace that comes from God when facing death. The Bible has a wonderful passage that proclaims '...Death is swallowed up in victory. O death, where is thy sting? O grave, where is thy victory?' (2 Corinthians 15:54-55).

The ultimate test for a philosophy is the way it prepares you for death. I stumbled across the dying words of Thomas Paine while writing this chapter. Paine, a leading atheist, whose works are still honored by atheists today, said while he was dying:

> "I would give worlds if I had them, that *The Age of Reason* had never been published. O Lord, help me!... No, don't leave me; stay with me! Send even a little child to stay with me; for I am on the edge of Hell here alone. If ever the devil had an agent, I have been that one."[59]

Compare this with the dying words of Sidney Cooper, a member of the Royal Academy of Science:

> "I have full faith in Thy atonement, and I am confident of Thy help. Thy precious blood I fully rely on. Thou art the source of my comfort. I have no other. I want no other."[60]

Of these two men, Cooper was best prepared for death. These are not exceptions to the rule, but they are the rule: evolution offers no hope during this life, or once this life is over.

Secondly, I am confident about this life. The Bible tells us that the great God who made this vast complicated universe is interested in each individual. The scriptures teach 'cast all our cares upon Him, for *He cares for you.*' (1 Peter 5:7). Even if you are not a Christian He cares for your soul and desperately wants to save you, but He leaves it up to you. If you are already a Christian, you are a Child of God and He cares very much for you.

Whenever I have a problem, I take it to the LORD and have often seen Him answer my prayers. Before I was a Christian, I had to struggle alone; It's different now. Jesus has never let me down where it counts. He doesn't take away problems, but helps me through them. That is what the Christian life is all about – strength in the storm. As the Scriptures relate, 'My grace is sufficient for thee: for my strength is made perfect in your weakness.'[61]

Thirdly, I have a peace that passes understanding. An atheist will have no idea what I am talking about. Until you have experienced it for yourself, you will

---

59   V. Ferrell, *Other Evidence,* Pilgrim Books, p. C-24.
60   Ibid p.C-20
61   2 Cor. 12:9.

not understand. Some say 'A problem shared is a problem halved' but with God it's different. It becomes 'A problem shared is a problem gone'. He will help us through by taking it on Himself.

Lastly, I have a responsibility. My friends sometimes ask me 'Ok, Lee, you're a Christian now and you're going to heaven, so why don't you just do what you want?' The Bible says that I am bought with the precious blood of Christ and no longer own my life because it belongs to God. The Bible teaches 'The blood of Jesus Christ His Son cleanseth us from all sin [past, present and future sins]' (1 John 1:7). If I sin, God can punish me, and there are some sins that God will remove His Children for committing, called a 'sin unto death'. But for the obedient Child, God has a storehouse of blessing. The Bible promises that '...eye hath not seen, nor ear heard, neither have entered into the heart of man, the things that God has prepared for them that love Him' (1 Cor. 2:9) and that God 'is able to do exceedingly abundantly above all that we ask or think' (Ephesians 3:20).

Before I became a Christian, I was extremely selfish, did what I wanted to, and didn't care about anyone else. Determined to get rich, I wanted to live a life of luxury, and was pushing to achieve that goal. Those are no longer my goals. My goal now is to serve the Creator by introducing Him to as many people as I can. Although I may not hit the mark of a million in this life, God has promised me riches untold in the next life. I have spoken to children, teenagers and older groups, for Christ!

I have also had a change of attitude. Before, I was extremely proud of myself and my achievements. I now know that I am insignificant compared to the Creator of the universe. Interestingly, (and unfortunately for the evolutionist) I have also had a change of attitude towards science. Before I became a Christian, my teachers and scientists were almost gods. I believed everything about science that I was taught. I have now learned to be more cautious and to study things more before I accept them as truth. I would encourage you to do the same, and yes, that includes Christianity.

More importantly, I now have a different worldview. As an evolutionist I looked at things from a completely different viewpoint than from what I do as a Creationist. This is clearly demonstrated by looking at the five fundamental questions of life that every religion in the world, including atheism, tries to answer. They are summarized as follows.

Who am I? If evolution is true, then we are not only unimportant but are a major part of 'the problem'. We are the environmental polluters and the fewer humans the better.

Where did I come from? If evolution is true, then we are the results of a huge explosion, approximately 20 billion years ago and millions of years of billions of accidental mutations.

What is the purpose to life? If evolution is true, then there is no ultimate purpose to life but we were simply the lucky ones to make it. As evolutionists say, 'Your main purpose in life is to pass on your genes.' If they are right, then what's the point to struggle besides to survive? What about people with disabilities? This is one reason why evolution is linked to the horrible crime of eugenics.

Where am I going when I die? If evolution is true, then we will go into the grave and be recycled into a worm or plant.

How do we tell right from wrong? If evolution is true then there is no sure way to tell. Natural selection demands cruelty and ruthlessness, and death is the hero of the plot. When one animal evolves a little higher than the others, the rest will eventually die by natural selection, avoiding the good genes from being blended back into the population. 'Mother nature' doesn't have any morals.

Now let us answer these questions from a Biblical worldview.

Who am I? You were made in the image of God, and He thinks you are very important. He loves you so much that He sent His only begotten Son to die on the cross for you.

Where did I come from? We were created by the God of the universe.

What is the purpose to life? We have a responsibility to the creator, and we also have a choice to make whether to obey or disobey Him.

Where am I going when I die? This depends if you have accepted Christ as your savior. If you accept him you will spend an eternity in heaven. If you reject Him you spend an eternity in the lake of fire. Ultimately, you are in charge of your eternal destination.

How do we tell right from wrong? The God of Bible has set down rules but since we have all broken his rules God has sent His Son in our place that we might receive the free gift of eternal life. We have a choice either to receive the free gift of salvation, or to reject it.

Which set of answers is most satisfactory? I hope you would agree that the Biblical answers are the best. Indeed, the naturalistic 'answers' are not really answers at all. They are cold 'facts' that have little meaning. Questions of the soul cannot be answered by evolutionary theory.

Allow me to end this chapter by discussing what I believe is one of the best evidences for the existence of God, what I call 'The Ultimate Experiment'. If I were to ask you what the ultimate experiment to support the existence of God might be, what would your answer be? Would it be the Miller attempt to make life in the laboratory? I believe the ultimate experiment is the Experiment of Changed Lives.

Although a daunting thought for the atheist, go into a Christian Bookstore and look at the Biography/Testimony section. It is full of the accounts of men and women who have performed the ultimate experiment: Those who have put their trust in the creator of the universe. The Bible tells us that when we put our trust in Christ, then he will perform a miracle in our life. We are promised, 'If any man be in Christ, he is a new creature: old things are passed away; behold all things are become new.' (2 Corinthians 5:17). We are also told, 'Whosoever shall call on the name of the Lord shall be saved.' (Romans 10:13).

Every experiment has predictions, and those are Gods predictions. God is saying, "If you call unto me for forgiveness, then I will save you from your sins and I will make you a new person." Those predictions been verified a million times over: God has proven himself to millions throughout the centuries. This short essay is only one of many stories of people who have come to realize that God is real, not just on a cosmic level, but on a personal level as well.

I originally rejected belief in God because I thought that I was turning from 'faith to facts'. However, I was to learn that the facts point towards a God and the Bible. After a long struggle, I turned to the living God and asked Him for forgiveness. Since then my further studies have strengthened my belief in God and in Creationism.

This short essay may not convince any hard-line atheists, but hopefully will encourage you to look at the subject with an open heart and mind. If you do, you will discover that God was correct when he said, '...seek, and ye shall find...' (Matthew 7:7).

If God could transform someone like me, then He can transform someone like you. God didn't promise us an easy life, but an abundant life. I have had abundant life, and when I pass from this life to the next this sinner who once was only fit to hear the words 'Depart from ye, ye worker of iniquity I never knew you' (Matthew 7:23), will finally hear the precious words, 'Well done thou good and faithful servant, enter into the joy of thy Lord' (Matthew 25:21).

Insects Bug Evolutionists!

Karl's Christian life had very little power until he began reading literature produced by the Institute for Creation Research. As a junior high school math teacher, he recounts how he confronted the evolutionary science curriculum that was being adopted in his school. The result was a national debate about teaching evolution.

My first home was an apartment above a used clothing store run by the Union Mission in downtown Charleston, West Virginia. My parents had met at the mission where my father was employed. After a few years living in that apartment and the Mission's summer camp, we moved to the Orchard Manor housing project on Charleston's West Side. The "Manor" was known as the South Bronx of West Virginia. That was where I grew up.

It was a rough life. As a third-grader I witnessed street fighting with knives and chains. Although my parents were good people who often attended church Sunday mornings, the neighborhood had a strong influence on me, and I started smoking and skipping school. Few of my neighbors had a normal two-parent family, and most of those who did were alcoholics. Crime and violence were almost a daily occurrence and I was involved in some of both. During that time, I experienced several incidents that could have led to my death or imprisonment, but the Lord preserved me through all of this.

I joined the Navy and served on the USS Wright (CC-2), which was a floating command post for the President and Joint Chiefs in the event of a nuclear war. One day, when I was alone in a Bainbridge, MD barracks between duty stations, I accepted Jesus Christ as my Lord and Savior. Before this I had joined my buddies in laughing at another sailor who was praying over chow. Not long afterwards, I ran into that Christian sailor in the laundry room. My uneasiness was soon put to rest as we talked. He invited me to attend a military Christian group meeting in a nearby home.

The first night two Christian truck drivers stopped in for fellowship. Through the witness of these men who I saw as genuine, the Holy Spirit opened my heart to my lost condition. I experienced this just before I was to leave the Navy. The political climate had forced President Johnson to declare that the Vietnam War was winding down and he was releasing thousands of active duty personnel. My orders to the Philippines were canceled and, as a new Christian, I became a college student.

Each day after morning classes, during the 40-minute drive to work, I listened to a preacher on the radio. Though he believed in the Gap Theory, he spent a lot of time refuting evolution. This caused me to rethink the theistic evolution position I had held by default until then. In my first year as a sixth-grade teacher I used science supplement booklets published by the *Institute of Creation Research* and got on their mailing list. The ICR material soon convinced me of a literal creation in six 24-hour days about 6,000 years ago.

Unfortunately, my Christian life had very little power during that time. Local evolutionists removed any reference to Creation Science from county schools without any resistance. When my daughter began college, she took a class in biology taught by an aggressive evolutionist. She appealed for my help in dealing with the situation, motivating me to write to the *Institute for Creation Research*. At the same time, Dr. Bert Thompson was teaching a local seminar on the creation-evolution debate.

Dr. Thompson's lectures and literature gave me material to share with my daughter. ICR literature and their devotional, *Days of Praise* affected me profoundly. It was like placing a few drops of water on the tongue of a man dying of thirst. Much of that devotional is made up of Bible verses thus, in effect, God's Word was again nourishing me. It naturally led me back to the Bible itself. It was like the transformation (metamorphosis) of a butterfly. A lot was happening unseen, and all of it was part of God's plan.

I began to read my Bible again and get back into a close relationship with God. At the same time, I saw the need to start a local creation group. I started promoting the group but no one responded. A local youth pastor who had a degree in biology met with me a couple of times but did not persevere in forming a creation ministry. I went to the public library meeting site alone for a few weeks and finally decided that I must have misread the Lord's direction.

The week I decided to quit, a fellow who had seen our group's announcement on the library entrance called. I had not even known that the announcement was there! He became a great leader in the local group, and a few others soon joined us. All had great testimonies about how the Lord had led them to the group. We were invited to speak at events hosted by local intelligentsia at two universities and we made a solid showing.

The Lord gave me a ministry (www.insectman.us) using my insect collection to present the truth of Creation to local groups. I made a 60-minute presentation, using transparencies that would take the audience through the fallacies of evolutionism as revealed by the wonders of God in the amazing facts and details of insects.

As Romans 1:20 declares, we can know much about God by what He created. Nothing in creation compares to insects in variety of size, color, shape, and behavior. The more I study and talk to professional entomologists, the more I realize how little is known about the insect world. Functional designs found in insects have inspired many wonderful products and technology. Just to name a few: Micro Air Vehicles, super-resilient material for medical purposes, better cameras, cell phones, and television monitors, robotics, and hearing aids. If it were not for insects, mankind would soon starve or die from decaying debris. When God created those wonderful creatures, He did not make a mistake.

Karl working with Christian high school students during a field lab on entomology.

Even insects that are considered pests (or worse) are not absolutely bad. I am not sure what bedbugs did in the original perfect creation that God called "good," but bedbugs have some benefits. *Compounds including crushed bedbugs were once used for pharmacological* purposes.

Ants have so many fascinating features that scientists (whether they want to or not) really do "consider her ways" (Proverbs 6:6 KJB). Ant behavior,

Karl with mother and son at a Bible School insect presentation.

metabolism, and structural design is studied to improve Internet traffic routing, deciding human medication dosage, products to assist cleaning up oil spills, making better antibiotics, and studying human aging—just to provide a few examples.

Bees are unquestionably crucial to the very survival of mankind due to their pollination activities, but their venom is studied to treat cancer. Hornet exoskeletons may contribute to designs to harvest solar energy and provide other energy benefits. Wasps are used to sniff for drugs, bombs, and bodies.

Mosquitoes, roaches, termites, and aphids may make you cringe, but further study may change your mind. Mosquitoes (only females bite and only at certain times in their lives) are an important part of the food chain, serve as pollinators, and their flight ability is envied by aerodynamics experts. Roaches are integral to ecology and their ability to get around astounds mechanical engineers. Some skyscrapers have a climate control system inspired by how termites build their mounds. Aphids are potential resources for understanding how to make drugs that do not harm "good" bacteria while attacking "bad" bacteria. Interplanetary space flights likely will carry insects as food.

The irritating fruit fly has contributed to so many inventions, products, and genetic insights that it would take multiple pages just to list them. Also, other types of flies truly cause the ointment of evolutionism to stink (Ecclesiastes 10:1a KJB). "Medical maggots" and other facts establish that we should "Thank God for Insects"[62] on this subject.

After I had spent over 24 years teaching at the elementary level, God used pressure at work to cause me to consider transferring to teaching junior high school. There, one of my students told me about a play she was rehearsing. It turned out to be a local production of *Inherit the Wind*. Soon our group became involved in writing letters-to-the-editor exposing it as evolutionist propaganda. God used this to launch our group as a bona-fide defender of Christ the Creator. It gave us public exposure and provided us with confidence that we could engage evolutionists without embarrassment.

After fighting that battle, one day I noticed a discarded memo below the faculty mailboxes directed to science teachers about the new science curriculum that was being adopted. This led to a brand new confrontation. I appeared at a board of education meeting and asked that the county allow Darwinism to be taught critically and not as scientific fact. I was told to seek redress from the state. The state sent me back to the county. During those several weeks, I polled county science teachers and found that they wanted guidance on what they could do regarding criticism of evolution in the science class. I went back to a board of education meeting with my survey results. The board now had to face objective data from a population of professionals directly involved with the issue.

Board member Betty Jarvis took up the cause to direct the board attorney to write a resolution permitting a critical approach to the teaching of evolution in county schools. The local media, led by a nationally published atheistic editor, began to run hostile editorials. Soon we were in a major battle that came to be known as the "Evolution Resolution" that got national media coverage. Board meetings were crowded with citizens voicing their opinions. During this time, I was exposed to many devious and downright vicious tactics by evolutionists in their relentless protection of the dogma of evolutionism.

The resolution was voted down in December of that year. Soon, however, I was placed by Ms. Jarvis on the text selection committee, as a citizen, and was able to persuade the science teacher committee members (fully supported by the county science supervisor) to recommend *Of Pandas and People* as a supplementary book for teacher use.[63] The local newspaper published this amazing item: "Karl Priest, a member of the Kanawha Creation Science Group, presented the book to the science teachers. 'I want to thank Karl Priest for bringing this to

---

62   http://www.insectman.us/articles/karls/thank-god.htm.
63   Percival Davis and Dean H. Kenyon. *Of Pandas and People*. 2nd Ed. Dallas, TX: Haughton Publishing Company, 1993.

my attention,' said Bob Seymour, who oversees science programs for the school system. 'This follows science to the letter.'"

A well-known Christian law firm offered to represent the board of education pro bono against any legal action by those seeking to censor "Pandas." Once again, the same foes led a malicious campaign to defeat this effort. Using the Freedom of Information Act, I found out that the committee science teachers had been flooded with propaganda from the National Center for Science Education. The purchase of "Pandas" lost on a 3-2 vote with a retired chemist board member voting with Ms. Jarvis and a professed Christian board member voting against the measure. Ms. Jarvis subsequently lost an election after being ridiculed and lied about in the local media.

I filed a grievance, stating that I felt professionally threatened without a clear policy about what could be done to criticize evolution in the classroom. Dr. Joseph Mastropaolo, after an all-night drive from Atlanta due to a missed flight from his home in California, supported me at an all-day hearing. Dr. Mastropaolo used his masterful logical and scientific arguments to support the hard evidence I brought. During the hearing Dr. Mastropaolo exposed the woeful reasoning used to defend evolution from any form of criticism.

Before a previous visit Dr. Mastropaolo began by challenging the atheist editor of the *Charleston Gazette* to debate. The editor responded that Dr. Mastropaolo and I would pack the auditorium with busloads of Christians. Dr. Mastropaolo replied that the atheist editor would control the key to the door. Next, the atheist editor attacked Dr. Mastropaolo as a mere gym teacher because Dr. Mastropaolo's doctorate is in kinesiology. That dodge was countered by Dr. Mastropaolo telling the atheist he could say Dr. Mastropaolo was a dropout of a one-room schoolhouse in the foothills of the Adirondack Mountains, real hillbilly country. With such impoverished credentials, Dr. Mastropaolo should be a pushover.

When he arrived in town, Dr. Mastropaolo challenged the Unitarian atheist pastor who had led the opposition to debate. That man declined using the excuse that he was not a scientist. Dr. Mastropaolo told him he could bring all of the local scientists he wanted as part of a team. I was amazed that neither man accepted the challenge and continued to use censorship and authority to defend Darwinism. I realized that many boisterous evolutionists are full of hot air. That realization was manifested during this hearing.

For the hearing Dr. Mastropaolo questioned the board president (an engineer) with scientific questions that quickly placed the man in a corner and demonstrated that Darwinism cannot be defended.[64]

---

64   Dr. Mastropaolo's material is available in a booklet titled *Biology for the 21st Century*.

In a nutshell, Dr. Mastropaolo pointed out that in order for evolution to be considered a theory, it must have numerous successful experiments to its credit as well as numerous unsuccessful experiments to disprove it. Evolution has none of each, so it cannot possibly qualify as a theory.

To qualify as a hypothesis, evolution must have at least one successful experiment to its credit. All experiments to prove evolution have been 100 percent absolute failures; so it cannot qualify as a hypothesis. To qualify as a speculation it must be harmonious with the laws of physics, chemistry, and biology. Not only is it out of harmony with those laws, it is exactly the opposite. Devolution, the exact opposite and excluder of evolution, is the rule in the entire universe. If evolution is not a theory, nor a hypothesis, nor even a speculation, then what is it? It is an inverted fantasy, like the moon jumped over the cow.

Therefore, Dr. Mastropaolo concluded, evolution is a zillion times more impossible than the Tooth Fairy and the mathematical definition of impossible put together. An administrative law judge denied the grievance. She did rule, however, that teachers have a right to express criticism of evolution in the classroom.

After that, I was able to convince a fellow Sunday school class member to file a citizen's complaint as a parent about the inaccurate material in state science textbooks. Dr. Jonathan Wells, who also testified by telephone, helped us describe the flaws that included:

1. The 1953 Miller-Urey experiment reporting that conditions on early earth could have led to the beginning of life is questioned by many geochemists who now believe that the conditions on early earth were not at all like those that were assumed nearly a half century ago in the Miller-Urey experiment. No mention is made in the text of the scientific community's current understanding of the chemical composition of early earth's atmosphere and oceans. Nor is there any mention made of the hundreds of other experiments that have reached different conclusions.

2. Darwin's observation that finches on the Galapagos Islands were similar to each other but different from finches living along the South American coast to the east, thus purportedly demonstrating that a "single species can accumulate enough differences over a long time to become two separate species" — is also scientifically invalid, a fact that has been known for 30 years now. Darwin neither studied the Galapagos Islands finches in a scientifically correct manner because his system of identification was flawed, at best — nor did he personally observe the finches along the South American coast with which he was attempting to compare the Galapagos Islands finches.

3. The text asserts that the relatedness of two animals (e.g. rabbits and humans) can be partly determined by "look[ing] at the structure of its body and the way it develops as an embryo at the very beginning of its life." The drawings, used in the text for support, illustrate that proposition, however, were simply copied from drawings that had been made in the 19th century and those drawings are now known to be inaccurate.

4. The text also asserts that the major animal phyla are related, and undertakes to present the approximate order that each appeared on earth (jawless fishes first, primates last). Fossil evidence, however, strongly suggests that the major animal phyla all appeared at about the same time, fully formed. The fossil evidence does not show that the animal phyla came from a common ancestor or, much less that they branched off in a different order from each other (e.g. birds branching off, or evolving from, reptiles).

5. The theory of evolution cannot fully explain or account for the complexity that is observable at the biochemical level.

After a battle of several months, once again with national media interest, the state board of education dismissed this complaint. The next year two students, who needed help with science projects with a creation theme, contacted our creation group. This gave birth to a Creation Club at school, which still functioned even after my retirement.

Next, West Virginia revised state Science Standards, and we entered another battle joining national leaders of the Intelligent Design movement. Despite overwhelming public support for our request to teach science objectively, the West Virginia Board of Education rejected our request. Currently there are other plans in the works to free public school students from evolutionist chains.

Evolutionists attempted to discredit me, not by clear evidence, but more often by calling me names, such as a liar, buffoon, and idiot. My colleagues and administrators received anonymous letters and phone calls attempting to ruin me professionally. I was even investigated by the State Police due to a complaint filed by an evolutionist. Those years required many sacrifices of finances and time. I thank God I was counted worthy to offer them. Like an ant, I just keep moving and am amazed at how God directs my paths.

God the Creator has transformed my Christian life through revealing Himself through His creation. Not only did God use my interest in science to revive a lukewarm sinning man, but He has also allowed me to share a little bit of persecution in His name. I encourage everyone to find a way to serve God. It will transform your life.

Grand Canyon Raft Experience

In 1980, Tom was managing the corporate computer center for a Fortune 500 company when he took a vacation that would transform his life. His rafting trip through the Grand Canyon changed his life in two phases, first to take him out of the corporate world, and then, 15 years later, to bring him to the Lord. He now runs Canyon Ministries (www.CanyonMinistries. com), leading Christ-centered rafting trips through the Grand Canyon, and is also a contributing author to the *True North Series* of guidebooks, which provide a biblical understanding of our National Parks.

"Let's go boatin'!" is the call that echoes off the walls of the Grand Canyon during my guided tours. It gets people moving and ready to head down river. In my over 30 years as a guide, I've had the privilege of taking thousands of people through the Grand Canyon, which I now believe is one of God's true, created wonders.

I was born and raised in the Los Angeles area. My father was a Safety Engineer for a construction company and my mother a homemaker. My parents met at church and up to the time I was about eight years old, we went to church on a fairly regular basis. But at some point my father had a falling out with the church, and we started going camping instead. After that, I do not remember going to church except for weddings and funerals, though my home was a very wholesome place … just without the obvious presence of God.

After graduating from high school, I spent about a year operating a gas station with my brother. It was the Vietnam era and my draft number was coming up fast. Since the station was not really supporting both of us, I decided I would dictate the timing and volunteer for the draft, a two year commitment. After basic training, I went to jump school at Fort Benning, Georgia, followed by parachute rigger school, and was soon a jump school instructor.

When I got out of the Army, I took a position as an entry level computer operator with the oil company with whom we had owned the station. Thirteen years later when I left the company, I was managing the corporate computer center for this Fortune 500 company. I was living what I thought was the good life with most of my leisure time spent in the outdoors – biking, camping, skiing, or boating. I had a nice boat and all the toys.

But, I was living a very "secular" life. I had already been through two failed marriages and God was nowhere to be found in my life. So…how does one move from managing a large corporate computer center to a 30-year career as a rafting guide in the Grand Canyon? My love for the Canyon started in 1980 when I took a life-changing vacation – my first Grand Canyon river trip. We were on a raft that required three boatmen; one of them did not show up. Although I had no whitewater experience, I got drafted to man one of the oars and rowed my first trip through the Canyon. About halfway through, I was hooked! The following year, I started working as a part-time guide and, in 1983, left my corporate life to work in the Canyon.

For the next 15 years, I led trips through the Grand Canyon and taught that natural processes were responsible for forming the exquisite and varied rock layers found in the Grand Canyon. The evolutionary interpretation is that millions of years of slow particle-by-particle deposition interspersed by long periods of erosion created these massive formations, and later the Colorado River carved out the 900 cubic miles of missing material from the Grand Canyon.

But deep in my heart, I had lots of questions about how these processes could have created what we see today. There were too many totally unbelievable things that had to happen for this process to work. I knew about the biblical story of Noah's Flood, but it was just that … a story. The profound significance of the Canyon was not yet embedded in my mind, let alone my heart. I was being prepared, though, for a major shift in my thinking.

A Sovereign Appointment

One day in July 1994, a lady got off a plane at Marble Canyon, Arizona. She was going on a Grand Canyon rafting trip, and I was one of her guides. Little did I know how much she would end up guiding me. My worldview was about to be turned upside down.

She was a native North Carolinian, a professional pilot, and an ex-gymnast who had owned a gymnastic school. An avid tennis player and marathon runner, she was about to hit one of those 'big' birthdays, the kind women don't like to see coming. So under the threat of a black balloon birthday bash, she gathered up three of her friends and got out of town.

We didn't hit it off at first. In fact one of the first things she said about me to one of her friends was, "I don't think he likes me." But soon, long hours were spent under the starlit nights talking about everything under the sun. On the second night of the trip, she started her ministry on my lost soul – not an easy project. I vividly remember a very philosophical conversation about the meaning of life. My view was that the meaning of life was to have fun, while hers was

172 • Transformed by the Evidence

this strange idea of having a personal relationship with Jesus Christ. During our nine days together, she continued to gently share the Gospel, enough to get me thinking.

The Lord obviously had His hand in our meeting, even though I didn't think so at the time. Because if we had not been trapped in the Grand Canyon, we would not have given each other much of a second thought. For one thing, this lady was way too "religious" for me. And as for me, I was not quite what she had in mind. I was not a Christian, I drank a little too much at times, my language was not always Godly, and I was divorced. But because He had scheduled enough time in this very magical place, we were able to see past those few "minor flaws" we both had.

Remember, I was immersed in evolutionary thought, which, contrary to what you might have been told by evolutionists themselves, seeks to eliminate God from all reality. The logical extension of this – that we are not responsible to anyone, that there are no absolute truths in life, that we set our own rules and this life is all there is – was the backdrop for my lifestyle.

After the trip, this lady, who read her Bible and believed it, sent me a Bible. That October, I traveled to the Himalayas in Pakistan with friends to manage the base camp for their climbing expedition…and the Bible went with me. The weather did not cooperate, and the months of planning were for naught; no base camp was ever established. But it did allow lots of "tent time" as we waited for the weather to clear. So in my little tent at about 12,500 feet above sea level, in zero degree weather, I started to read the Bible, and slowly things started to come together. The lady had told me to start reading in 1 John, which I did. But, wondering why I was starting to read towards the end of the book, I started reading Genesis as well.

The Genesis account seemed to strike a nerve in me, but I wasn't quite sure which nerve. Maybe it was from some small seed planted by a Sunday school teacher in my youth, or maybe it was just an intrinsic knowledge that what I had been teaching was a lie. My eyes kept falling on a prayer this lady had written in my Bible. It read:

Dear Lord,

I know I have done wrong, that I miss the mark of perfection.
I am willing to turn from my sins.
I believe Jesus Christ died for me.
Please come into my life and forgive me.
I receive you in my life as my Lord and Savior, as best I know right now.

I read this prayer tens of times before it really started to sink in, but at some point, I started to mean it. I made a conscious decision to believe in the Gospel, and to accept Christ as my Lord and Savior. And in November of 1994, I returned from Pakistan a child of Christ. That was when the love of my Creator started, a love for the Lord that will continue to grow and unfold for the rest of my life.

This choice impacted not only my heart, but also my head. The uniformitarian view of life, the belief that what we see is the product of billions of years of gradual change, doesn't jibe with the biblical account of origins. The way I saw the Canyon – this place that I love and that draws me back year after year – was changing in the most profound way.

As to the lady who sent me a Bible, her name is Paula, and to make a long story short, it took me about a year to get her to say "Yes," and we were married the following October, on the day the Lord had planned all along.

The Creation of a Creationist

The following year (1996), we were living in North Carolina. Paula was flying for an airline out of Washington, DC, and I commuted to Arizona to run river trips. That summer, I took our pastor and one of his sons on a river trip. On the third night of that trip he said, "Tom, you need to figure out a way to share this place with fellow believers." That seed grew into Canyon Ministries, which Paula and I started the following year to provide Christ-centered rafting trips through the Grand Canyon. We led our first Christian trip through the Canyon in 1997.

At the time, I could not have called myself a creationist. I was a baby Christian and far from understanding the significance of the Canyon from a biblical perspective. But I had learned that Genesis told an altogether different story from what I had been sharing with my river guests. As I studied the creation model, things started to make sense, and I started sharing it with the folks on my trips. The creation interpretation of the Canyon was much more logical, was easier to believe and understand, and it answered more questions than the million-of-years, molecule-to-man theories of evolution. I came to believe that it took more faith to believe in evolution than in creation. I was being transformed by the evidence.

One of the things I realized was how the evolutionary model had changed considerably. When I first went to the Canyon in 1980, the general consensus was that the Canyon was 70 million years old, and over the years, that number worked its way down to just 6 million years. Recently that story has been questioned again, suggesting 70 million years is closer to the correct age. But the bottom line is that the evolutionary/uniformitarian geologists have neither a consensus on the age of the Canyon, nor how it was formed.

The Persuasive Evidence

The Grand Canyon is often called "Exhibit A" in support of a young earth. But why did the Lord create this magnificent place? The Bible says, *"For since the creation of the world His invisible attributes, His eternal power and divine nature, have been clearly seen, being understood through what has been made, so that they are without excuse."* (Romans 1:20); and the Grand Canyon confirms that. What we see in the Canyon only supports and upholds what we read in the Word of God. And only from down in the Canyon can so much of it be seen.

So is the Grand Canyon there to provide the skeptics with evidence that may be "clearly seen" if only they are willing to see? I am often asked, "What are the main evidences you see in the Canyon that support creation and the global Flood?" There are many, but here are four of them:

Formation of the Grand Canyon: Stretching 277 miles through the Southwestern portion of the Colorado plateau, the Canyon is carved through sedimentary layers of limestone, sandstone, and shale, and into the basement of schist, granite, and gneisses. It descends over a mile into the earth and is 18 miles wide at some points. How could the Colorado River carve through the 8,000 foot Colorado Plateau when the river, in its upper reaches east of the plateau, is less than 4,000 feet? As demonstrated at Mt. St. Helens, catastrophic processes provide a very plausible explanation for rapidly carving out canyons like the Grand Canyon. A global flood would provide just such a catastrophic mechanism.

Layering of Grand Canyon: The Grand Canyon exhibits 5,000 feet of geologic layers. How the sedimentary layers of the Canyon were deposited is a key difference between the two models (creation vs. uniformitarian). The upper layers are divided into 10 formations, with the lower formations containing 9 layers. Creation geologists consider the upper layers to be Flood deposits laid down as a single sequence during Noah's Flood. The uniformitarians believe these layers were laid down by at least seven different regional events over a period of an estimated 300 million years with millions of years missing between each layer. Each of these events would have required the entire region, several thousand square miles, to

rise and fall several thousand feet as a single unit. However, there is no significant sign of movement within the formations.

Contact point between sedimentary layers: Known as unconformities, many of these contact points between the layers form a distinct line which can be seen even from the rim of the Canyon. If these unconformities represent from 5 to 125 million years of "missing time," which is the uniformitarian interpretation, there should be signs of either physical or chemical erosion  between the layers. There is no sign of channeling, canyons, or valleys, as we see with erosion of present-day topography. Only Flood geology, on a global scale, accounts for this.

Folding: Folds, or bends in the rock, are found in some sedimentary layers, sometimes seen across multiple layers. Uniformitarian geologists interpret these folds as the result of heat and pressure, but the rocks show no signs of the heat required to fold rock. The folding of the rock, without  cracking or showing the effects of heat, indicates that the folding had to happen while the layers were still soft and pliable. Thus these folds show that the deposition and upheaval responsible for the folding were, in fact, one event. That event is described in the Bible in Psalm 104:8.

As I examined these evidences, along with additional factors like radioisotope dating and the fossil record, I personally came to see that what the Bible teaches is supported by the testimony found in the layers of the Canyon. But more importantly, this is not about the Grand Canyon, or the debate about creation versus evolution. It is really a battle over worldviews.

The Creation of a Creation Ministry

In 1996, two years after I had become a Christian, Answers in Genesis (AiG) held a seminar in Greensboro, North Carolina. I naturally wanted to attend the seminar, mostly to hear Dr. Gary Parker's talk on the Grand Canyon. After his talk, I introduced myself to him and told him about Canyon Ministries. He in turn introduced me to Ken Ham and that led to our running trips for AIG in the following years.

In 2000, we were asked to outfit a research trip for the Institute for Creation Research. It gave Paula and me the incredible opportunity to spend 14 days with 13 creationists from three countries exploring the Canyon. It was during that trip I really began to fully understand the creation model and its biblical significance. It also introduced me to some of the world's top creation scientists, many of whom have been incredible resources and encouragers in my work.

Canyon Ministries' first truly creation-based trip was with Answers in Genesis, and Dr. Gary Parker was the lead interpreter. AiG's singer, songwriter, and general adventurer, Buddy Davis, was also scheduled to be on the trip, but Buddy had heart surgery about a week before the trip. His replacement was the Sr. Editor for Master Books, Jim Fletcher. Shortly after the trip, Jim wrote to me about his idea for a book about the Canyon from a biblical perspective. About halfway through the letter, there was a one line paragraph that read, "And we want you to write it."

Well, the first thing I did was check my resume and, sure enough, it didn't say "author" anywhere on it. It took some time for me to agree to do it, mostly because it was way outside my comfort zone. But that was a place I would find myself a lot over the next few years. The book started off as a little six-month project with six contributing authors. It took two years and the contributors' list expanded to 23 before *Grand Canyon, a Different View* was published in May of 2003.

Shortly after the project started, Paula and I led an *Experiencing God* Bible study in our home. In the study, Henry Blackaby asked the question, "How have you seen God working in your life?" As I looked back, I could see how God had put me in a very unique position to do the book.

- First, He allowed me to learn the wrong model, so I would know it.
- Then, most importantly, through His grace, He brought me to Himself.
- He put us in the paths of some of the world's foremost creation scientists.
- He timed Buddy's heart problems to allow Jim to be on the trip. (Buddy didn't think too much of that part.)
- He also gave me a godly wife who supported and encouraged me through the entire process and it was to her the book was dedicated.

Shortly after its release, the book, which is carried in the bookstores within Grand Canyon National Park, came under considerable fire from the evolutionary camp. The problem started in December of 2003 when the presidents of seven major scientific organizations from across the country jointly signed a letter to the National Park requesting the book be removed from the bookstores because it "advances a narrow religious view about the Earth."

The story was carried on the Associated Press wire shortly after that, and it exploded from there. The Alliance Defending Freedom (ADF), a legal organization dedicated to defending the rights of Christians, quickly agreed to assist us in what they saw as a simple first amendment issue. About three days after it became public, I met with Gary McCaleb, Senior Counsel for ADF. I'll never forget meeting him for the first time in front of his office. We were shaking hands and he said, "I want you to know we are with you all the way to the Supreme Court if necessary." I was thinking "SUPREME COURT? *What* is this guy talking about? I just want to sell my book; I don't want to go to the Supreme Court."

I cannot say enough about what a blessing ADF has been to Canyon Ministries and to us personally. They gave me a crash course in how to deal with the media, and, when needed, dealt with them for us. Before my first TV interview, they put me in front of a camera and showed me what I looked like on screen. And whenever a new attack was made on the book, they were right there in my defense. I was overwhelmed by the surprise attack of the enemy and without ADF's help, the secular media would have made mincemeat out of me.

Over the next year, the book became entangled in a controversy which was international news. It was in most of the major newspapers across the country and on at least three other continents, as well as several television and dozens of radio programs. AiG was the first to come to our aid with the launching of a very successful letter-writing campaign. ICR and several others joined in, and thousands of letters were sent to the Secretary of Interior in support of the book. I'm happy to report the book is still being sold in Grand Canyon National Park.

This controversy reminds me of the story in Genesis of Joseph being sold by his brothers. Years later when they met again he told them, *"As for you, you meant evil against me, but God meant it for good in order to bring about this present result…"* As with Joseph, I believe the Lord has used this little book to bring glory to His creation. Because of the controversy, many people have considered the scientific validity of creation for the first time or, for those who already believed, were strengthened in their faith.

As I said, this was a time spent way outside of my comfort zone, and it was only through God, our church and the help of His people that Paula and I survived. And I say "we" because in the heat of this battle, Paula stood steadfastly by my side, and, on occasion, in front of me. My dedication of the book to her was well deserved.

What's all the Fuss About?

Why is it a debate at all? Why is one little book such a threat? I believe it is because it attempts to shine some light into this darkened world in which we live, light in the form of Truth. The message of the Grand Canyon is one that is clear and unmistakable and points directly to a global Flood and ultimately to the Lord Jesus Christ. It is also a message that supports and upholds the Bible, the inerrant Word of God. And it is a message that is supported by the science currently being done in the Grand Canyon.

But it is not a message received well by evolutionists or by those who have put their faith in the uniformitarian misinterpretation of the Bible. They have bought into a lie, one that is clearly predicted in God's Word. Several verses from the Bible speak to the issue, but to me the most profound is Colossians 2:8. It reads: *"See to it that no one takes you captive through philosophy and empty deception, according to the tradition of men, according to the elementary principles of the world, rather than according to Christ."* It is our prayer that Canyon Ministries can help open the eyes of those who have been taken captive by the philosophies of the world.

Years Later

It has been quite a few years since Paula first stepped a foot on my boat. I am no longer a working guide in the Canyon, since I was let go from my job in 2004. As I look back on that release, though painful at the time, I see now how it was God's way of getting me out of my comfort zone once again. It has allowed me to focus more on Him and to provide a better interpretation of the Canyon to our guests.

Canyon Ministries runs about a dozen trips a year through the Canyon, varying from three to nine days in length, for about 250 guests a year. In 2005, we also formed a non-profit entity to create a scholarship fund which allows us to provide trips for pastors, Christian teachers, and ministry leaders, allowing them to see the Canyon and the evidence it holds.

The scholarship fund, in cooperation with Answers in Genesis and The Master's Seminary, launched the first Christian Leaders Trip in the summer of 2008. Through donated funds, the program provides scholarships to 24 Christian leaders and professors on an eight-day rafting trip through the Grand Canyon to show them the evidence which supports and upholds the truth of God's Word. As of 2013, we have completed six trips and taken almost 150 men from seven countries, representing 75 institutions, including many major seminaries, universities and Bible colleges. The ripple-down effect occurring from these men passing on to our future Christian leaders what they learned, is having an effect on how the first few chapters of Genesis is interpreted and taught.

Public speaking was not on my resume either, but sharing the message of the Grand Canyon with churches and creation groups has taken me out of my comfort zone the furthest. And since my resume now says "author" on it, I teamed up with Mike Oard, John Hergenrather, and Dennis Bokovoy to produce the *True North Series* of guidebooks to our National Parks. Three guides are currently available including *Your Guide to the Grand Canyon, Your Guide to Zion and Bryce Canyon National Parks,* and *Your Guide to Yellowstone and Grand Teton National Parks.* Our goal is to produce guides for many of our National Parks in order to provide visitors with a biblical understanding of what is found in these national treasures.

God's purpose

The Grand Canyon is an awesome spectacle of the Lord's creation, a classic example of erosion unequaled anywhere on earth. As you look at this amazingly beautiful hole in the ground, not only is the Canyon a testimony to creation, but it also presents evidence of God's judgment on the world. It is a vivid reminder that *"…the world at that time was destroyed, being flooded with water."* (2 Pet 3:6). The Canyon is an incredible witness to that biblical truth which has not only transformed my thinking, but the beliefs of many others as well.

It was because of man's sin, originating with Adam, that God judged the world with a worldwide catastrophic flood. And that message of judgment is clearly seen in the Grand Canyon for those who are willing to look. The Canyon is also a reminder to Christians that God's Word is true and can be relied upon. It demonstrates that the accounts of the Flood found in the Bible are true, and therefore the Judge of Genesis is also coming as the Redeemer so gloriously revealed in the book of Revelation. That's the fundamental truth found there.

That profound truth humbles me, as I am always humbled when the water carries me forward on another trip through God's grand cathedral. And if you travel the river, you can see it, the Canyon, reaching out to the hearts of those passing through. It can truly be a life – and heart – changing experience. One of the recurring comments we hear from those who join our trips is, "The Canyon has brought the accounts of Genesis from black and white into living color." We praise the Lord for the ministry God has given us.

Oh yes, "that lady." Well, she was right. The true meaning of life is to have a personal relationship with the one true and living God – Jesus Christ.

Creation Message to Russia and Belgium

Kerby found church boring, and wasn't interested. He was amazed when a Sunday school teacher told him that the theory of evolution was wrong. But later, a part-time pastor and professor at the local university challenged him to read several classic Christian books, and he found he could not get around their implications for his life. He came to realize the great Achilles heel of evolutionary theory—its need for millions of positive mutations in sequential order, all of which had to happen by lucky chance. This proved to him that atheistic evolution was not just unlikely, but was impossible. Kerby is now a missionary to Belgium and has also served in Russia.

When I was 15 years old, my mother began attending a Baptist church in our little town of Williamston, Michigan. My sister and I had to go with her, and worse, we had to go to Sunday school. I was not interested in church then. I found it boring. What I was interested in was girls and popularity. That was about it.

Our Sunday school teacher was only 18 years old and didn't seem that confident. Still, I was amazed to hear him say one Sunday that the theory of evolution was wrong. I couldn't believe my ears. I was a good student, and I knew history and science. I was dumbfounded that anyone in our modern age could actually speak against the theory of evolution. I couldn't believe he had never heard of the Scopes monkey trial. How could he be so ignorant? Evolution was proven science!

Every year new discoveries of fossils in Africa were proving Darwin's theory. I had read about them in National Geographic. Why would any intelligent person hold on to the ridiculous theory of creationism? I could see in my mind's eye the black and white photo of old William Jennings Bryan, soaked in sweat in the Tennessee heat, with his suit coat off and his suspenders showing, trying unsuccessfully to make his case against modern science—an old man's futile fight against the modern world.

That was in 1925, and yet here in this Sunday school class, some diehard was still speaking as if Darwin had never written *On the Origin of Species*. This was just too tempting of a target, and I began to ridicule and tease our teenage teacher in class about his old-fashioned beliefs. If it got under his skin he didn't show it, but my sister was uncomfortable with it and told me after class that I was going too far.

It didn't bother me, although I was not trying to be mean. I just was amazed that people could hold onto beliefs that so clearly contradicted hard science. Apparently having had enough of me, my teacher, Steve Jones, invited me to hear a Christian rock group one Friday night with some friends. I kind of knew it was his way of trying to silence me. I went and took the opportunity to share some of my best dirty jokes but he refused to listen to them.

After the concert, he drove me home and shared with me the four spiritual laws. I could not argue with them. They seemed right and clear. He asked me if I wanted Christ to be Lord of my life. I didn't, and I told him so. I was just totally, completely uninterested in being a Christian. It was not anything I wanted to do. I liked girls, and parties, and lots of things that were very far from Christian.

As he left, though, I realized that if I died, there would be no doubt where I would go. I had had an opportunity to be forgiven and accept Christ as Lord of my life, and I had rejected it. I believed, and still believe, that there is a heaven above and a hell below. So, perhaps for the first time in my life I knew I was going to hell and it scared me.

I privately struggled with this for months. Finally, I decided that it was time for me to turn my life over to God, alone on my knees in my room. I told no one of my prayer or my decision. I was embarrassed to be a Christian. But I began to notice changes in my life. Bad habits were just dropping away. My cussing went. My anger went. My pornography collection went in the trash. I quit getting drunk. I enjoyed being at home, whereas before I could not stand being at home—I was always going to a party somewhere. I enjoyed reading the Bible and was shocked to find that it somehow spoke to me in a way it never had before. I found myself reading the Psalms and there was something in me that was new and good and wanted to do what was right. I could hardly believe it. I was transformed. I knew it was not because of anybody or any church, as we rarely went to church, and I had told no one of my repentance.

After another year, I had enough courage to go forward and be baptized at a new church my mother had started attending. The part-time pastor, Dr. Bill Bowen, was a full-time professor of philosophy at Michigan State University. He was brilliant. There were five of us new believers in the church and he got us together in a class and gave us several deep books to read: *The Screwtape Letters* and *Mere Christianity* by C.S. Lewis, *A Place to Stand* by Elton Trueblood and *The Normal Christian Life* by Watchman Nee.

I was deeply affected by these books. I could see that these were very intelligent men who wrote them. They had no doubt about the truth of what they were writing. Dr. Bowen, my pastor, was also himself no lightweight intellectually.

So I realized that Christianity was not based on shoddy backward beliefs, but was extremely profound and based on solid facts. I could not deny the amazing improvements occurring in me, and the answered prayers I was getting regularly. Before I became a Christian I had often been depressed and had considered suicide. But now I had a deep peace in my life and it was like I was coming alive again. Instead of being a desperately bored Christian, I was doing very well and happier than I had ever been.

Hal Lindsey's book, *The Late Great Planet Earth*, also helped me. I could see that the Bible was a prophetic book, predicting the future (such as regarding the restoration of the nation of Israel in Isaiah 11:11). I also could not deny that the Bible passed the test of empiricism – it was not just theoretical, but it worked on a practical level in my daily life. Everything it said about a person becoming a new creation after accepting Christ (2 Cor. 5:17) was true in my life.

I had intellectually and personally found the Bible to be true. If it is right on predicting the future, and on the need of each person to be born again, who was I to reject the other parts of the Bible that say that God created the world and everything in it? It seemed to me that if God exists at all, creating the world is not a big challenge for him – whether it is in six days or one day.

I thought then, and think now, that we humans are to God as an ant is to a human. An ant cannot see how acres of farmland can be turned upside down and ground into powder in an afternoon. Millions of ants could not do it. But to a farmer and his tractor, it is an everyday thing. Thus, it is no problem for God to create the world.

Nonetheless, I was surprised to find scientists, like Henry M. Morris, who actively researched the geological and biological evidence for the creation of the world. I had accepted the theological possibility that God could create the world, but to follow that up with hard science had never entered my mind. But these men were doing it. I bought some of their books and was amazed to find things I had never considered—like the serious errors in evolutionary logic.

I soon discovered the great Achilles heel of evolutionary theory—its need for millions of positive mutations in sequential order, all of which had to happen just by lucky chance. Positive mutations are extremely rare and difficult to support, especially when they are accompanied by negative side effects. This proved to me that atheistic evolution was not just unlikely, but was impossible.

I found that even Charles Darwin, the popularizer of evolutionary theory, conceded this point in his autobiography. He referred to the "impossibility of conceiving this immense and wonderful universe, including man...as the result of blind chance or necessity...I feel compelled to look at a first cause having an intelligent mind in some degree analogous to that of man; and I deserve to be called a theist."[65]

The book, *The Genesis Flood* also impressed me with its careful research into geological strata. I realized for things like multi-strata fossils to exist, a massive flood was the only logical explanation, exactly as the Bible posited.

The book's explanation of the shortcomings of carbon 14 dating was very helpful because I had always wondered how creationists could reconcile the large differences between carbon 14 dating and their own timetable. I realized that evolutionary theory was based on an assumption that the levels of carbon 14 have always remained the same.

I learned that a vapor layer, mentioned in the Bible as having existed before the flood, limited the creation of carbon 14 by sunlight. Thus the levels of carbon 14 in bones would have been reduced, making all fossils before the flood seem much, much older than they were, thus throwing off carbon 14 measurements of everything from before 5000 B.C.

I also could not deny that for dinosaur eggs to have been preserved in large numbers worldwide required them to be quickly and rapidly buried by floodwaters. Eggs just don't keep well otherwise! The same is true for the preservation of entire dinosaur carcasses. Normally they rot or are eaten. To be fossilized they had to be instantly buried in mud, and lots of it—which is what happens in a massive flood.

The fine detail in many fossils, showing even feathers, spoke of rapid inundation. I knew that the dating of strata by evolutionists requires millions of years of very stable climatic conditions and gradual wearing down of rock. But the Bible speaks of massive and sudden climatic change in the flood. This is supported by discoveries of dozens of entire frozen mammoths in Siberia. These are still being discovered, with undigested forage in their stomachs. Other books, like *The Revolution Against Evolution* revealed the problems evolutionary theory has with out-of-order strata.

Also very convincing to me were Bible verses that showed impossibly advanced understanding of the universe, such as Job 26:7, showing that the earth is suspended on nothing. At the time this was written, more than 3,500 years ago, people thought the earth was sitting on the shoulders of Atlas in Greece, or on the back of a giant turtle in Mexico, or on an elephant in India. No one really understood the vacuum of space or weightlessness, but the Bible had it down quite accurately.

Probably the most convincing evidence to me was, and is, the total lack of an evolutionary explanation for the problem of abiogenesis—the creation of life. Since

65   p. 85, *The Autobiography of Charles Darwin*. (Nora Barlow edition). Also found at http://darwin-online.org.uk/content/frameset?itemID=F1497&viewtype=text&pageseq=1

it involves nonliving matter, evolutionary theory does not apply to it. Darwin is of no help at all here. Evolution has no real answer to this problem. Its response defies the second law of thermodynamics (entropy) and statistical probability.

While a student at Michigan State University my understanding of these issues deepened. I had many chances to hear the beliefs of professors and other students and to share my own. It amazed me that so many were unbelievers, not because of science, but in spite of it. I discovered, in talking with people, that their reasons for not being Christians often had almost nothing to do with evolution or science, but everything to do with their own preferences. They had not come to their beliefs by research, but simply by choice.

I found this out simply by asking people for evidence proving atheism was true. We both soon discovered that they had no valid evidence for their atheism. It was something they believed, with little basis in facts. It was a religion like any other, only one remarkably lacking a solid foundation. It was something they had accepted by faith.

One day I spoke to a Jewish student. Every objection he had to Christianity was resolved in the course of our conversation, yet I could see that he had no intention of becoming a Christian, so I asked him why. As a very honest person, he told me it was simply because it was against his family's traditions. In other words, facts and proof had no effect on his decision. Science played no role. His family's traditions and opinions were more important than the truth. I was amazed by this, perhaps because such honesty is rare, but it fit in with what I had discovered over many years.

After graduation, I landed a position as a newspaper reporter, and then became an editor for the State of Michigan. After 11 years, the time came when God called us to be missionaries, and we were sent to the world capital of atheism and evolution—the former Soviet Union. Russia even has a museum in Moscow dedicated to Darwin and evolution.

Russia at that time was about 25 percent atheist, the US about 5 percent. I wasn't sure what I would find when I got there; after all, these were people who had been born and raised on atheism and evolution. They didn't have a shred of religious upbringing. Atheism was taught in their schools. They had turned churches into museums of atheism. Surely if there were people who were deeply convinced atheists because of science, I would find them there. Instead, I found that many were ready to abandon their atheism, and were closer to weak agnostics.

I read a translation of the official atheist's manual produced by the communists, expecting to find powerful arguments proving that God does not exist. Instead it was just a mocking of Christians, and showed very shallow thinking.

In our 14 years in Russia, I discovered not one single sincere atheist. One conversation illustrates this well. I was speaking one day with the father of a church member, Sergei Sergeiovich, about God. He was a captain in the Russian military. He smiled condescendingly, and said that I believed in mythology—fairy tales.

I asked him if I could ask him a question.

"Sergei Sergeiovich," I began, "have you ever, in your military career, been in a situation so dangerous that you prayed?"

He thought a moment, and then told me that, yes, he had prayed.

"Then you are not an atheist, Sergei. When you have troubles you know who to go to!"

He smiled, and admitted it was true.

I found atheism and atheistic evolutionary theory to be much like the emperor's new clothes. The man was naked, but no one was brave enough to say it publicly.

Richard Dawkins himself has stated that atheists cannot prove that God does not exist, and that they do not know how life began. It is therefore based on faith. It tries to prove it is correct by showing the fallacies in other religions.

Criticizing another person's house, however, does not build your own. Atheism cannot make its own case. Nonetheless, it argues that religion is the root of all evil, and that we all would be better off without it. Wars would cease, religious terrorism would cease, etc. But in Russia, over the course of 14 years, I had the unique privilege of seeing what a society was like after it had eliminated religion from public life. Communist Albania even proclaimed itself the first officially atheist state after closing all churches and mosques in the entire nation

The result is that the countries of the former Soviet Union have some of the highest levels of suicide, alcoholism and abortion. The devaluation of life is a natural and unavoidable result of atheistic evolutionary theory.

On a tour I took of the former KGB headquarters in Vilnius, Lithuania, we were taken into the execution room. I saw the bullet holes in the wall where priests and other Christians were shot for not believing in the religion of atheism and evolution. Bones of hundreds of unidentified victims were on the floor, covered by Plexiglas, so you can walk over them.

Many Russians told me of friends and relatives who were sent to concentration camps because they were believers—never to be seen again. The millions killed by atheistic communism and atheistic fascism are ignored by those who say that all would be bliss if we only exterminated religion.

Atheism claims not to be a religion, a claim that is smoke and mirrors. Atheism is a religion, or a belief system, with recognized popes (Richard Dawkins), evangelists (Bill Maher and Christopher Hitchens) and departed saints (Darwin, Madalyn Murray O'Hair, Nietzsche and Bertrand Russell). It has its own body of holy literature ("Positive Atheism" and "Skeptic" magazine), and it has its own organizations that work to convert the world to the "true" religion of atheism ("Atheist Alliance International", "International League of Non-religious and Atheists", "Rationalist International", etc.)

The closest atheism can come to actual science for what it believes is Darwin's theory of evolution. Despite its evident shortcomings, they cling to it tenaciously, as the only other alternative is belief in God, with all that entails. This is something they are not willing to accept, so year after year this false science presents itself to the world as fact.

This became very clear to me in the course of a lengthy e-mail dialogue I had with an atheist, after I wrote an op-ed piece on the flaws in evolutionary theory published in the *MSU State News* that was read by many worldwide. I received several letters from that, one of which was from a man named Issie in California.

Issie seemed to be, at first, the one truly sincere atheist I had ever met. He said he was simply an atheist because it was true. I had always believed after many years of conversations that atheists do not exist—down deep everyone believed. Madalyn Murray O'Hair, for instance, went to séances throughout her life, showing that her "atheism" was not very real, and that she believed in the supernatural world.[66] So I was intrigued that, perhaps, I had found someone who truly was an atheist.

One day I asked Issie if he had ever prayed. He replied that, yes, he had. I asked him when the last time was that he had prayed, and for what. He said it was when he was 14, when his mother was dying of cancer. He had asked God to heal her. But she died and Issie decided he would never pray again. He was mad at God for not healing his mother.

I pointed out to Issie that it seemed to me his atheism was simply a form of belief in God. He was still mad that God had "refused" to heal his mother, so he was punishing God by being an atheist. So once again I had to conclude that there are no real atheists. And evolution is still what it has always been—a bad theory.

As the years have gone by, I have continued to see God move miraculously in my life and the lives of others. And at the same time I have seen the increasing wealth of evidence for intelligent design. The intellectual weakness of the challenges to the intelligent design of the universe, such as that of Richard Dawkins, is itself one of the strongest evidences for creation. If the best scientists in the world cannot come up with better arguments than they have, clearly intelligent design is correct.

The conclusion for me is simple: The Bible is true, not just spiritually but practically and scientifically. God is alive and well, and everything the Bible says about him is just plainly and simply true.

---

66   from *My Life Without God.* by William Murray, son of Madalyn Murray O'Hair.

The X-Axis and Creator Christ

Paul G. Humber taught mathematics for over 30 years—most of them at the college preparatory Haverford School – just outside of Philadelphia. In this chapter, he points to the simple, mathematical concept known as "The Number Line" that is more profound than many realize. He also touches on such topics as the Swanscombe Skull, the Chapelle aux Saints Skull, Jehovah Jesus, Reasons to Affirm a Young Earth, and "The LORD Our Righteousness" (Jeremiah 23:6). He currently directs CR Ministries (http://www.cr-ministries.org/).

In a speech he gave at Macalester College in St. Paul, Minnesota, Dr. George Washington Carver is reported to have said the following to God in prayer: "Oh, Mr. Creator, why did You make this universe?" Dr. Carver reported that God answered, "You want to know too much for that little mind of yours … Ask me something more your size."

After more exchange, Dr. Carver finally came down to this, "Mr. Creator, why did You make the peanut?" Dr. Carver also reported that God said, "That's better!' and continued, "He gave me a handful of peanuts and went with me back to the laboratory and, together, we got down to work."

This richly pigmented, humble American then went inside the laboratory, "closed the door, pulled on an apron and shelled a handful of peanuts. That whole day and night, he literally tore the nuts apart, isolating their fats and gums, their resins and sugars and starches. Spread before him were pentoses, pentosans, legumins, lysin, amido and amino acids. He tested these in different combinations under varying degrees of heat and pressure, and soon his hoard of synthetic treasures began to grow: milk, ink, dyes, shoe polish, creosote, salve, shaving cream and, of course, peanut butter."[67]

---

67   The reader may request a fuller article about Carver by writing to the author of this chapter, paulhumber@verizon.net.

My "Peanut" and Transcendence

For three decades, I taught mathematics on various campuses, including the University of Phoenix (Philadelphia), the Haverford School (24 years), Rutgers University (Camden), Abington High School (both campuses), and the University of Pennsylvania (Dept. of Human Resources).

The course that I enjoyed teaching the most was integral calculus. After drawing a three-dimensional object on a two-dimensional surface, I would, using integration, explain how to calculate, within certain boundaries, the volume of a sine (or logarithmic) curve formed by rotating the function about the x or y-axis.

The x-axis by itself, however, is mind-boggling! Another name for it is the "number line." Just that simple concept helps me get a better glimpse of God's majesty and glory. Both testaments of the Bible point us in the direction of God's mind-boggling infinity. The Old Testament, for example, says: "For my thoughts are not your thoughts, neither are your ways my ways," declares the LORD. "As the heavens are higher than the earth, so are my ways higher than your ways and my thoughts than your thoughts (Isaiah 55:8-9).

In the New Testament, we read, "Oh, the depths of the riches of the wisdom and knowledge of God! How unsearchable his judgments, and his paths beyond tracing out (Romans 11:33)!

The word "higher," in Isaiah, suggests dimension, and the word "paths," in the Apostle's letter, suggests the "number line." First-graders, for example, can understand a ruler and the idea of measuring how tall they are when standing up against a wall. Placing that same ruler onto a sheet of paper, they can trace-out a horizontal "number line."

Marking a point in the center, a student can label it as zero. Then he can mark off inch-segments or intervals (e.g. 1, 2, etc.). This is an imperfect number line, and there are two aspects about it that point to the infinity of God—to His transcendence and to His immanence. The first is infinity on a macro-scale.

The elementary-school student, coming to a mark for 4, discovers that the ruler runs off the edge of his page. In other words, he cannot mark off the point having "coordinate" 5.[68] He can very easily understand, however, that he could mark down 5 if he had a larger sheet. In fact, continuing on theoretically forever is not impossible for even a young person to sense. He may be

---

68   Perhaps without realizing it, the first-grader has just entered into the realm of algebra and geometry. Algebra speaks of numbers, and the coordinate 1, 2 and 5 are all numbers. He is doing algebra when he places numbers onto the sheet. The number line itself, however, involves geometry. Whereas algebra deals with sets of numbers, geometry deals with sets of points. The number line is a set of points and is, therefore, geometry. The student is beginning, in other words, to learn about coordinate geometry (or algebraic geometry).

aware of the word, googol, for example, that it is a very large number. Specifically, it is 10 to the hundredth power. This will probably be beyond the grasp of a first-grader, but seeing it as follows can impress even this young person: 10,000,000,000,000,000,000,000,000,000,000,000,000,000,000,000, 000,000,000,000,000,000,000,000,000,000,000,000,000,000,000,000.

A googolplex is ten to the googolth power, a number that is too large for a first-grader to comprehend, or even to write out. Even math teachers' despair and it is impossible to obtain a sheet of paper large enough to measure a googolplex number of marks on our number line.

Even a child, however, can look at the stars in space and imagine a kite-string (number line) reaching from where he is to the closest star. It's mind-boggling to consider that dimension, but at least it is a faint, mental image of what is required. The Old Testament text says, "As the heavens are higher than the earth, so are my ways higher than your ways." We get a glimmer of the majesty of our God by considering the extension of a simple number line.

God's Infinite Immanence

Another aspect of God's infinity is His immanence, and this is perhaps more mind-boggling and even harder to envision. Just as it is good to appreciate the "transcendence" (the far-away-ness) of our God, it is also important to appreciate the infinite "immanence" (detail and closeness) of our God.

Deists, for example, allow for the transcendence of God (He is, in their mind, distant), but they deny His "immanence" (the notion that God is very near and involved in every detail of life). The simple number line can help with this, too.

We say that the number line is infinitely dense. By dense, we mean it is thickly crowded. Let me help the first-grader to understand.

One may point to any interval on the one-page number line. He can take the inch-interval between 3 and 4, for example. It is not difficult for the child to make a mark that is more or less half-way between 3 and 4. The mark he puts down is geometry, but the number, 3½, is algebra. The space between 3 (or 4) and this new point can now also be split in half, and this process of splitting segments in half can go on infinitely (at least in theory—if not visually). In short, there is an infinite number of points between any two points on the number line—however small! If one chooses any two integers, 3 and 4, for example, is it possible to find a coordinate exactly between them by adding the numbers and dividing by two. This is true for any two rational (fractional) numbers, however close.

Humans tend to think of small things as unimportant, but germs and fertilized embryos are both small and important. We must be careful to wash our hand after caring for a sick patient, and we should be careful not to discard a human being from the moment of conception just because he is hard to see.

In fact, scientists are discovering the very complex machinery in every cell of our bodies, and the Lord controls the "paths" of every electron (small thing) in the universe (big thing). "Oh, the depths of the riches of the wisdom and knowledge of God! How unsearchable his judgments, and his paths beyond tracing out!"

Some skeptics might say that the number line is just a human construct, but Creator Christ spoke the following words to Job before His taking on human flesh: "Where were you when I laid the earth's foundation? Tell me, if you understand. Who marked off its dimensions? Surely you know! Who stretched a measuring line across it (Job 38:4-5)?

That "measuring line" is our number line. We are, in other words, thinking God's thoughts after Him—even with respect to the simple "number line." He knew all about it long before we did, and calculus is a piece of cake for Him.

When Young

Though it seems I was always "good" in math, I did not realize the application of the number line to God's infinite transcendence and immanence until maturity. Nevertheless, my study of the Creator and the creation transformed me at the tender age of seven. I did not understand about the beauty and wonder of His perfect robe of righteousness, but I sure felt it. What a refreshingly clean feeling it was and is—to have Christ's perfect righteousness covering over my unworthiness.

He transformed my whole life. Someone, for example, encouraged me, at that very early age, to pray for a wife. I married that woman 17 years later, and we have been a married-team for over 45 years. Our cups still overflow with manifold blessings.

When I took biology in high school, I remember going during off hours to convince my biology teacher of the follies of evolution. He said that in the future we would evolve big heads and thumbs—the latter to push buttons. I liked him; he liked me—but we were on opposite ends.

I continued my education at the University of Pennsylvania. After graduating in 1964, I pressed on for a Master of Science in Education degree at the same institution—specializing in mathematics.

While at the Haverford School, the bulk of my teaching years, I put on various Upper School assemblies, promoting biblical truths and challenging evolutionary indoctrination. Students would come to my room, as I was sort of the local "Bible Answer Man." Colleagues would invite me to speak to their classes. One headmaster told me that he would not want a school full of Paul Humber's but was glad for one.

All was not rosy, however. On one occasion, a speaker came and spoke to the Upper School students in assembly; creationism was then characterized as pseudoscience. I complained to the headmaster that it was not fair presenting only one side of a debate. He agreed and gave me permission to get a speaker to present the

Paul Humber is seen here putting on an assembly at the Haverford School, near Philadelphia.

other side. Consequently, I invited Dr. Austin Robbins, who had served on the faculties of Georgetown University School of Dentistry, Temple University Dental School, and University of Pennsylvania School of Dental Medicine. Much fossil evidence consists of teeth and the study of dentition.

Soon thereafter, the chairman of the science department came to my room and indicated either that he had, or was about to, complain to the headmaster regarding the objections of his department to decisions that had been made without their consent. Somewhat angered by this obfuscation, I told the Chairman then and there that he was promoting indoctrination rather than science. The objections of the department, however, prevailed, and Dr. Robbins never came to the school to present the other side of evolution. This is part of the reason why I put on various assemblies myself.[69]

Evolutionary Hypocrisy

While still on the faculty of the Haverford School, I invited a professor of anthropology at the University of Pennsylvania to participate in a creation vs. evolution debate that eventually took place at Westminster Theological Seminary on April 20, 2001. Approximately four hundred people attended.

The same professor, though permitting the debate to be videotaped, did not want it be sold (or even distributed) because his opponent, Dr. Jack Cuozzo, offered evidence that the professor disputed. Dr. Cuozzo had claimed in the debate that he had found a missing piece of the famous Swanscombe (Neanderthal) Skull and was for the first time, at the debate, announced publicly.

He stated that the mastoid piece (near the temple area of the skull) fits a model of the Swanscombe nicely and that there were possible trephination (surgical) marks on the fossil. This, he indicated, suggested that Neanderthals were much more advanced in medicine than evolutionists believe. Along the same

---

69   Two of these assemblies are now available on YouTube.

line, the possible file marks on the La Chapelle tooth may suggest more sophistication in dentistry than is normally attributed to Neanderthals.

As moderator of the debate, I sensed a responsibility to try and resolve this impasse. On the one hand, it seemed that one debater was trying to censor the other; while I myself was not interested in promoting falsehood.

As Dr. Cuozzo's piece had been submitted to the British Museum, I contacted Professor Chris Stringer, Head of Human Origins, Department of Paleontology, The Natural History Museum, London. He wrote to me a number of times during the summer and fall following the spring debate.

Dr. Stringer wrote regarding Dr. Cuozzo's artifact from Swanscombe that "It is of course possible that there are, say, Mesozoic fossils in the Swanscombe gravels." Earlier he had indicated that the artifact was only gravel, but subsequently Dr. Cuozzo pointed to evidence that the piece was a true fossil.

Previously, Dr. Stringer had written: "I do consider that Dr. Cuozzo acted in good faith in this case, and did the right thing in returning this material for examination. The pieces in question, particularly the mastoid, were suggestive of human bones in their shape, although I think he would not have considered them to be fossil human bone if he had been able to make direct comparisons of their appearance with genuine fossil bone from Swanscombe."

Dr. Cuozzo, to use Dr. Stringer's words, "acted in good faith" by submitting the samples to the proper authorities for examination. There remains dispute as to whether Dr. Cuozzo's piece is from the Swanscombe Skull, but is this really just cause for tapes of the debate to be censored? Do not debates, by their very nature, necessarily involve dispute? As a creationist, Dr. Cuozzo undoubtedly discounts much of what his opponent had to say, but he was not attempting to disqualify a videotape involving his evolutionary opponent's views.

It may be very difficult to prove the truth concerning Dr. Cuozzo's artifact. There are arguments on both sides, but to obstruct the distribution of a videotaped debate because one party believes the other is not accurate, seems like censorship. One could well argue from this type of reasoning that most debates should be censored. This seems somewhat like nit-picking or straining at gnats. I am happy and willing to hear what an opponent has to say, but do have difficulty reconciling the professor's criticism of Dr. Cuozzo while at the same time, seeing the same professor pass off to me a reconstruction of a deliberately altered model of the Chapelle aux Saints Skull.

After the debate, I wrote the following words to the professor: "Regarding the matter of honesty, when I visited the Musee de l'Homme this past summer, I purchased a postcard of La Chapelle aux Saints. In the model you gave me, there are sixteen teeth in the upper jaw. The postcard, however, reveals no such number. You told me over lunch that the model you gave me was of La Chapelle aux Saints, but I don't believe you informed me that ... the teeth were added. Don't you think that giving a deliberately altered model is a bit misleading?"

I never received a response to these words and had received many previous ones. I hold open the possibility, therefore, that this professor may be a little embarrassed by the inconsistency of distributing and possibly selling misleading models of the La Chapelle Skull while at the same time forbidding the sale and distribution of a videotape containing a claim by Dr. Cuozzo that he disputes.

Christian Released Time

After leaving the Haverford School, I did two things—taught for a while with the University of Phoenix and promoted Christian Released Time classes for public school children. Creation, as well as Gospel-salvation, the deity of the Lord Jesus, and His return to earth, may all be taught during such sessions. I am still involved with this ministry.

Approximately 20 public schools in and around Philadelphia, have become involved over the years, and my efforts to facilitate such has been affirmed in *WORLD* magazine and *The Philadelphia Inquirer*.[70],[71] One of my books, *Evolution Exposed*, has a whole chapter on my efforts to reestablish Christian Released Time in the Philadelphia area.[72] Additionally, I am the author of *Jehovah Jesus*, a book containing 157 passages from both Old and New Testaments showing that the Lord Jesus Christ is indeed God the son in human flesh, the Creator of heaven and earth!

For many years, I wrote devotionals for *Days of Praise*, an Institute for Creation Research publication. Several of my articles/booklets have been translated, and many are available on the Internet.[73]

Working with members of the Creation Research Society, I edited three booklets: *Reasons to Reject Evolution*, *Reasons to Affirm a Young Earth*, and *Reasons*

---

70   The article was titled, "Law ensures there's room for religion; In PA, students can be released for lessons off school grounds," and may be found at http://www.religionandsocialpolicy.org/article_index/article_display.cfm?id=1013&SiteTopicRequest=17&TOPIC_TITLE=Education%20Programs/Schools/After%20 School%20Programs/%20Day-Care.
71   Readers may check my website, www.CRMinistriesPhilly.com. My email address is paulhumber@verizon.net.
72   See six positive reviews of it at www.amazon.com (so far no negative ones).
73   Here is a partial listing: Evolutionist Kenneth R. Miller's "Evidence" for Increasing Information, Uncle Tom, Harriet Beecher Stowe, and Creator Christ, Evolution fails predictability-Creation passes, The Failure of Gould's "The Most Impressive Statement," Comparing creation and evolution, Debating Dawkins, Woe to teachers of evolution, Creator Allah or Creator Christ? A "Moron" and a "Liar," Cancer and War from God's Hands, Natural Selection--A Creationist's Idea, Advanced placement coordinator questions evolution, Evolution and the American Abortion Mentality, Columbus and His Creator, Hitler's Evolution Versus Christian Resistance, Stalin's Brutal Faith, and The Ascent of Racism.

to *Affirm a Global Flood.* The second of these two has been translated into Spanish and French and reprinted in India. The third booklet, which came out in 2011, is available at Amazon.com, and is now in its third printing.

Conclusions

My father named me, Paul, after the Apostle, who wrote: "no one will be declared righteous in His sight by observing the law." We need to be declared righteous if we are to have any hope of heaven. Where can we get it? All that we have is polluted. It makes no difference if we are creationists, evolutionists, church-goers, or atheists. We all flunk in righteousness. Not even Adam and Eve qualified before they sinned![74] Only One Person ever passed the test, and He did so perfectly.

The Apostle added, "But now a righteousness from God, apart from law, has been made known, to which the Law and the Prophets testify. This righteousness from God comes through faith in Jesus Christ to all who believe." But exactly how did God's righteousness get down "from God" to us?

Mary received Him into her womb and placed Him in a manger. Hundreds of years prior, the prophet Jeremiah prophesied that the coming Messiah would be called (notice especially the third word) "The LORD Our Righteousness."

How does Jesus become "Our" Righteousness? Isaiah experienced it in anticipation —"I delight greatly in the LORD; my soul rejoices in my God. For He has clothed me with garments of salvation and arrayed me in a robe of righteousness" (Isaiah 61:10a).

Consider the following, magnificent exchange. Our sins covered Jesus on the cross, but this is only half the picture. Many seem to have missed the second half! Jesus' perfect righteousness must cover over us—as a garment. Arrayed in

---

74   One reader wrote: "Is this what you mean to say? Romans 5:14 seems to say that our sinning is different from Adam's, which I understand as that he fell from a sinless condition to a sinful condition whereas we are born into a sinful condition due to his original sin. If my understanding is correct, then had Adam died before sinning, he would have died righteous. To state it another way, before the original sin, he had not sinned at all and so would have been qualified for heaven." This is a good question, but I did mean what I wrote. He is correct in saying that we are born in sin. The original sin of Adam is imputed to all "in Adam." However, Adam was tested by God. Not only did he not prove himself righteous before God, he proved himself unrighteous. For us to qualify as righteous, therefore, we have to have two things happen to us. First, our sins (including our sin "in Adam") need to be washed away—cleansed by Christ's cross, as it were. But that only gets us back to where Adam was before the fall. Adam never obeyed God by experientially rejects Satan's temptation, but that also is where Jesus enters our picture. Jesus resisted three temptations of Satan in a wilderness (not garden) when He was starved (not full, like Adam). He became "our Righteousness" (Jeremiah 23:6). If we are "in Christ," therefore, then we are clothed in His righteousness. Christ's righteousness is imputed to us, even as prior to the sin of Adam had been imputed to us. The Lord Jesus Christ is, consequently, a total savior. Not only does His blood cleanse us from sin, but His perfect righteousness covers over all who are "in the Beloved One."

Jesus' righteous robe, heaven's gates will burst off their hinges when we arrive clothed "in Him"—so perfect is He!

The Apostle added, "For if, by the trespass of the one man, death reigned through that one man, how much more will those who receive God's abundant provision of grace and of the gift of righteousness reign in life through the one man, Jesus Christ" (Romans 5:17).

Over and over again the Apostle wrote of our being "in Christ." To be "in Him" is to be clothed in His righteousness. The Apostle wrote, "God made Him who had no sin to be sin for us, so that in Him we might become the righteousness of God." The prodigal's father: "Quick! Bring the best robe and put it on him." That robe is Christ's cloak of perfect righteousness!

Elsewhere, the Apostle wrote: "What is more, I consider everything a loss compared to the surpassing greatness of knowing Christ Jesus my Lord, for whose sake I have lost all things. I consider them rubbish, that I may gain Christ and be found in Him, not having a righteousness of my own that comes from the law, but that which is through faith in Christ—the righteousness that comes from God and is by faith" (Philippians 3:8-9).

In celebration of this truth, William Cowper wrote: "Let others in the gaudy dress of fancied merit shine; the LORD shall be my righteousness, the LORD forever mine."

I do not know how much longer I will live on this earth, but it has been a wonderful privilege—experiencing His grace at age 7 and also learning of His infinity—even by way of the "number line" and other events that transformed me into an active creationist. The future, however, is much brighter! Imagine living forever with the Creator of the Universe—the inventor of the number line and calculus—just to mention a few things! He created all things and covers those who enter Him by faith with the Perfect Righteousness of the Lord Jesus Christ!

Evidence from the Grand Canyon

Though he gave his life to Christ in seventh grade, Jonathan didn't pay a lot of attention to the first few chapters of Genesis and, furthermore, evolution was simply not an issue for him. He came from a family of engineers, and the idea of life arising by chance seemed absurd. But he never questioned the evolutionary time scale until evidence from the geology of the Grand Canyon caused him to consider flood geology. His view of earth history is now based on creation and the flood of Noah, and has had a transforming effect on his faith.

I grew up in a conservative evangelical Methodist church. I've also known the stories in the Scriptures my entire life. In seventh grade, I gave my life to Jesus Christ. Even before this, I accepted the general theme of Creation. I believed that God created everything, but I was very non-specific in that belief. You might say that I took Genesis 1 figuratively. But a more precise description might be that, between Genesis 1:2 and Genesis 2:4, I just didn't care to pay much attention. Learning and understanding what was in Genesis transformed me.

I never believed in evolution at any time in my life. It simply wasn't an issue for me. I come from a family of engineers, and my dad taught me the basics of computer programming shortly after I learned to read. The idea that the entire diversity of life arose without engineering or design seemed absurd and the idea that Nothing could engineer Something made even less sense.

Furthermore, I never questioned the timescale of evolution and had no reason to believe that the earth was thousands of years old, that dinosaurs went extinct because of a great meteor millions of years ago, or that mammals are relatively recent. That isn't to say that I had detailed knowledge of these things - in fact, the lack of detail in my knowledge was probably one of the reasons why I continued to believe these ideas. For instance, if I had known that modern geology puts human's arrival several hundred thousand years ago, I may have asked more questions. But that wasn't part of the curriculum, or perhaps I just wasn't paying attention.

In college, I tested out of all of my science requirements through the advanced placement program, so neither my belief in an old earth or my disbelief in evolution was an issue. However, during college, I met a young earth creationist for the first time. I had never seriously thought about the possibility that the earth was a recent creation. I thought that this person must not be thinking clearly about the issue. I never talked with him about Creation again because I felt he obviously did not know what he was talking about.

I had a good knowledge of biochemistry and genetics for quite some time - at least compared to most lay people. I had completed various chemistry and biology courses that focused on common biochemical cell pathways. In addition, due to illness in my family, I was forced to be engaged in biochemistry and genetics from an advanced lay perspective.

After some time, I began to wonder about the Creation/Evolution debate, and whether, as an educated layperson, I might be able to contribute anything. I started reading books, engaged in online conversations, and eventually started a blog about what I was learning about Creation/Evolution. When I began to study the issue I was warned to stay away from the Answers in Genesis website because they were the mostly deceitful creation group. This played in well to my existing biases, because I did not share their "young earth" view.

However, as I engaged in more and more debate, I realized that the evolutionary side would often resort to misrepresentation and name-calling to make their case (this was true of both sides, but was most pronounced by the evolutionary side). In fact, I realized that in many cases evolutionists either had not read or had not understood the opposing material. I began to wonder if maybe this same sort of smear-first, maybe-respond-intelligently-later strategy was also being used against Answers in Genesis. So I started reading their site.

I was surprised by the quality of the content. Not everything they claimed was valid, nor all of their conclusions correct, given the evidence, but that is true with all information sources, even articles in the leading academic journals. As I began to go through their material, I realized that there actually were very intelligent people who believed in a young earth.

During this period I also visited popular evolutionary science blogs. One author claimed in a recent article that a young earth creationist was lying about dinosaur blood found in bones that were supposedly millions of years old. After reading the article in detail, I discovered that they were not lying - only disagreement existed. All of the evidence was correctly portrayed by the creationists. The evolutionist seemed to be taking advantage of the fact that Christians are strongly opposed to lying in order to turn Christians against each other. I challenged the evolutionist to point to the specific lie. After continual probing, it turned out that the only "lie" was that the evolutionist disagreed.

About that time, Answers in Genesis held a seminar in my hometown. At this time I did not think that Genesis 1 could be regarded as history. However, the Answers in Genesis conference showed that there was a whole lot more in the Bible that was based on the youth of the earth than I had previously realized. In addition, there was legitimate evidence that the earth (or at least the geological column) was indeed young. That was when I first began to take the young earth creationist position seriously, though I had not yet fully made up my mind.

Ultimately, what led me to become a creationist was a picture of the Grand Canyon, described in two different ways. The cross-section of the Grand Canyon's geological strata shows the very bottom starts out with tilted rock layers. These layers are then cut straight across by a horizontal layer. Then, layer after layer is horizontal. Finally, at the top, while the layers are still mostly horizontal, they are significantly eroded into very irregular shapes and patterns.

In the evolutionary view, each stratum represents large time scales spanning millions of years. In most creationary views, the layers are described in terms of their relationship to Noah's flood in a system known as "flood geology." Flood geology interprets a large portion of the geologic column by Noah's flood. Geological formations are generally classified as being "pre-flood," "flood," or "post-flood." Therefore, the Grand Canyon gives you not a picture of millions of years of God being silent, but rather a direct picture of God's hand on world history. It is a picture of the flood itself.

In this view, the tilted layers at the bottom are the layers that existed before the flood. The contact between the tilted layers and the horizontal layers marks the beginning of the flood – the catastrophic onset of the floodwaters simply takes rocks of all types and erodes them flat. After this, the flood washes in sediments in horizontal layers stacked one on top of the other and completely parallel. But at this point the top layers are no longer completely flat. This is because, first, when the flood ended, the receding floodwaters carved out deep trenches and valleys. Then, in the post-flood world, deposits are characterized by normal erosional patterns – very localized and irregular.

After understanding this, I realized that the difference between these two paradigms is your worldview. It was at that moment that I decided that my worldview was going to start with Scripture, and not with the world's conception of truth. Colossians 2:8 says, "See to it that no one takes you captive through hollow and deceptive philosophy that depends on human tradition and the elemental spiritual forces of this world rather than on Christ." My view of earth history had been based on human tradition, now it was going to be based on Christ.

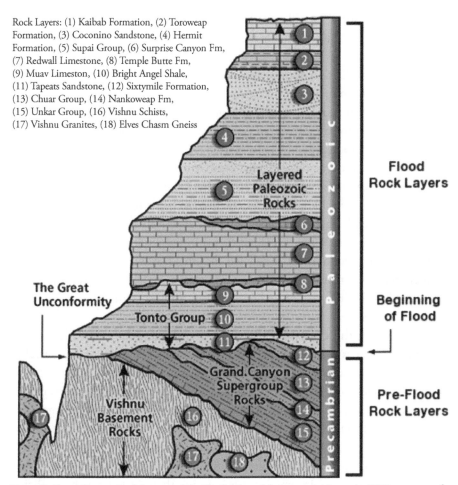

Rock Layers: (1) Kaibab Formation, (2) Toroweap Formation, (3) Coconino Sandstone, (4) Hermit Formation, (5) Supai Group, (6) Surprise Canyon Fm, (7) Redwall Limestone, (8) Temple Butte Fm, (9) Muav Limeston, (10) Bright Angel Shale, (11) Tapeats Sandstone, (12) Sixtymile Formation, (13) Chuar Group, (14) Nankoweap Fm, (15) Unkar Group, (16) Vishnu Schists, (17) Vishnu Granites, (18) Elves Chasm Gneiss

Flood Rock Layers

Layered Paleozoic Rocks

Beginning of Flood

The Great Unconformity

Tonto Group

Grand Canyon Supergroup Rocks

Vishnu Basement Rocks

Pre-Flood Rock Layers

Figure 2: Grand Canyon Rock Layers and the Flood (adapted from material From the US Department of the Interior)

Once I realized that my entire view of the earth history had been based on human traditions, I started a process of re-evaluating my life, to see if there might be other parts that are based on human tradition instead of Christ. As I started to examine myself, I realized that most of the way that I viewed the world was actually based on secular ideas and philosophies. It wasn't that I intended to adopt these philosophies – on the contrary, I have been trying to live my life according to Christ from a very young age. But it is difficult, without careful reflection, to see just how much influence the world has on your thinking. I was transformed.

As a simple example, I had never realized how secular my view of modern history was. I had always framed my understanding of history in terms of people, movements, and cultures. However, it never dawned on me to ask, "What is

God doing in history?" I still don't have a complete answer, but knowing that I was leaving the question out made me realize just how secular my understanding of the world was.

In my re-evaluation of the evidence, I discovered numerous treasures about the world around me. As a software engineer, I realized that there was a difference between what people could do as programmers, and how much one can get a computer to automate. There are some tasks, such as true creativity, that are inherently non-programmable. I also started realizing that the reason for the difference between these activities is that creative tasks have a spiritual dimension, and therefore cannot be automated using physical mechanisms.

In addition, this idea can be systematized to help programmers understand which tasks need human input to be handled effectively and which ones can be faithfully automated. When I realized that spiritual wisdom can be transformative to software development, I decided that this was worth investigating even further and more rigorously. This led me to start a conference titled "Engineering and Metaphysics" to explore how spiritual realities can help us in our day-to-day practices.

In biology, this caused me to ask additional questions about life, such as human tradition is focused on the "how" questions (i.e. what are the mechanisms by which organisms work). While these are certainly interesting and worthwhile questions, there are also numerous other questions that deserve intense and scholarly investigation. For example, one could ask "why" organisms are constructed the way they are. It is tempting to piously leave this as simply an unanswerable question, assume that we don't need to know, and say "I don't know why God did it this way but He did." Even though such a view gives a nod to God's purposes, in practice it is ignoring them just as much as atheists do. Instead, we need to pursue a study of God's purposes in making life the way it is as intently as we study the mechanisms by which life works and changes. It is not enough to know taxonomy names or the organisms that belong there. We must also search out why God made it that way with the same vigor.

When I decided to base my views of earth history on Creation and the Flood, it transformed my view of nearly everything. It was the starting point that helped me understand just how much my mind had been given over to secular philosophies. From there, I realized that every aspect of life has a spiritual dimension, and we must retrain ourselves to see it. In addition, this view has also had transformative effects on my faith. In the old earth view, God was largely silent for most of earth history, and His word was not helpful in understanding any but the briefest moments of history. He is absent from most of the Creation, and everywhere you look are fossils and geological features from times when God had nothing to do, or at least nothing to tell us about.

The flood view shows God has been active in his creation from the very first, and He has left evidence of His wonders and miracles everywhere. Nearly every dinosaur fossil discovered is one more reminder of God's great judgment in the flood. Everything from the bones in the ground to the shape of the continents is a daily reminder of God's providence. Instead of having faith on one hand, and science on the other, I have an integrated understanding of how they work together. Instead of understanding God's amazing handiwork, I can now see it. I can also see how spiritual principles apply to every area of life, not just the isolated questions of morality and belief that I used to restrict them to.

Interestingly, understanding how Creation worked also helped me understand evolution better, too. Evolution is not a dirty word - it simply means change. As a Creationist, I know that the world has changed. The world that was destroyed in the flood was not the world we live in today. So the question is, "how has God equipped life to handle such changes?" The reason that Creationists have been skeptical in the past of changes within and between species is many Creationists had assumed that the evolutionists were right about the mechanism of change - that is, random mutation coupled with natural selection. However, Creationists are not as constrained in their possibilities as evolutionists are. Evolution has little place for guided or preprogrammed changes. As a Creationist, however, I see the propensity of the genome to change in self-consistent ways as an obvious evidence of design.

When I believed in an old earth, it meant that most of history was disconnected from the Biblical narrative. Now, when I think of the Paleozoic, I think of the onset of the flood; when I think of the stars, I think of the fourth day of Creation; when I think of the K/T boundary (the geological layer above the dinosaurs with very few fossils), I think about the end of the flood, and Noah releasing the animals to repopulate the earth. Christianity becomes not just one part of my life, and one part of the history of the world, but rather a total truth about the whole history of the earth.

Many people today view the distinction between science and faith as the difference between "fact" and "value". This distinction also holds that the "facts" are public - meaning that they are available to everyone. Faith, since it is a "value," is personal, and therefore private. If something is personal, then its applicability to others is limited. For instance, my hankerings for cheeseburgers are personal - they have no place in public decision-making. However, the fact that food-borne diseases kill is a public fact, and therefore has relevance to public policy, even though good people may differ as to what that relevance is.

If faith is a private value, then it is improper for it to be part of public discussions. As long as we keep spiritual and Biblical ideas as mere doctrines, they will remain a personal belief, and we have left ourselves no legitimate reason why Christian principles should ever be considered in making public policy. However, Creation bridges the gap between fact and value. If the world shows evidences of Creation, then God's Creation is a public issue. The spiritual nature of the world is also a public issue, and must be considered in public decisions. This is true whether or not everyone agrees about Creation. The point is not that we can prove Creation to everyone's satisfaction, but that the evidence, data, and implications are all publicly available and, therefore, public discussion is possible. We are not debating a private value, but the history of the earth and the nature of reality and their associated implications.

My hope is that God's creation can also inspire others to begin transforming their lives. When I understood the relationship between the world and Biblical history, it became evident that knowing Christ was essential for a proper understanding of the world, and even of life itself. Even though being a devoted Christian for most of my life, I didn't realize how much I was missing because I lacked an understanding of creation. Now I spend my time diving deeper into a Christian understanding of the world, and helping others do the same.

CHAPTER 26: DR. RICHARD BLISS

Good Science Program[75]

This interview took place in September 1994 on the Revolution Against Evolution TV show just two months before Dr. Bliss went to heaven. Dr. Bliss was the founder of the Good Science program at the Institute for Creation Research, and during this interview he recounts the steps he took that moved him from an agnostic evolutionist to a Bible believing creationist.

Dr. Richard B. Bliss spent over 23 years as a science educator, first as a classroom teacher, then as director of science education for the Racine Wisconsin Unified School District. He also serviced as an Adjunct Professor at the University of Wisconsin. Dr. Bliss has a B.S. in Biology, a M.S. from the University of Wisconsin, and a doctorate in Science Education from the University of Sarasota in Florida, now known as Argosy University. Argosy was formed in September 2001 by merging three separate academic institutions, including The University of Sarasota, which for more than 30 years has offered degree programs.

At the University of Wisconsin all of his training was in science. He also attended the University of Colorado, and Florida State University. Because all of his academic science training was in evolution, it was very difficult for him to make the transition to scientific creation. His mind was programmed for evolution. Until he became a Christian in 1951 he had no interest in creationism.

At the time he began to consider what the Bible taught, he had a four-year National Science Foundation post-Masters Fellowship at the University of Colorado. Then he took a course in animal species and evolution under one of the leading evolutionary biologists. He asked the professor if he could do a study to resolve the evolution-creation question scientifically. His professor felt evolution had to be the explanation for the existence of all life, so Bliss asked him if he could explore evolution for the paper he was required to submit for the course.

His professor replied, "Dick, you are not going to find anything in the scientific literature to change your mind." To this Bliss answered, "I know, but I just have to research this question." The University of Colorado has a mammoth library, the Guggenheim Library, where Bliss did his research. When looking in the card catalog under evolution, he found the title *Implications of Evolution*, by G. A. Kerkut. Bliss checked out the book and couldn't believe what he was reading. Professor Kerkut first explained what evolution was, and then effectively

---

75   Based on an Interview by Doug Sharp and Richard Geer.

critiqued it. Bliss specifically remembered the evolution of the horse example. In that book Kerkut explained seven basic assumptions that evolutionists must make. These assumptions, the essence of evolution, are assumed, then the data are interpreted to fit the theory. These assumptions are

1   Non-living things gave rise to living material.
2.   Spontaneous generation could occur only once.
3.   Viruses, bacteria, plants, and animals are all interrelated.
4.   Protozoa gave rise to multi-cellular organisms.
5.   Invertebrates are interrelated.
6.   Invertebrates gave rise to vertebrates.
7.   All vertebrates are related.

As he was reading this book Bliss's thinking was locked into the evolution of the horse, so he did an intensive study to determine if this scientist was correct. Bliss concluded that the assumptions of evolution are magnificent, but the evidence for them from science is close to zero. Conversely, he found there exists much evidence to show that a God of Creation had to be involved in the creation.

Bliss also read other books on creation and evolution, including *The Genesis Flood*. A short time later, a very learned man came into his life, a Michigan State University natural science professor named Dr. John Moore. Dr. Moore came to Racine, Wisconsin, where Bliss was a science teacher at the time, to give a presentation at the University. At this time, Bliss was sharing his growing knowledge with the Science Investigation group at the University of Wisconsin, Parkside. He was then an adjunct professor on the campus, so could invite speakers to address the class. After Dr. Moore's presentation, he stayed at Bliss's home and they talked for hours. Bliss didn't know if Dr. Moore knew that at that time he was still in the "evolving" stage, but was rapidly starting to put things together with Moore's help. It took him about three years of intensive study to reject Darwinism and accept creationism. When he was finally convinced of the creationism worldview, he began to work in that area full time, and later even published several books on the subject.

He once reviewed a book by anthropologist Dr. Geoffrey Goodman, an evolutionist. His review was favorable, although it pointed out some areas of disagreement. Years later Dr. Goodman got in touch with Bliss, who thought

Oh no, he's discovered something, and he's going to make me look stupid. But I shouldn't have been concerned. He said, 'Richard, I've got something to tell you! I found Jesus Christ as my Savior. I believe in Jesus Christ. I believe that the Bible—every jot and title—is true!'[76]

---

76   January, 1995 *Acts & Facts*.

His Work in Creationism

One of the first books Bliss published with Professor Moore's help was called *Origins: Two Models*. At this time he was director of science education for the Racine Unified School District, a large district with over 40,000 students. Bliss first researched the two-model approach for teaching science in seven junior high schools, and this study turned out to be his doctoral dissertation. He did the pilot study in the junior high, and his dissertation research was done in the high school. Bliss saw that students who were part of the two-model project were much more involved in learning, and learned far more than the control group who were taught only evolution. His staff also recognized that he was on the right track. After the success of this approach was documented, Dr. Bliss thought "everyone's going to accept the two model approach because it worked so well to motivate students to study science."

When the evolutionists learned about his research, particularly the professors at the University of Michigan, Bliss started to encounter major problems. He didn't have any problems at the University of Wisconsin because he had some very close friends there, but the University of Michigan professors were absolutely intolerant: "Two models, they yelled! We believe in only one model, the evolutionary one, and refuse to believe in the other." As far as Bliss knows, his was the first attempt to research a two-model approach in the United States. And his book was the first one based on the two model approach.

The Goals of the Good Science Program as Taught by Dr. Bliss

The two primary goals of the Good Science program are to teach children how to recognize the evidence for intelligent design, and to understand that the Bible contains historical facts. He found that once children are able to recognize how to achieve these goals, it brings excitement and meaning to learning. It is also important to teach them how to recognize the miracle of creation all around them. Miracles are so commonplace that we often do not recognize them as such. People must consider the fact that the creator's power affects practically everything, but people miss this fact and continue to live their lives as if He doesn't exist.

Effect of Evolution on Teaching

Dr. Bliss concluded that Darwinism has contributed little to science except in a negative sense. Historically, many of the great scientists, including Isaac Newton, James Maxwell, and Robert Boyle, were all men of strong Christian faith. They were the Nobel Prize winners of their day. Many scientists today have accepted a no-God philosophy and then jammed their Darwinian god into public school kids. These kids are forced to believe something that is scientifically false.

And a lot of the kids know this. Students should not have to challenge those dogmatic teachers. Bliss knew that many great Christian teachers are working in our schools today, and stressed that if you are a Christian teacher, you should also be a missionary for creationism. Many Christian students have to face much prejudice against their Christian faith. Christian teachers are often required to teach a curriculum that they know is scientifically false. An example is embryonic recapitulation is still taught using Haeckel's falsified drawings, in spite of the fact that they were exposed as false in the early 1900s.

Fortunately, many Christian children are now being home schooled, and many Christian schools are teaching objective science. In his seminars, Bliss teaches the students not to regurgitate facts, but to think at the higher levels of reasoning. The public school children that are being taught evolution are often not given the freedom to think at the higher levels, but are forced to think within a Darwinist box. Bliss stressed that evolution is a worldview, and there never was a more thoroughly devastating worldview than evolutionism.

Bliss noted that the Bible book of Romans talks about when we do not retain God in our thinking, God gives us over to a reprobate mind, and we end up doing a lot of things that are harmful to us. There is no excuse for not believing in the Creator because the evidence all around us screams a creator God has made us, and all life, and has given us a purpose in living. Unfortunately, Bliss noted, many people have rejected the clear evidence and conclude, "I don't want to accept the obvious implications of this knowledge that God has put into his creation. The Scriptures teach that the visible things in the creation of the world are clearly seen, even His [God's] eternal power, so they [atheists] are without excuse. There is today, no excuse for someone rejecting the existence of the creator God."

After Dr. Bliss's death, the good science program was taken over by retired biology teacher Fredrick Albert Willson, who died on September 8, 2011. Willson taught biology at South High School in Torrance, California from 1959 to 1988. Since then, unfortunately, the program has ceased to exist.

Have you Considered that the Flood Formed Most of the Fossils?

As a child, Jonathan loved science, and made up his mind to read a science book every day. His childhood interest in science conflicted with his Christian upbringing but, without clear answers from either side, he began to accept evolutionary concepts and concluded that the Bible and evolution must both be true. Finally, his father challenged him to consider the view that the Flood formed most of the Earth's fossils. This idea transformed his thinking, and he now uses the science he learned throughout his education as a tool to present the gospel.

It is very encouraging to look back at my life and remember how God has led me from my very young years, into my work as a college professor. I was raised in a Christian home by creationist parents. My mother in particular took the time to explain the Genesis creation account to me. My dad was a civil engineer and a university professor who also enjoyed enticing me into the ways of science. I earned a B.S. in Chemistry from the University of Alabama, an M.S. in Chemical Engineering from the University of Alabama; and a Ph.D. in Chemical Engineering from the University of Kentucky. My professional experience includes being a Process Engineer for Conoco-Philips, an Associate Professor in Physical Science at Tennessee Temple University, and now as Professor of Natural Science at Clearwater Christian College.

My Journey from Evolutionist to Creationist

In the early 1960s, Time-Life began issuing a series of books on various science topics. My dad bought me many of the books in this series. This was about the time that President Kennedy made putting a man on the moon a national priority, and one of the Time-Life books was about the space program. How fascinated I was reading that book!

I was the oldest brother with four younger sisters. Our parents believed in the power of good books to enrich our lives. During the summer months when school was out, the rule was that we could read almost anything we wanted to for an hour a day – but no comic books! Our parents also limited our TV viewing to an hour a day, teaching us early to rely on the printed word for entertainment and information.

Our home always had many bookshelves crammed with books. We read profusely, and to this day reading is a major enjoyment for me. To relax, all I need is a good book. I have visited many homes with few or no books, and wonder, where does this family get its information? From sound bites on the radio or TV? From web sites? While still a youth, a love of reading was instilled in me that has been very beneficial in my college teaching.

When I was in fifth grade, I spent many beautiful summer afternoons reading articles in the *Book of Knowledge*, a children's encyclopedia. The Doubleday-Anchor science series, which my dad collected and encouraged me to read, was also an important reference. It included topics such as the history of mathematics written by Professor Morris Klein, and a book on crystals and crystal growing. At the public school I attended my K-12 teachers reinforced my parents' love of books. They said things like, "Books are the treasures of our civilization, treat them with care and respect. And read them carefully and often."

Starting in fourth grade I made up my mind to read one science book a day. I began with the *All About* books, a children's science series published by Random House. After school I read about Roy Chapman Andrews' expeditions in the Gobi desert where he discovered some of the first known dinosaur eggs. How fascinating that was! But these books also taught me evolution – human, biological, geological, and cosmic evolution.

I gradually began accepting evolutionary concepts. My mother had led me to the Lord at a young age, but I was now faced with the claims of the Bible on one side and evolution on the other. My parents had taught me recent fiat creation, but now I was learning that evolution is true. None of the books I read directly challenged, or even mentioned, the Bible, so I concluded that the Bible and evolution must both be true.

One evening in fifth grade I was on the living room couch reading the *All About* book on how the horse evolved. The book included the usual diagrams with the terminology of the time showing the progression from Eohippus (the "Dawn Horse") to the modern Equus. I remember wondering, *How do I know that this book is true and that the horse really evolved from some non-horse animal?* My answer was that it must be true, because how else could this book have a diagram of horse evolution so clearly and precisely sketched out? My next question was, *How can evolution be true if the Bible is true?* My answer was: *They must both be true. God must have used evolution to create all life.* I had read nothing about theistic evolution, and my parents had not warned me about it, so on the couch one evening in fifth grade, I was becoming a theistic evolutionist in my effort to harmonize the Bible with the books I was reading.

At this same time, our school, Wardcliff Elementary in Okemos, Michigan, sponsored periodic family fairs with food, fun, games and contests – but mostly these were *book* fairs because, in addition to the tables of books for children and parents for sale, all the prizes were books. The contests ran the gamut from athletics to art. I entered the art contests because I liked making imaginary drawings of unseen cosmic places.

In those years, no one had yet seen close-ups of the surface of most planets including Venus and Mercury, so I drew them out of my imagination based on what I had read. On school mornings I would get up at 5:30 am and, if I wasn't looking at the pictures and reading articles in the *National Geographic* my parents subscribed to, I would work on one of my space drawings. I eventually won an award for my "Surface of Mercury" drawing.

One of my award books was about primitive man. On one page there were two pictures, one with a primitive man running down a path, and the other with the man and a dinosaur running together. The caption asked "Which of these pictures is true?" Of course I knew the answer: the picture without the dinosaur, *because dinosaurs and man lived many millions of years apart!*

The previous summer I had read about the geologic ages in the *Book of Knowledge*, so about the same time as the book fair, I asked my dad to help me make a mural of the geologic ages. We lived in a big sprawling two-story farm house, and our dining room had a blank wall about 8 feet by 20 feet long. This was where I would hang my mural. I had taped together lots of paper bags from the grocery store, and my mural showed the evolution of life from the Precambrian to the Holocene *in neat progression.*

As I was small for my age, I needed my dad's help to hang this huge mural. I thought he would help me right away – after all, he had been giving me books to read and encouraged my reading – but now he made excuses to put off hanging the mural, which never went up! Later, I realized that my reading had taken me in directions that he probably didn't expect. *Let no one believe that young children cannot be profoundly led astray by what they read, even in a Christian home!*

But God was at work in my life. The geologic age concept teaches that the ages of rocks span a vast gamut. Some sandstones are quite young, but others might be hundreds of millions of years old. The age depends on the geological layer in which each is located . *That's fine*, I thought, *but what is the difference in appearance or physical structure or chemical composition of a "new" sandstone versus a very old one?* That summer, I searched through the twenty volumes of the *Book of Knowledge* to find the answer.

To my amazement, far from providing an answer, the *Book of Knowledge* never even acknowledged the question! It was as if they were implying that rocks do not really "age" as they grow older. *How could this possibly be?*, I wondered. After all, a person's appearance changes as he ages over only a few decades. An old house looks a lot different from when it was new, especially if it is not properly maintained. Thus God planted into my mind the first seed of doubt that evolutionism could be true.

In the same years, I enjoyed looking through my microscope (a Christmas gift when I was eight), my telescope (a birthday gift when I was ten), and doing experiments with my chemistry set (a Christmas gift when I was 11). My sisters and I took "nature walks" in the countryside around our farm to collect plant and insect specimens. But mostly I enjoyed my chemical experiments. Although the quintessential Space Age nerd, I exemplified the very scientific spirit the educational system sought to engender in the post-Sputnik frenzy to get a man on the moon before the Russians did!

As the "space race" heated up, my dad was hired to do contract work on the Saturn V rocket engine at Redstone Arsenal in Huntsville, Alabama. He would travel to Huntsville early Monday morning and return Friday evening with slides of the Saturn V tests completed during the week. So in our Friday night "family parties," we got to see one of the most powerful rocket engines ever developed being put through impressive performance runs.

One set of slides showed a Saturn V engine clamped in place running at full blast. To dissipate the heat, the exhaust gases were directed toward a reservoir holding millions of gallons of water. We were amazed to see all that water vaporize into steam in a matter of seconds! Looking back today, I can see that God was packing my memory with many personal experiences and factoids that I am able to use to make my teaching come alive.

In high school I began cataloging chemical compounds, both their structure and properties. I amassed a filing system with thousands of entries, facts that I now use in teaching. Today's students are less "nerdy" than many of us in the 1960s, because the Cold War fears that provided a rationale for science emphasis in education are gone. But God was also tearing down the last shreds of my belief in evolution. I had realized that the easiest way to talk about Christ as Savior was to begin with Christ as Creator. Evolution was a clear obstacle to this.

Finally, as I was studying one Saturday afternoon, my dad sat down on my bed and gently asked, *Have you ever considered that the Flood formed most of the fossils?* In my mind's eye this was almost as if a great flash of light suddenly illuminated the scenery, and I saw things the way they really are. Never has evolution tempted me again. I was transformed. I also believe that my mother and dad had been praying for me that God would work in this way.

I now knew that Darwinism is wrong, but knew almost nothing about the positive case for biblical creation. In college I attended a Philosophy of Science class team-taught by three professors who skillfully presented a positive case for biblical creation. I thought, *I would like to do this someday!* Graduate school and work in the chemical industry came next. However, I then had little time to explicitly study origins issues. However, my graduate school studies involved coal science, geology, and atmospheric science. Each of these were essential to understanding the effects of the Flood.

Finally, at age 26, I came to the point of surrendering to God's will for my life. Up until then I had tried various things to see if each was His will, but now was the time for real commitment. One Saturday afternoon I cried out to God for guidance. That guidance came slowly, but definitely, over the next few years. God called me into Christian education as definitely and as explicitly as He has ever called any missionary to the field, or pastor to the pulpit. Christian education is not a career for everyone – we need Christian creationists in secular settings too – but it was God's call for me.

Through the years, God has intersected my path with that of other fine creationists. I taught alongside Dr. Gary Parker for a time. Before that, I was privileged to work alongside Dr. Allan Davis, one of the professors whom God used to help Dr. Parker to understand the failure of evolution. Dr. Bill Davis, co-author of the book *Of Pandas and People*, has also been one of my academic colleagues. It has been a privilege to work with these godly people as well as others, and each one of them has been a blessing and an encouragement.

I enjoy enormously the classes and students that I teach. I recently completed a textbook for Earth Science Survey, and another for Physical Science Survey classes. Both are written on the college level, but from a recent, fiat creation view. In projects like this, I find myself fondly going over scientific facts and my experiences. Now I seek to pass these truths on to the next generation. My wife and I have home schooled our four children – Faith, David, Daniel and Charity – and have had the privilege of passing these same truths on to them.

I am writing these words a few days before Christmas. Of all universally recognized historical events, Christmas and the Resurrection most dramatically demonstrate God's ability to work in history for man's good and His glory. But in my own personal and academic life, I can look back and see God working in the same wonderful way in my life.

In a world beset by trials and uncertainty, knowing that the cosmos is the product of a loving, all-powerful Creator gives me confidence that no natural disaster or geopolitical crisis is beyond His control. This confidence has developed gradually as I have better understood biblical creation over time. As a result, I can read and hear sensational headlines without being fearful, and I can pass along this confidence in the God of creation to my students and children. Rather than fearing what may come, I can depend on my Creator instead! For me, this has been a slow, but a very real, transformation.

How to Scientifically Destroy Darwinism in Four Seconds Flat!

After Russ saw that real science doesn't support Darwinism or old-earth beliefs, he realized that these false teachings are undermining the world's faith in the Lord Jesus Christ. Armed with the knowledge that kinds will only bring forth after their own kind, and that a global flood destroyed the old-earth belief, he knew something needed to change in his life.

Though I was raised in a Christian home, like many Christian-raised kids, as is common I strayed from God when I went off to college. I was an all-conference college baseball player, and after graduating I began my own business. God simply did not register in my plans during that time. In fact, it is fair to say that I was on my road to Damascus only when, at the age of 28, I heard the Holy Spirit, who sounded a lot like my wife, Joanna, nudging me to return to God.

I began attending church and growing as a Christian believer. Sixteen years passed as I grew in my faith and became a Trustee. However, I believed God had used evolution and billions of years to develop His creation. After all, I reasoned, billions of years leading to Darwinism is taught as science in our schools and textbooks, and they would not contain lies.

During this time frame my business became very successful. My game plan was to retire at the age of 49 and spend my remaining years golfing, traveling the world and doing other things I enjoy. However, God had other plans for me.

During the summer of 1997, an event took place that would forever change the fortunes of my family. Joanna obtained a video, *Lies In The Textbooks* by Dr. Kent Hovind, that exposed many misinterpreted evidences, as well as several out-and-out frauds, used to support billions of years leading to Darwinism. These examples included the facts which had fooled me into accepting the view that Darwinian evolution had occurred.

I was surprised by the lack of viable evidence in support of either billions of years or Darwinism. Before long, I realized that these are two religious-based beliefs that have somewhat of a symbiotic relationship, a term generally applied to plants or animals.

A symbiotic relationship exists when one, or both, entities are dependent on the other to survive. Though a belief in billions of years can exist without Darwinism, a belief in Darwinism cannot survive without billions of years of time.

I soon came to the realization that billions of years leading to Darwinism undermines the foundations of the Gospel message by placing death before Adam. These foundations are laid down in the early chapters of the book of Genesis. This is where we learn that God made a perfect creation; Adam's sin corrupted the creation, allowing death to enter while separating man from God. This required our redemption with Him through our Lord and Savior, Jesus Christ.

As a result, the idea that death occurred prior to Adam undermines the foundation for our need of a redeeming Savior. What a blessing it was to me when I discovered that observable science is a Christian believer's true friend.

Biology: Kinds after Kind

A key to my obtaining a grasp on biological issues was learning the difference between micro-adaptation and macro-evolution. Because the definitions of these terms can vary, allow me to define them.

Macro-evolution is Darwinian-style change that leads to the origin of totally new kinds of plants or animals. A dog begetting a non-dog would be a good example.

Micro-adaptation is variation within the same kind of plant or animal. That is, micro-adaptations are kinds bringing forth after their kind, such as a white dog birthing a brown dog. Ten times in the book of Genesis we are told that plants or animals bring forth only after their kind.

> And God made the beast of the earth after his kind, and cattle after their kind, and every thing that creepeth upon the earth after his kind: and God saw that it was good (Genesis 1:25).

Millions of examples of biblically correct kinds bringing forth after their kind can be found. Meanwhile, Darwinists teach that one kind, such as bacteria, will bring forth a different kind, eventually leading to humans. However, no viable example of Darwinian change taking place has ever been scientifically documented. This was eye-opening for me.

Geology: The Global Flood

The key to my understanding the age-of-the-earth issue was the realization of the role of the global flood in the billions of years view. This is vital for

Christians to understand since old-earth beliefs undermine the Gospel message by placing death before Adam.

I had been led to believe that radiometric dating techniques were reliable and accurate. Actually, this is far from the truth: isotope dating methods yield a wide range of dates. The fact is, the published dates the public sees are usually only those ages that match the Geologic Time Scale.

When I realized this fact, a light came on: Old-earth ages are based on a belief that the earth's crust of stratified rock layers formed slowly over never-observed millions of years of time! Thus, a global flood erodes old-earth beliefs! God's Word tells us that God has judged man's sin using a global flood, and such an event erodes old-earth beliefs.

And the waters prevailed exceedingly upon the earth; and all the high hills, that were under the whole heaven, were covered (Genesis 7:19). One of the great prophecies in the New Testament is found in 2 Peter 3:

> Knowing this first, that there shall come in the last days scoffers… For this they willingly are ignorant of, that by the word of God the heavens were of old, and the earth standing out of the water and in the water. Whereby the world that then was, being overflowed with water, perished.

The Bible told us ahead of time that scoffers would deny the global flood in the last days. So, why do scoffers deny the global flood? Because such an event would explain how earth's strata formed quickly, undermining the old-earth interpretations of the earth's crust.

CreationMinistries.Org

Occupationally, I am a General Manager and make logical decisions based on facts. After I learned that science doesn't support Darwinism or old-earth beliefs, I realized that these false teachings are undermining the world's faith in the Lord Jesus Christ. Armed with the knowledge that life will bring forth only after their own kind, and that a global flood destroyed old-earth beliefs, I knew something needed to be done. This transformed my life.

I began to intently study the creation-evolution issues, obtaining knowledge from Creation speakers, scientists and even the die-hard Darwinian faithful. After three years of study, I felt God's calling to do something more important than making money and, in December of 2000, I gave my business to a valuable co-worker and began CreationMinistries.Org to confirm biblical Truth and expose misinterpretations of God's creation in order to exalt Jesus Christ as our Creator, Judge, and redeeming Savior.

In studying the issues, I was amazed by the overwhelming facts that demolish Darwinism and old-earth beliefs. God soon led me to explain how to destroy Darwinism in four-seconds flat and to share undeniable proof of a global flood.

How to Scientifically Destroy Darwinism in Four-seconds Flat

First, I will need to explain a few things. Back in 2002, I discovered that adaptations and mutations within any particular kind of plant or animal are caused by the sorting or loss of genetic information. This is known as Gene Depletion.

Darwinists must explain where the original genetic information came from. Scientists know of no way for complex information to come about on its own in a natural environment. All observations show that complex information must be derived from extreme intelligence.

Darwinian evolution has failed due to its inability to provide a naturally occurring mechanism that could add massive amounts of new and beneficial genetic information to existing gene pools. Nothing was known about genetic information in Darwin's day but we now have a basic understanding of genetics and are beginning to understand the extreme complexity of genetic data, and its ability to function. We can no longer think that life developed by time, chance, natural law and random accidents.[77]

Lacking a way to generate the needed genetic data, Darwinists came up with what is called *Neo-Darwinism*. This is the belief taught as science in schools today that genetic mutations create the new and beneficial genetic data needed to power paramecium-to-pine tree evolution. The story continues that the improved mutant takes over the population as Natural Selection eliminates their weaker, non-mutated colleagues. Then, *over billions of years*, mutations changed that first single-celled organism into every living plant or animal that has ever existed on the earth.

This belief holds that all parts of all living beings came about piece by piece. Whether we are talking about the bluebird's beak or the central nervous system of an evolutionary biology professor, Neo-Darwinists believe everything came about due to random mutations adding massive amounts of new and beneficial genetic information to the ancestor's gene pools.

Since this belief is taught as if it were science in schools around the world, it is fair to require Neo-Darwinists to present thousands of undeniable examples of nature adding new and beneficial genetic information to pre-existing gene pools.

---

77   Miller, Russ, *It's About Time*, 2012, page 91.

However, there has never been a scientific experiment or observation that has shown a single viable example of a natural process adding appreciable amounts of new and beneficial genetic information to a creature's DNA.

Gene Depletion

In fact, all observations show that most all mutations cause the loss of pre-existing genetic information. Furthermore, all variations or adaptations are also caused by the sorting or loss of the DNA inherited from the parents. This is a principle known as *Genetic Depletion*.

Note that I said there has never been a *viable* example of a natural process adding appreciable amounts of new and beneficial genetic information to a creature's DNA. I did not say that Darwinists do not present examples. There is a big difference.

The lack of viable examples is due to the fact that mutations in the DNA strand occur due to the sorting or loss of the parent's pre-existing genetic information (Gene Depletion), not from the gain of new and beneficial genetic data.

Beneficial Mutations

Darwinists will often point to a mutation that may have resulted in some type of benefit to the mutant as proof of nature's having added new and beneficial genetic information to the mutant's DNA. This is simply dishonest. Even in an extremely rare case where a mutation benefited the mutant, the change was still caused by the sorting or loss of genetic information, not by the gain of new and beneficial data.[78]

For example, if a wild boar living on a brush-choked island were to lose the genetic data to form its parents' sixteen inch long legs due to a mutation in its DNA, and instead had legs just 15 inches long, that mutation would be a benefit if the shorter legs allowed it to duck under the brush faster to escape the leopard hunting it. Though this mutation would have resulted in a benefit for the boar, like virtually all observed mutations, it would have been caused by the loss of genetic information, not from the gain of new and beneficial data.

Natural Selection

Neo-Darwinism also predicted that biology would find that Natural Selection, acting on new and beneficial genetic information added to a plant or animal's gene pool by mutations, caused a bacterium cell to eventually improve and evolve into all of the millions of life forms ever to have lived on the earth.

---

78   Miller, R., Dobkins, J., *The Darwinian Delusion*, 2010, pages 132-134.

However, as previously pointed out, observable evidence proves mutants are mostly the weaker of their kind. Again, this is due to Gene Depletion: mutations and variations are caused by the sorting or loss of the parent's genetic information. Gene Depletion is why mutations are the ones most likely to be removed by Natural Selection which can only select from traits that are actually exhibited in any given population. This is exactly the opposite of what Neo-Darwinists claim.

For an example, suppose a wild boar living on an island experienced a genetic mutation that resulted in losing genetic data to form its parent's four sixteen-inch-long legs. Instead, the mutant boar developed three 16-inch-long-legs and one leg that was just 14 inches long. The result would be that the mutant is the slowest pig on the peninsula and when the leopard comes along, the mutant is likely the first of its kind to be removed by Natural Selection. By putting these principles together I came up with how to scientifically debunk Darwinism in 4 seconds flat.[79]

Gene Depletion + Natural Selection make Darwinism a scientific impossibility.

The lack of viable evidence in support of Darwinism is due to Gene Depletion and Natural Selection combining to make Darwinism a scientific impossibility.

Gene Depletion fits well with the *Second Law of Thermodynamics.* This scientific law holds that all material things are losing energy, wearing down. This is the most accepted law in all of the fields of science, except for in evolutionary biology. Darwinists have to go against scientific principle because they do not wish to admit their belief is not scientifically viable.

Since 2001 I have developed 14 popular-level PowerPoint messages. These are designed with an average of 150 visuals each so folks from age 8 to 98 can follow the teaching. I have also put together a DVD Study Series with a Study Guide, radio programs, a website, written five books and illustrated our *'Noah's Ark & Dinosaurs'* and *'Endowed By Their Creator'* coloring books. I do not copyright my DVD's and encourage folks to make copies to pass on to others. We are challenging people worldwide to believe the Bible—cover to cover.

I published *It's About Time* in 2012, which presents the top ten old-earth beliefs along with the evidences that have been misinterpreted to support old-earth beliefs. I then take the same facts and interpret them through a biblical worldview. This demolishes the old-earth interpretations while revealing the truth and reliability of God's non-compromised Word.

---

79 CreationMinistries.Org presentation, *50 Facts versus Darwinism In The Textbooks*, 2002-present, visuals 100-112.

I also cover the top ten Darwinian beliefs and the top ten evil fruit growing from the tree of old-earth beliefs in *It's About Time*. After reading the book, one pastor sent me this note: *"I read It's About Time and Wow! What a tremendous read! You've changed so many of my long held beliefs - including the Gap Theory. Thank you!"*

God has allowed me to share service messages in hundreds of churches. I have also spoken on college campuses, at national conferences and appeared on worldwide Christian television programs many times.

After I presented *'50 Facts versus Darwinism'* at Northern Arizona University, a high school biology teacher quit her job and began teaching science in a Christian school. Northern Arizona University's response was to begin an accredited course attacking both me and biblical creation. Our messages are powerful and life-changing!

God also led me to develop Bible-based **Grand Canyon Rim** and **Grand Staircase** bus tours. At the south rim of the chasm I point out original creation rock from days and three, pre-flood layers and what I refer to as the judgment layers, the strata laid down during the global flood. Then, what really brings God's Word to life is that I also take people to where they can put their hands on each of these evidences, making God's Word relevant to the world we live in!

I give an *on-the-rim* talk during our Grand Canyon Rim tours. As we stand on the Kaibab limestone that makes up the rim of the gorge, I tell folks, *"If you're looking down into the Canyon and you would like to see the best proof of the Truth of God's Word anywhere in the world, then you're looking the wrong way!"* This is because the best evidence of the global flood that erodes old-earth beliefs, is not found in Grand Canyon. It is found above the Canyon's rim.

Cedar Mountain and Red Butte tower 900 feet above the Kaibab limestone. These buttes consist of 600 feet of the Moenkopi layer and 300 feet of the Chinle formation. Both layers were laid down by water and formerly covered the entire region, yet have been removed for thousands of square miles. We know this because the layers are picked up if you drive to the northern border of Arizona or east into the Painted Desert.[80] While Grand Canyon represents over 900 cubic miles of missing sediments, these missing layers represent tens of thousands of square miles of missing materials.

Once the folks on our tours realize that these layers formerly existed on top of where they are standing I then ask them, *"How can a 900 foot thick layer of strata be removed for thousands of square miles, yet leave no trace of where the displaced sediments are?"* The only logical response is that the missing strata were removed and dispersed the last time the flood waters rushed off of the area.

---

80   Miller, Russ, *It's About Time*, 2012, pages 100-101.

So how does the National Park Service explain Cedar Mountain and Red Butte? Their first line of defense is to ignore the scientifically observable evidence as it destroys the *billions of years* foundation of the secular worldview. Since 99.99 percent of visitors do not know anything about the buttes, silence is all that is needed to conceal the truth. If pressed for an explanation of these two buttes the Park's fallback position is to claim the two formations are volcanic up-lifts in spite of the fact they consist of stratified layers laid down by water! Most Park Rangers and geologists are only repeating the secular interpretations of the evidence that they have been taught.

The best proof in the world of the global flood

As stupendous as the missing 900 feet of strata is, it is almost nothing when compared to the 4,000+ feet of strata layers that are missing from above them! There used to be 4,000+ feet of strata on top of the 900-foot thickness of rock layers that make up Cedar Mountain and Red Butte. In total, layers a mile thick have been removed from above the rim of Grand Canyon and these missing layers represent tens of thousands of square miles of missing sediments.

In case you are wondering how we know the layers once covered the area, it is because the strata layers are picked up in northern Arizona and southern Utah in what is known as the ***Grand Staircase***.

The primary steps of the Staircase are seen at the Vermillion Cliffs, Zion and Bryce Canyon. The Bryce hoodoos are remnants of a large sapping structure rather than a canyon formation. A sapping structure forms when water suddenly rushes away from an area causing the area to collapse downward, and from Bryce south the mile of strata layers have been removed in a stair step pattern.[81]

This is mind-boggling support of the global flood, since the only logi-cal interpretation of the removal of a mile-deep thickness of strata over such a vast region, is that the layers were removed the last time the global floodwaters surged across the continent at the end of the flood.

Grand Canyon (A), Chocolate Cliffs (B), Vermilion Cliffs (C), White Cliffs (D), Zion Canyon (E), Gray Cliffs (F), Pink Cliffs (G), Bryce Canyon (H). National Park Service image: public domain.

Because the global flood erodes *billions-of-years* beliefs that provide the foundation for Secular Humanism, and as secularists own the park system and the educational establishments, these observable facts are glossed over or kept out of geology courses and books. False secular teachings have undermined sci-

---

81   Miller, Russ, *It's About Time*, 2012, page 54.

entific education and research, along with the eternal salvation of billions of unsuspecting people.[82]

This is one of the reasons why I have also developed and lead biblically-based Grand Staircase tours. These tours include one day each at Zion and Bryce Canyon National Parks along with a day of Colorado River rafting. Experiencing these areas through a biblical view leaves little doubt that God's Word is true cover to cover.

On a recent tour, a young man approached me and said, "*Russ, my mother is a Christian and got me to come on your bus trip but I'm an avowed Atheist and evolutionist, and I have no interest in your god.*" However, as we were getting off the bus at the end of the day he grabbed me by the shoulder and said, "*Russ, this day has changed my life. Now I know there was a global flood; that Darwinism is a lie and the Bible is true!*"

God also led Tom Vail of Canyon Ministries to ask me to lead several of his creation-based river rafting trips through Grand Canyon. This is another great way to incorporate this bastion of Secular misinterpretations to remind folks of God's past and coming global judgments of sin, as well as His grace and mercy toward us all.

I now spend more time at Grand Canyon than I could have ever imagined. Again, God's plan for our lives is usually much different than our own plans. Learn more about our ministry's efforts, our messages and our God-honoring tours at www.CreationMinistries.Org.

Summary

Joanna and I have dedicated our lives to confirming biblical Truth, exposing misinterpretations of God's creation and exalting Jesus Christ as our Creator, Judge and redeeming Savior.

Whether we are speaking in a church or hiking along the rim of Grand Canyon, the purpose of *CreationMinistries.Org* is to ensure Believers and true seekers that they can put their faith in the Bible – Word for Word and cover to cover.

"All scripture is given by inspiration of God, and is profitable for doctrine, for reproof, for correction, for instruction in righteousness" (2 Timothy 3:16).

---

82 Miller, Russ, *It's About Time*, 2012, pages 54-55

Transformation

Many Christians miss much of the second half of the Gospel. Let me illustrate. Have you ever been sweaty on a hot day and then took a cool refreshing shower? When in a shower, it's great to have the cleansing waters lavishing all over us, but that's only part of the picture. This next part is extremely important as well. When you step out of the shower, you want to put on clean clothes. It's not enough to have our sins washed away. We need something else.

In the Garden, the Lord wanted our first parents to prove themselves obedient. Not only did they fail the test, but they became filthy in the sweat of sin. An animal sacrifice was required – an anti-type of Christ on the cross, but they needed more. They needed a covering. They knew they were naked and they sewed fig leaves together to cover themselves.

In Luke 18:18 a certain ruler asked Christ, "Good teacher, what must I do to inherit eternal life?" He was contemplating making some fig-leaves to cover over his spiritual nakedness. "Why do you call me good?" Jesus answered. "No one is good—except God alone. Jesus was challenging the man's idea that it is possible for people to be good.

We do that, saying, "Oh, he was such a good man!" or "I'm not all that bad." Jesus knows otherwise. John 2:23 says, "Now while He was in Jerusalem at the Passover Festival, many people saw the signs He was performing and believed in his name. But Jesus would not entrust himself to them, for he knew all people. He did not need any testimony about mankind, for He knew what was in each person."

Jesus continued: "You know the commandments: 'You shall not commit adultery, you shall not murder, you shall not steal, you shall not give false testimony, honor your father and mother.'"

Jesus was not saying that we can get to heaven by obeying God's Law, but the law was a mirror to remind the young man that he was a sinner. "All these I have kept since I was a boy," he said. The man was saying that his fig-leaves were in pretty good shape. When Jesus heard this, he said to him, "You still lack one thing. Sell everything you have and give to the poor, and you will have treasure in heaven. Then come, follow me."

Jesus was not going to let this man get away with his idolatry of wealth and self. When he heard this, he became very sad, because he was very wealthy. He wanted to keep his idol and still be saved. Jesus looked at him and said, "How hard it is for the rich to enter the kingdom of God! Indeed, it is easier for a camel to go through the eye of a needle than for someone who is rich to enter the kingdom of God."

Jesus is saying that all of our fig-leaves won't work. We all fail God's test – His Law.

What did God do in the Garden? He gave our first parents what they needed. We read in Gen. 3:21: "The LORD God made garments of skin for Adam and his wife and clothed them."

And He's done something more precious for us! In the parable of the prodigal son in Luke 15, Jesus tells us "But while he was still a long way off, his father saw him and was filled with compassion for him; he ran to his son, threw his arms around him and kissed him. "The son said to him, 'Father, I have sinned against heaven and against you. I am no longer worthy to be called your son.' "But the father said to his servants, 'Quick! Bring the best robe and put it on him.'"

That "best robe" is the robe of Christ's perfect righteousness (Jeremiah 23:6). Hundreds of years before Jesus came, He proclaimed His own name: "The days are coming," declares the LORD, "when I will raise up for David a righteous Branch, a King who will reign wisely and do what is just and right."

This means that you must have His robe of righteousness surrounding you. "In Him we have redemption through his blood, the forgiveness of sins in accordance with the riches of God's grace that he lavished on us."

Jesus said, "Unless your righteousness surpasses that of the Pharisees and doctors of the law, you will never enter the kingdom of heaven." This is like saying you have to be better than the best person you ever met. You have to be *perfect*, and Jesus is the only One who was, and is, perfect.

In Romans 3:19-20 we read: "Now we know that whatever the law says, it says to those who are under the law, that every mouth may be silenced and the whole world accountable to God. Therefore, no one can be justified by observing the law, but by law we become conscious of sin."

The rich young rule was an idolater, and his fig-leaves wouldn't work. Our so-called righteousness won't work. But Isaiah 61:10f says: "I delight greatly in the LORD; my soul rejoices in my God. For **He has clothed me with garments of salvation and arrayed me in a robe of *His* righteousness**."

Romans 3 (verses 21-22) adds: But now, apart from the law the righteousness of God has been made known, to which the Law and the Prophets testify. This righteousness is given through faith in Jesus Christ to all who believe."

Romans 5:17 notes: "For if, by the trespass of the one man, death reigned through that one man, how much more will those who receive God's abundant provision of grace and **the gift of righteousness** reign in life through the one man, Jesus Christ!

Philippians 3:8-9 says: What is more, I consider everything a loss because of the surpassing worth of knowing Christ Jesus my Lord, for whose sake I have lost all things. I consider them garbage, that I may gain Christ and be found **in Him**, not having a righteousness of my own that comes from the law, but that which is through faith **in Christ—the righteousness that comes from God** on the basis of faith.

CPSIA information can be obtained at www.ICGtesting.com
Printed in the USA
BVOW11s2154130414

350498BV00001B/2/P